Advance Praise

"Through a careful reading of urban strugg̶l̶e̶s̶ a̶n̶d̶ b̶y̶ p̶u̶t̶t̶i̶n̶g̶ s̶o̶c̶i̶a̶l̶ a̶n̶d̶ urban theory in the service of the most profound questions of collective transformation, Stavros Stavrides demonstrates the 'spaces of possibility' present in our cities and our daily lives."
—Silvia Federici, author of *Caliban and the Witch* and *Revolution at Point Zero: Housework, Reproduction and Feminist Struggle*

"Grabbing back for the common the spaces taken by capital and the State, which aims to turn them into spaces of order for their various operations, is one of the main achievements of the social movements of the urban peripheries. Thus, these movements not only place limits on the accumulation of capital and power by the 1 percent, but they turn the territories of the common into territories in resistance, a process that Stravros Stavrides knows and analyzes in depth, from a view that places the tension for emancipation at the center of his reflections."
—Raúl Zibechi, author of *Dispersing Power: Social Movements as Anti-State Forces* and *Territories in Resistance: A Cartography of Latin American Social Movements*

"Threshold spaces are like portals to new dimensions of sociality and doing, in which subjective experience is enriched by being part of a collective emergent process that pulverizes hierarchies and restores joy and hope into the territory. In this insightful book, Stavros Stavides pushes us to think of the modern city as having many immanent heterotopic threshold spaces which could be bridged to expand the commons and challenge the despotism of late neoliberal urban crises. A must read for organizers, intellectuals, and revelers worldwide."
—Massimo DeAngelis, author of *Omnia Sunt Communia: On the Commons and the Transformation to Postcapitalism* and *Beginning of History: Value Struggles and Global Capital*

"Combining innovative theoretical arguments with the concrete spatial sensibility of an architect, Stavros Stavrides shows us how people are breaking down urban barriers and opening the city to new and exciting interactions. This book teaches us how to make the metropolis into a common space."

—Michael Hardt, coauthor of *Assembly* and *Commonwealth* with Antonio Negri

"In a sense, *Towards the City of Thresholds* has already crossed a threshold: the threshold between us sensing the emancipatory potential of cities and actually realizing this. Through these dark hours of counter-revolutionary waves crashing onto our cities and communities the world over, it is imperative to keep this message alive: that a common world of liberation is still within reach. *Towards the City of Thresholds* is a must-read."

—Antonis Vradis, coauthor of *New Borders: Migration, Hotspots and the European Superstate* and *Athens and the War on Public Space: Tracing a City in Crisis*

Towards the City of Thresholds

Towards the City of Thresholds
Stavros Stavrides

Common Notions
commonnotions.org

Towards the City of Thresholds
Stavros Stavrides
This edition © 2019 Common Notions

ISBN: 978-1-942173-09-0
LCCN: 2019936532

Common Notions
c/o Interference Archive
314 7th Street
Brooklyn, NY 11215

www.commonnotions.org
info@commonnotions.org

Design and typesetting by Morgan Buck and Josh MacPhee
Antumbra Design | www.antumbradesign.org

Special thanks to Andrea Mubi Brighenti and professionaldreamers of Italy, publishers of an earlier edition of *Towards the City of Thresholds* which inspired this expanded edition.

professionaldreamers is a small, independent publisher that collects and promotes essays on space and society (www.professionaldreamers.net).

Printed in the USA on acid-free, recycled paper.

Contents

Illustrations

Acknowledgements

The idea of a city of thresholds has been central to my research and involvement with urban movements for many years. Appearing sometimes as an inspiring image or promising concept, this idea has sustained a probably ambiguous, always precarious, and undoubtedly unfinished effort to think about the emancipatory potential of existing, emergent, and possible spaces.

This book aims to expose important facets of a theoretical argument in the making. Parts I, II, and III comprise the book as it was first published by professionaldreamers in 2010. Part IV includes three more recent texts that serve to connect my work on urban commons developed in *Common Space: The City as Commons* (Zed Books, 2016) and *Common Spaces of Urban Emancipation* (Manchester University Press, 2019). They indicate how my ideas about the social meaning of thresholds can be integrated with a theorizing of urban commons that understands commoning as a threshold-creating process.

Chapter 1 contains selections from a paper presented at the Seminars of the Aegean (Organized by NTUA, AUTH and Harokopio University at Naxos, 2003). A reworked version was published as part of the book *Suspended Spaces of Alterity* (Athens: Alexandria, 2010). For the present publication the text has been further developed.

Chapter 2 contains parts of two texts published in the corresponding catalogues of the Greek participation in the International Exhibition of Architecture – Venice Biennale: 10th Exhibition, 2006 ("Living in Exile in the Archipelago") and 11th Exhibition, 2008 ("Inhabiting Rhythms").

Chapter 4 contains parts of a paper presented at the Living in a Material World Conference (Brighton, UK 2001) and published in the short-lived e-journal *Journal of Psychogeography and Urban Research*, which is unfortunately no longer accessible.

Chapter 5 is a revised and developed version of a chapter of my book *From the City-as-Screen to the City-as-Stage* (Athens: Ellinika Grammata, 2002). The chapter's title is "Distance as a condition and means of approach."

Chapter 6 is based on a paper published in *Utopia* 72 (2006) as "The space of order and heterotopias: Foucault as a geographer of otherness."

Chapter 7 is a revised version of a chapter of my book *Suspended Spaces of Alterity*, originally titled "Following the traces of a heterotopia: in Zapatista Chiapas."

Chapter 8 is based on ideas developed during a presentation at an RC21/International Sociological Association Conference in São Paulo, Brazil (2009). The presentation's title was "The December 2008 Youth Uprising in Athens: Glimpses of a Possible City of Thresholds." A version of this chapter can also be found in the e-journal *Spatial Justice/Justicespatiale* no. 2, available online at http://issi.org/06.php.

Chapter 9, "Squares in Movement," originally appeared in *South Atlantic Quarterly* 111(3), Summer 2012. Special thanks to Michael Hardt for granting permission to publish it here.

Chapter 10 is based on the afterword to conference proceedings I wrote for *Crisis-Scapes: Athens and Beyond*, May 9–10, 2014.

Chapter 11 is a revised version of "On Urban Commoning" in *Make_Shift City: Renegotiating the Urban Commons* (Berlin: Jovis Verlag, 2014). Special thanks to the editor and publisher for their permission to include this essay here.

The book's main ideas were and are still being tested in both academic and activist environments. I owe a lot to my students in the postgraduate course "Experience, Representation and Meaning of Space" that I have been organizing for the last eight years. The remarks and criticisms of my students have always been inspiring.

A lot of people have also contributed to the "city of thresholds" idea by commenting on lectures given in the context of specific urban initiatives in various neighborhoods in Athens.

My participation in the interdisciplinary Critical Research Methodology group in Athens—which combines engaged social criticism with a truly collaborative dialogue on social science methods beyond academic formalities—has had a tremendous influence on my research. Sotiris Dimitriou, the soul of this open group—who also inspired so much of my work over many years—unfortunately passed away in 2016. I feel that his existence as an engaged, generous, and antihierarchical intellectual has left its deep mark on my research and thinking.

Eftichios Bitsakis, Andrea Mubi Brighenti, Oliver Clemens, Karen Franck, Costas Gavroglou, John Holloway, Sabine Horlitz, Demetres Karydas, Maria Kopanari, Jenny Robinson, Quentin Stevens, Fereniki Vatavali, the late Annie Vrychea, and Andrew Wernick have in different times and places expressed stimulating opinions and offered helpful suggestions on the ideas elaborated in the book's original chapters.

Brighenti has also generously and consistently supported this work from the very beginning, meticulously and creatively commenting on the final draft.

Anna Holloway has translated the texts on which chapters 5, 6, and 7 are based.

Special thanks to Alexandria Publications for granting permission to use material from the published book *Suspended Spaces of Alterity*.

Evgenia Michalopoulou has always been inspiring in her caring criticism and in her insistence on the power of collective dreams. She and Zoe Stavrides Michalopoulou had to once again face the alternating disappointments and enthusiasms that always accompany my attempts to think and write. I really appreciate their patience and their unlimited support. I cannot promise them, I am afraid, that it will be easier next time.

Unless otherwise specified, all pictures were taken by the author. Special thanks to John Davis, Babis Louizidis, Stamatia Papadimitriou, and Ioannis Papagiannakis for allowing the reproduction of their works.

Since its initial publication, *Towards the City of Thresholds* has traveled to many activist and academic venues and met with encouraging criticism and suggestions for which I am really thankful. Its translation into Turkish and Spanish helped me clarify some thoughts and their expression. I am thankful to the corresponding translators and editors for that.

For this expanded edition, I chose not to rewrite parts of the book or to update the references to literature. A different choice might mean writing a new book on thresholds in light of my recent research adventures.

Accommodating this choice, Malav Kanuga of Common Notions kindly suggested the inclusion of the three texts of Part IV in the book. It was a very good idea and I thank him for that. I also thank him for his enthusiastic support of this project and Erika Biddle-Stavrakos for her careful editing of the text.

Preface to the US edition

Critical thinking seems to be an obvious task in current times of cynicism and phobic individualism. It becomes even more urgently needed as the discontent of those who suffer from predatory policies and aggressive privatization of public resources is dangerously courted by religions fundamentalisms and racist mentalities. If critical thinking has any meaning in such difficult times, it is to be found in attempts to show that another future, one based on solidarity, equality, and justice, is possible.

There have been times when utopian visions seemed the most appropriate way to illustrate a radically different future. And surely, criticism of the present was their propelling force. Realism and pragmatism have always been extremely strong opponents of utopian thinking, and their power to convince people that the experienced reality is the only one possible is always augmented by the ruling elites.

Moving forward we need something more than visions. We may argue that concrete critical ideas for an equalitarian future will provide a realist alternative to the utopian nightmares of pervasive capitalism. We can dream of a different future by constructing it in, against, and beyond the unjust societies we live in.

This book is meant to be a modest contribution to the study of existing struggles that gesture towards an emancipated and emancipatory society. It combines critical thought with concrete experiences, the power of political imagination with the inspiring thrust of acts that produce new relations between people. A large part of it is focused on criticizing obsessive efforts to defend identities which, more often than not, trap people in roles and habits that prolong their attachment to the dominant values of individualization. The core argument of the book is developed around the issue of otherness: how do we deal with otherness in ways that produce exchanges and encounters without effacing differences and without merely establishing tolerance?

By carefully studying the inventiveness of people in struggle, as well as the potentialities hidden in many everyday routines and habits, this book suggests that experiences and symbolizations of space play a crucial role in the construction of bridges towards otherness. Differences that are either augmented in order to be exploited (as the differences between locals and immigrants) or effaced so that possible resistances are eliminated (such as the differences between "Western" and Indigenous value systems) need to be offered the possibility to negotiate on an equal basis in the search for a shared world.

This is where the idea of the city of thresholds becomes not just one more smart term for something but an emblematic condensation of a different social world of human emancipation. Thresholds unite as they separate. Thresholds mark areas of potential change. Thresholds create areas of communication out of differences that do not cancel each other.

Today's important struggles arise out of collective experiences of deprivation and poverty as well as of stigmatization and discrimination. Indigenous peoples' struggles; struggles for collective and individual dignity in work, education, and health; struggles in support of different forms of sexuality, belief, and culture; struggles for the defense of common goods and resources; struggles for gender equality; struggles against the ruling elites who destroy nature (and us, as part of nature). All of these struggles need to explore bridges, thresholds, and passages between themselves in order to construct networks of solidarity and shared hopes.

All-encompassing plans for an emancipatory future have often turned into nightmares, possibly because the richness of practices of transition was either ignored or suppressed. Transition is not simply a means to an end; experiences of transition unleash potentialities of change that are experienced in the present. In place of borders between a capitalist present and a liberated future, today's struggles create passages towards an emancipating beyond. They show people—beyond those who participate in them—that another kind of social relations is possible. In small-scale thresholds towards the future, as in the everydayness of neighborhood relations based on mutual aid, as well as in large-scale thresholds like those briefly opened by the occupied squares movement or, more permanently by the struggles of the Zapatistas, the lives of real existing people become open to change. The search for ways to take hold of lives wasted in cruel divisive societies (if not in cruel wars) makes people inventive. As members of societies in movement, orienting this inventiveness towards the construction of thresholds might be our task. And sharing, as a multileveled process of equalitarian solidarity, will have to be invented anew—not only as a practice that defies antagonism and egoistic reasoning but also as a process of constructing alternative social relations.

Is the city of thresholds one more canonic utopia? Is it a conceptually neat utopia, perhaps? I hope not, because I experienced it in the Syntagma Square occupation in 2011and I keep sensing its flavor in everyday actions of mutual aid in crisis-ridden Athens. I also saw it emerging previously in the heterotopias of the 2008

December uprising. And I believe we may trace its characteristics in the many spaces of contemporary urban commoning that develop within and against the city of enclaves.

Approaching otherness and creating shared worlds may indeed be developed through concrete urban experiences. Otherwise, dreams, no matter how urgently needed, tend to cover up reality. To explore the possible existing beyond capitalism and domination, we might need to develop new ways to enact the possible. Not in enclaves of heroic otherness but through metastatic thresholds in which human liberation is developed and tested.

Athens
March 2018

Introduction:

spatiotemporal thresholds and the experience of otherness

While attempting to consider the role space has in the potential emancipatory transformation of society, radical thinking and action tend to take for granted that space contains, delimits, and thus identifies social life. Spaces of emancipation are mostly envisaged either as freed strongholds to be defended or as enclaves of otherness. It is important, however, to think of space not as a container of society but as a formative element of social practices. Imagining a different future means trying to experience and conceptualize spatialities that may help create different social relations.

People experience space but also think through space and imagine through space. Space not only gives form to the existing social world (experienced and understood as a meaningful life condition), but also to possible social worlds that may inspire action and express collective dreams.

Seeking to explore, then, the ways space is potentially connected to processes of emancipation we cannot be satisfied with the discovery of alleged "spaces of emancipation." If emancipation is a process, it has to generate dynamic transformations and not simply institute defined areas of freedom. Spatial characteristics rather than concrete spaces become the focus of such an exploration. It is exactly at this level that the idea of threshold emerges to convey the spatial dynamics of emancipation. As will be shown, thresholds mark and give meaning to the act of crossing as productive of change.

This book's main argument is that emancipatory spatiality emerges in the creation and social use of thresholds. Social struggles and movements are greatly influenced by the formative potentialities of thresholds. Fragments of a different life, experienced during the struggle, take form in spaces and times with threshold characteristics. When people collectively realize that their actions are becoming different from their usual collective habits, then encountering boundaries becomes liberating.

It is in everyday encounters with otherness that people develop an art of negotiation based on the collective creation of in-between spaces, i.e., thresholds. During periods of liberating change, this art is practiced to its maximum potentiality. Struggles that implicitly or explicitly aim at changes in common life may merely create temporary enclaves of otherness. However, otherness may also be experienced as the inhabiting of in-between spaces and times, i.e., thresholds. In a self-organizing neighborhood these spaces and times are created in assemblies, demonstrations, or common meals. In a rebellious Zapatista municipality, thresholds become the means to invent new tactics of collective self-determination.

Encountering otherness can be potentially liberating as long as it invents passages from self to other. This means approaching otherness as a process rather than a state. Movements need to investigate an "art of doing" that helps people discover, create, and appreciate otherness. We can think of the city of thresholds as the always-emergent work of a collective effort to create a liberating future. An emancipated "public culture" will hopefully be created out of these thresholds to otherness, bonds of solidarity, and new forms of common life.

Beyond borders

Many assume the imposition of boundaries in human settlements is a natural phenomenon. Observing animals in the process of defining their territory, some suggest that a kind of natural will compels marking boundaries of an area where a single being or group reigns supreme. Territoriality appears as a natural need arising from the urge to survive while fighting against enemies or rivals. Thus, the demarcation of an area goes hand-in-hand with its description as a potential site of fighting. Although the act of marking out an area seems to be an attempt to ward off a fight it necessarily constitutes a declaration of war.

However, humans create settlements not only to define boundaries in order to secure a community that senses the hostility of the surrounding environment; boundaries are also crossings. An often-complicated set of ritual acts, symbolic gestures, and movements accompanies the crossing of boundaries. Invasion is only one among many other possible ways to cross the borders. So we could agree with Georg Simmel that man is not only "a bordering creature" but also the "creature who has no border" (Simmel 1997a, 69).

The creation of an enclosure, in Simmel's words, contains the "possibility at any moment of stepping out of this limitation into freedom" (ibid.). If the bridge and the door materially exemplify this ability to separate and connect at the same time—since "the human being is the connecting creature who must always separate and cannot connect without separating" (ibid.)—then we must begin to understand bordering as an act that contains many possible meanings. It is not only the declaration of war on otherness but also the possibility of crossing the bridge towards otherness. It is not only hostility but also, perhaps, negotiation.

An exile, always feeling away from home, would probably describe an emphatically characteristic border consciousness. In the words of an activist who was forced to leave South Africa: "Indeed, the experiences and products of exile could be a dissolvent of border consciousness. It could be a way of reconnoitering, shifting and extending the limits" (Breytenbach 1993, 76).

An exile understands that borders possess the power to cut people off from the places that define them, their history, and their identity. But while away and not permitted to come back, the exile realizes that identity is not a totally circumscribed area marked by a permanently identified structure of characteristics.

Identities constructed in exile assimilate new experiences, discover new criteria, and check new targets. Identity thus becomes not an area defined by a boundary, but—to use a Bakhtinian term—it assumes a "chronotopic" quality (since it is being shaped inseparably by spatial and temporal indicators). Identity in exile is not only open to otherness, it is forced to face otherness.

Of course, the opposite experience is also possible. In a foreign land, an exile might attempt to seal off their identity. This attitude will freeze their identity in an imagined state of unpolluted innocence. Travelling mentally towards an imagined homeland, this exile is always absent, creating around themself boundaries even more rigid than those they have escaped or been expelled from. Fighting to preserve this small imaginary enclave of sameness from imaginary or real invasions, an exile of this mindset may thus strengthen the idea of borders as a site of clashing forces—forces that at the same time define and exclude.

What is it that the experience of an exile could reveal about border consciousness? Mainly that social identity is constructed through a process radically influenced by what could be called "the borderline of identity." This borderline can be permeable or extremely controlled, can be a limit or a starting point, a place to inhabit or the entrance to a no man's land extending between two opposing worlds that do not share common spaces, even when in contact.

The use of differing borders constructs the character of identity. A fixed and unambiguous identity is a closed identity with rigid borders. An open identity is one that that is enclosed in flexible borders offering meeting points with otherness. This kind of identity could, as we shall see, be described as possessing a threshold quality. Spatiotemporal thresholds would be the places where identities may negotiate encounters with otherness.

This line of thought would give new meaning to the words of David Harvey: "The relations between 'self' and 'other' from which a certain kind of cognition of social affairs emanates is always . . . a spatiotemporal construction" (Harvey 1996, 264). Indeed, not only because identities are understood as circumscribed areas defined by the quality and the specific place of their borders but also because concrete space and time relations make identities visible and materially effective. That is why the identity of persons or peoples can be forced to change via modulations of their spatiotemporal awareness.

Thresholds as social artifacts

As social constructions, different ways of defining and controlling space not only mirror different social relations and values but also shape them. Identities are not only sets of beliefs or ideas but are embedded in the social environment, influencing different practices and different ways of life, therefore producing material results. Studying different spatial arrangements as characteristics of specific societies one can discover not only the uses and meanings of space but also the logics of creating and sustaining different social identities.

Pierre Bourdieu observed that in societies lacking "the symbolic product-conserving techniques associated with literacy," social dispositions "are inculcated through an interaction of inhabited space with the bodies of societies' new members" (Bourdieu 1977, 89). Space then becomes a kind of "educating system" that creates what we have so far been referring to as social identities. But it is important to realize that such identities are the product of a socially regulated network of practices that weave again and again distinct characteristics.

So when Bourdieu studies the Kabyle house in 1960s Algeria, he does not study it as the material index of social symbols but rather as the sum of the possible practices that produce a world of values and meaning. The Kabyle house is a series of spatiotemporal conditions that define the meaningful movement of social bodies. The house endlessly teaches the body and is erected again and again as a universe of values by embodied performances.

To prove this double relation of the body with inhabited space in the creation of space's symbolic attributes, Bourdieu chooses to observe the symbolic function of the house's main door. This threshold is the point where two different worlds meet. The inside is a complete world belonging to a distinct family, and the outside is a public world where the fields, the pastures, and the common buildings of the community lie. The threshold acquires its meaning as a point of both contact and separation through the practices that cross it. These practices create the threshold as meaningful spatiotemporal experience, depending on who crosses it, under what conditions, and in which direction.

In Bourdieu's example, men cross the threshold of the main door only to leave the house, to go to the fields where they belong, facing the light of daybreak as the door faces east. Women cross the main door only to enter the house facing the wall opposite the main door called the wall of light. Both men and women perform their acts "in accordance with the beneficent orientation, that is from west to east." And this is possible, as Bourdieu demonstrates, because the threshold establishes a symbolic change of the orientation of the house; that is, in its relation to the outer space. The threshold then "is the site of a meeting of contraries as well as of a logical inversion and . . . as the necessary meeting-point and crossing point between the two spaces, defined in terms of socially qualified body movements, it is the place where the world is reversed" (Bourdieu 1992, 281–282).

As in the case of the Kabyle house, the spatiotemporal experience of the threshold is produced by this potential communication between two different opposing worlds. Existing only to be crossed, actually or virtually, the threshold is not a defining border that keeps out a hostile otherness, but a complicated social artifact that produces, through differently defined acts of crossing, different relations between sameness and otherness. If inside and outside communicate and mutually define each other, then the threshold can be considered as a mediating zone.

The anthropologist Victor Turner, following Arnold van Gennep, has described these in-between lands as possessing the status of liminality (from the Latin word *limen* = "threshold"). The condition of liminality is characterized by the construction of transitory identities. In Turner's words, "liminal entities are neither here nor there; they are betwixt and between the positions assigned and arrayed by law, custom, convention and ceremonial" (Turner 1977, 95).

Every passage creates the conditions of a threshold experience that is essentially the suspension of a previous identity and the preparation for a new one. Passing through a threshold is an explicitly or implicitly symbolic act. It is, therefore, also a gesture towards otherness: not only spatial otherness, as in the case of emerging from a house into the outside world, but also temporal otherness, as in departing from the present for a more or less unknown future.

"Rites of passage," as van Gennep has named them, accompany the passing of *initiands* from one social identity to another, and most of the times are connected with a ritually executed crossing of spatial thresholds (van Gennep 1960, 26). If this act of venturing towards otherness is performed in and through thresholds, couldn't we assume that thresholds are the place of negotiation with otherness? Thresholds can be the schematic system through which societies symbolically construct this experience of negotiation and, at the same time, materially allow the negotiation of identity to take place.

Approaching otherness

Approaching otherness is a difficult act. In all societies, it is represented as full of symbolic and material dangers. But approaching otherness is also a constitutive act of every social encounter. Every society or social group would appear to be characterized by the ways it controls and formalizes these acts of encounter. If the encounter is considered only as a necessary step to verify and deploy hostility between groups of people, then the act of crossing borders will only be an act of symbolic or actual war. This form of encounter characterizes communities that describe everything outside of them as potentially hostile. It is not by chance that these communities build shelters protected by material or symbolic walls with drawbridges that are drawn most of the time. Contemporary gated communities are an obvious example of such an attitude.

If, however, the encounter is part of an effort to embrace otherness without an intermediary phase of mutual recognition and negotiation gestures, we may end up with a virtual extinction or assimilation of otherness. In contemporary consumer culture everybody is forced to be on the move, chasing ever-new products, ever-new sensations. As Zygmunt Bauman points out: "Consumers are first and foremost gatherers of sensations" (1998, 83). What appears a new desirable sensation is a kind of fabricated otherness. Fabricated by the continuous, consumer-oriented education of the senses in the media and advertising images. Towards such an otherness, the citizen-consumer is all too eager to cross the borders. And with a similar attitude, guided by desire-propelling exoticism, the consumer assimilates otherness while touring in a foreign land, only to add new sensation-trophies.

In order to approach otherness in an act of mutual awareness, one needs to carefully dwell on the threshold. In this transitory territory that belongs to neither of the neighboring parts, one understands that it is necessary to feel the distance so as to be able to erect the bridge. Hostility arises from the preservation and increase of this distance while assimilation results from the obliteration of distance. Encounter is realized by keeping the necessary distance while crossing it at the same time. The wisdom hidden in the threshold experience lies in the awareness that otherness can only be approached by opening the borders of identity, forming—so to speak—intermediary zones of doubt, ambivalence, hybridity, and negotiation. As Richard Sennett remarks: "In order to sense the Other, one must do the work of accepting oneself as incomplete" (1993, 148).

These zones may require gestures that are not performed as indices of identity characteristics but mainly as acts of approaching. Therefore, the gestures will have an equally hybrid status, describing an intermediary identity offered as meeting place. This intermediary identity is perhaps what results from the "subjunctive mood" that Turner connects with liminality (Turner 1982, 84). Intermediary identities are performed only to test the other's will of contact. They are performed not to hide or to deceive but to offer ways to depart from a fenced-in self towards a self constructed through the encounter.

Sennett describes civility as the "treating [of] others as though they were strangers and forging a social bond upon that social distance" (1977, 264). If we understand civility as part of an art of building thresholds between people or social groups, then we can agree with Sennett and his defense of a new public culture. This culture would be characterized by this continuous effort to preserve otherness and to create in-between areas of negotiation. And a curious, difficult-to-define theatricality seems to be performed in such gestures of reconnaissance and mutual approach. Brechtian theatricality seems to dwell in thresholds. One departs from themselves to be an other. This temporary transformation is seen as a gesture—a *Gestus*, in Brecht's vocabulary—of seeking to understand what is other than him or herself. Theatricality is the common element in the behavior of liminal actors during rites of passage and contemporary strangers groping their way towards each other through a modern version of civility.

The human ability to become other is at the foundation of such an experience of a "subjunctive mood." This socially constructed ability helps people to meet others without forcing them into precast identities. Being able to become other, even if one returns again to one's former self, is being able to accept otherness and, potentially, a position from which to construct a relationship with the other as other. Isn't imagination after all this curious staging of reality that creates thoughts and feelings out of nonexistent happenings that are actually performed in the mind? And isn't this an exploratory encounter with otherness in its purest form?

An emancipating spatiality?

This book is divided into four parts that correspond to three inter-connected areas of research concerning the threshold spatialities of emancipatory processes. The first part is organized around the idea that contemporary urban space is discontinuous: to understand spatiotemporal experiences we have to work with concepts that may capture this inherent discontinuity. Chapter 1 explains how in this context, rhythm and exception are appropriate terms if we aim at finding not only the characteristics but also the potential-ities of the dominant urban model—that of a "city of enclaves."

The second chapter of this section reveals that both rhythm and exception are not only the means to establish a dominant spa-tial order but also forms through which spatialities of resistance are created. Focusing on experiences of the aftermath, exile, and immigration, this chapter explores spatiotemporal discontinuity as a possible ground of encounter with otherness. Otherness, un-derstood as a relative term, is shown to prosper in periods in which collective habits are destroyed or suspended.

The second part problematizes the encounter with otherness in the context of urban experience. Making use of Walter Benjamin's unfinished study of nineteenth-century Paris, the opening chapter attempts to understand the metropolitan experience as inherently dynamic and ambiguous, containing both nightmarish elements and liberating potentialities. Through his description of the bour-geois private individual and the flâneur, two distinctive attitudes towards public and private space are exposed. Both attitudes are compared in terms of their dependence on the manipulation of individualizing traces in metropolitan life as well as their par-ticipation in the creation of (private or public) "auratic" urban phantasmagorias. A precarious "study of thresholds" is evoked, considered as a knowledge constructed through the ambiguous experience of the flâneur-as-allegorist. This study explores the dynamics of urban experience by pointing to the revealing trace-aura dialectics that permit the surfacing of a third, in-between element: the threshold. A "city of thresholds" thus describes the possibility of a "redeemed" urban modernity.

The next short chapter focuses on walking, considered as a practice that exposes the experience of otherness in the city, to further explore the spatiality of threshold. Porosity becomes a spatial quality, passages become spatial artifacts, and the act of crossing creates thresholds and activates threshold potentialities.

The following chapter presents one of the most critical points of the book's argument: thresholds mark processes of transformations of social identity. Anthropology has theorized the difficult relationship between self and other as a culturally determined relationship. Approaching otherness (cultural as well as historical) is a crucial problem in social sciences and is equally so in the tactics of habitation. Having an appropriate distance of encounter is necessary for differences to persist without blocking negotiation and mutual understanding. The ability to recognize the appropriate distances in time and space critically influences the theatricality of social interaction. This ability is acquired and improved in the varied conditions of threshold creation. The in-between space of thresholds is explored in this chapter as a potential stage on which encountering otherness means visiting, rehearsing, testing, and exploring it.

The third part of the book brings together the findings of the two former parts to reveal the importance of threshold in understanding the spatial aspects of emancipating practices. The first chapter of the third part focuses on the threshold character of heterotopia. Reformulating Foucault's definitions of heterotopia, we can consider all spatial experiences that "rehearse" a future of human emancipation as heterotopic. Beyond and against the city of enclaves, heterotopic spaces mark thresholds in space and time where dominant order and control are questioned.

Testing the idea of heterotopias, understood here as thresholds towards radical otherness, the remaining chapters analyze the words, actions, and practices of two exemplary cases where collective identities were put into crisis: the Zapatista rebellion and the December 2008 youth uprising in Athens. Both cases are instructive of how multiple and ambiguous collective experiences—heterotopic experiences—connect with threshold theatricality to produce heterotopic spaces inside and beyond dominant capitalist spaces. This is what a potential city of thresholds may look like.

The social experiments that take place in heterotopias essentially construct the thresholds of otherness that lead into the future. These thresholds, these heterotopias, are bound to the twists of social change. In them, the radical otherness of human emancipation is confronted, approached, and explored. Think of the Paris Commune of 1871, think of the settlements of the *pobladores* [squatters] in the Chile of Unidad Popular, think of the Lacandon Jungle as a Zapatista heterotopia, or, perhaps, think of the streets of Seattle, Genova, or Athens at the time of huge social protests. All of them are temporary thresholds, all of them are heterotopic gestures towards an emancipating otherness. The city of thresholds becomes the spatial equivalent of collectively inventing the future.

Part I

Exemplary metropolitan rhythms and the city of enclaves

Rhythms, social practices, and public space

The idea that city-space does not simply contain social life but also expresses social values necessary for social reproduction is well documented in the social sciences. This idea underlies specific forms of social knowledge, for example, that of real estate vendors, municipal technocrats, advertising experts, and politicians.

The following questions can be useful in drawing a very different (or perhaps complementary) perspective: in what ways can the city-space express and support practices and values that are different or even opposite to the dominant ones? If space is formed by forces of reproduction can it also be formed by forces of resistance? What can we learn from spatialities in which social reproduction fails? Can we discuss how spatialities mold alternative cultural values? Are there spatialities in which new hybrid forms of public culture emerge?

To be able to search for such different spatialities, we must be able to locate practices that appear to secrete, express, or use spaces differently. We need to explore city-space by locating its dominant characteristics and its points of rupture. We must be able to establish where those characteristics are disputed, suspended or reversed.

The contemporary crisis of public space offers a useful starting point for our discussion. What is at stake here is not simply the actual or potential use of existing physical configurations but the ways space is created through practices of habitation and shared forms of projection (e.g., collective memories or dreams). Public space can be understood as a coordinated system of spatial distinctions that correspond to social distinctions (cf. Bourdieu 2000, 134). But we cannot effectively understand public space without observing social relations, and their political mediation, as produced and interpreted by social actors.

We need concepts for the ways public space is "performed" in everyday practices, ones that can reveal changes to spatial forms and in spatial practices. Those concepts must be suitable for capturing transformations in the public character of public space that leave no marks. How can we conceptualize temporary constructions, such as for instance the "red zones" defined as no-go areas in the exceptional circumstances of world leaders' meetings, only to be removed shortly afterwards? These spatial transformations affect public space even when they seem to be absent. How can we discern their possible or actual mutations?

In order to answer these questions, we need to integrate time and public space: to make a new social-space time. This is not simply the empty time of clocks but the socially meaningful time of performed practices. In the ongoing transformation of metropolitan public space, red zones are conceptualized as constructions of this radically new social space-time. Through the performance of red zones, a new model of citizenship and governance is enacted.

The logic of red zones

When Pierre Bourdieu insists that there is a distinctive "logic of practice," which is different from the logic we employ to interpret practice, he stresses the inherent temporality of every meaningful social action (Bourdieu 1977). Revealing the "fallacies of the rule" that tend to reduce practices to cause-and-effect relations, he shows how practices make use of time intervals. Practices, as series of interrelated acts, are defined by their tempo, by the way they unfold in time, and the ways they employ and simultaneously reproduce socially meaningful distances in time. Anthropologically, "making use of time" means understanding how rhythms of practices ensure a strengthening of human social relationships and how individual or collective performances can be based on differentiating variations of dominant rhythms. The return of a gift, for example, establishes a variable rhythm of reciprocity that can affect contestable power relations. Ritual acts can in general be considered as communal manipulations of social rhythms, despite the fact that these acts often appear focused on natural rhythms.

Rhythm seems a promising concept to connect a theory of practice with a meaningful performance of time and space. We can borrow this defining statement from Henri Lefebvre's "rhythmanalysis" project: "Every rhythm implies a relation of a time with a space, a localized time, or if one wishes, a temporalized place" (Lefebvre 1996, 230). Metropolitan experience can be understood as differentiated practices of habitation performed in distinct rhythms.

How can we understand places in which collective decisions are being negotiated (ancient agoras, post-1789 National Assemblies, modern forums, etc.) without knowing the rhythms of the assemblies, the connection of social rhythms with production rhythms, the interdependencies of these rhythms, and so on?

Using the concept of rhythm, we can understand the qualities and characteristics of public space that are created through recurrent social practices. Rhythmicality is a way of understanding the present and the future as being punctuated by defining repetitions. Space becomes a socially meaningful artifact in the process of being "temporalized" through inhabitation rhythms.

If we follow Lefebvre, there are two forms of repetition that define two major types of rhythm: cyclical rhythms and linear rhythms. "Cyclical rhythms" can be considered as the ways through which recurrent natural phenomena appear to obey laws of rhythmical repetition. These laws make them predictable and therefore socially usable. Cyclical rhythms have "a determined frequency or period" (Lefebvre 1996, 231). There is a tendency to identify these rhythms with traditional societies where social life is organized and understood as repeating itself. Social rhythms follow the rhythms of the seasons and their corresponding productive duties.

In his famous distinction between cold and hot societies—the former lacking the idea of history and therefore enclosed in a constantly self-repeating universe—Claude Lévi-Strauss considers rituals "a machine for the destruction of time." Alfred Gell is perhaps more accurate in noting that in such societies "it is not time that is destroyed, but its effects" (Gell 2001, 27). Cyclical rhythms use the experience of time in a way that coincides with the image a certain society has of itself. Cyclical rhythms produce social artifacts. The inhabitants of cyclical rhythms do not merely pay attention to the passage of time and its effects, but they give it specific social meaning by connecting the recurrence of social acts with specific forms of social reproduction.

"Linear rhythms," according to Lefebvre, are "defined by consecutiveness and the reproduction of the same phenomena, identical or almost at more or less close intervals" (Lefebvre 1996, 231). In other words, "the linear is routine" (ibid., 222). Regulated work rhythms (mechanical as in hammer blows or bodily, as in rowing) appear as linear rhythms that can be extended infinitely.

In modern societies, a concept of time connected with historical conscience can be attributed to a linear conception of time. This time is "empty" and "homogeneous" (Benjamin 1992, 252) because what defines it is the linear rhythmicality through which time is measured. The everyday experience of time regulated by clocks and routinized in measured, repeated acts, can only have quantitative historical differences. With this framework, we can speak of an alleged "tempo of history" speeding up.

In modern societies, the myth of novelty is offered as a substitute to the experience of routines. Rhythmicality is banished as restraining and anonymous, whereas originality appears as the true mark of identity. Yet, imposed working and living routines are methodically regulated. Imposed order in time and space is half-concealed behind a well-calculated randomness. In its prototypical form, this condition resembles the structure of the advertising message: you are urged to buy something you know is produced in massive numbers, by being convinced that it was created "especially for you." Your identity is supposedly verified and created through this act of buying.

The partitioned city and the "framing" of identities

In contrast to the supposedly modernist quest for universal order, public space in the "postmodern" metropolis appears to embody chaos and randomness. These characteristics have been elevated to key positive attributes of emerging urban environments. Privatization, and the consumer ideologies of individualistic hedonism that accompany it, transform practices used to "perform" public space into practices of self-gratification. These practices represent the city as a collection of chances (and places) for consumer satisfaction.

As Peter Marcuse, among others, has shown, the "postmodern condition" goes along with a new "partitioned city." Urban chaos goes along with a fragmentation of the city that is far from random (Marcuse 1995, 244). The contemporary metropolis is increasingly becoming a conglomerate of differently defined enclaves. In some cases, literal walls separate these enclaves from the rest of the city, as with large department stores and gated communities. Walls can also demarcate "pride and status of rule and prejudice" (ibid., 249). These are the invisible walls defining ghettos, suburban neighborhoods, and gentrified recreation areas.[1]

One of the basic attributes of the "partitioned city" is that it destroys the public character of public space. Public space, a creation of the practices that inhabit it, "is always contestable, precisely because whereas there are criteria that control admission to its purview, the right to enact and enforce those criteria is always in question" (Henaff and Strong 2001, 4).

The partitioned city is full of privatized public spaces in which public use is carefully controlled and specifically motivated. No contestation is tolerated. Users of these spaces must be checked and categorized regularly. They must follow specific instructions in order to be allowed access to various services and facilities. A shopping mall or a large department store, for instance, are such quasi-public spaces. A company-owned town or an enclosed community, separated from the network of public spaces that surround them (streets, squares, forests, etc.), controls local space by limiting its use to certified residents. Holiday resorts often exhibit former traditional public spaces in theme parks featuring rural or village communities. Public life is reduced to the conspicuous consumption of fantasized identities in a sealed-off enclave that mimics a "holiday city."

1. Loïc Wacquant's concept of "advanced marginality" attempts to understand contemporary ghettos as "isolated and bounded territories increasingly perceived by both outsiders and insiders as social purgatories, leprous badlands at the heart of the postindustrial metropolis" (Wacquant 2008, 237).

What defines these spaces as sites of "public life" is not the clashing rhythms of contesting practices (that create the political) but the regulated rhythms of routines under surveillance. The publicly exhibited identities of the users are enacted in accordance with those rhythms that discriminate and canonize them.

Social identities are performed in the quasi-public space of the partitioned city. The fact that different categories of people are allowed to enter the various enclaves and remain there is a critical indicator of their identity. Residential enclaves can exhibit recognizable collective identities, especially when inner or outer forces homogenize the residents. The suburban areas of American cities, the shantytowns of Africa, Latin America or Asia, the gentrified residential areas of different European cities, and the immigrant ghettoes all over the world equally exhibit visible urban identities. In these areas, public space is separated from the rest of the city and use is restricted to the members of the corresponding community of residents. Gated neighborhoods and impenetrable favelas take separation to the obvious limit.[2]

Identities are framed both spatially and conceptually. A frame is characterized by the clear demarcation of a contained space versus an outer space: what lies outside the frame does not contribute to the definition of the inside. Our experience of pictures, both in modern news coverage and advertising images, strengthens this socially inculcated intuition. A frame defines a situation, a subject, and eventually specifies information, attributing to it the status of a meaningful message. Framed messages are not connected to each other. Advertising messages float all around us on top of buildings, in magazines, and even on human bodies. News photographs appear next to each other in temporal or spatial jux-

2. For Teresa Caldeira, contemporary São Paulo, one of the most segregated great cities in the world, is characterized by "a new pattern of urban segregation"; "the fortified enclaves . . . are privatized, enclosed, and monitored spaces for residence, consumption, leisure, and work" (Caldeira 2008, 65).

Adjacent enclaves of rich and poor: Paraisópolis, São Paulo and Rocinha, Rio de Janeiro.

taposition, producing the image of a fragmented—or should we say partitioned—world. Framed identities correspond to the experience of a partitioned urban space where residential enclaves appear—or rather are fantasized—as completely independent of their surrounding public space.

The contemporary metropolis presents itself to its inhabitants as a network of flows rather than a structure of places. As Castells has shown, the "space of flows" constitutes the dominant ideology's structure of distribution of function and power in contemporary society (Castells 1996, 428). "The new dominant ideology" Castells explains, insists on "the end of history and the supersession of places in the space of flows" (ibid., 419). However, there still exist, albeit ideologically determined, experiences and practices of places as identity supporting spatialities. Besides describing a life divided between parallel universes (space of flows versus space of places), Castells is careful in describing an essential link between the mobility of managerial elites and their need to inhabit secluded enclaves, "establishing the 'in' and 'out' boundaries of their cultural political community" (ibid., 416).

The experience of urban enclaves appears only as an exception in a city where movement prevails over localized inhabitation routines. But, is this really so? First, we must distinguish between those for whom movement is a privilege and those for whom movement is an obligation (Bauman 1998). We must also distinguish between different kinds of movement, defining in each case the horizon that limits them. Is it inside an enclave, traversing the city, connecting home with work, connecting significations of status around the world (as in the case of travelling managers or academics), etc. (Castells 1996, 417)?

It is important to observe how each occurrence of potential or actual movement influences the formation of different urban identities. Not all identities become temporary because somebody is on the move; some of them are fortified when performed in transition. For example, the successful businessman or international politician. In this case, a spatial frame is also a defining structure. Even though these identities are not circumscribed by the space in which they are performed, a series of well-defined enclaves constitutes the urban space of businessmen and politicians. This series of enclaves (corporate buildings, select restaurants, lobbies, and so on) constitutes a topologically functional frame outside of which the rest of the city appears almost nonexistent.[3]

There is a whole range of contemporary urban spaces where the rules of urban identity formation do not seem to apply. People are always passing through such spaces, yet no one understands them as locations that define their inhabitants. In airports, supermarkets, motorway service stations or hotels, an apparent and generalized anonymity seems to prevail. Most people are in transit as if their lives were unfolding "in parentheses."

These places, where a solitary anonymity is performed, are nonetheless defining characteristics of contemporary urban identities. Those transit-identities of the motorway traveler, the supermarket shopper, and so on, construct the typology of the average modern city dweller. Explicit or implicit instructions for use always accompany these spaces, addressing each person individually, but eventually, as with advertising messages, they fabricate recurrent characteristics. Nonverbal messages are especially powerful, such as advertising images in department stores, company logos in fast-food restaurants or service stations. Transit identities are not the product of chance experience; on the contrary, they distill what is typical and recurrent out of what is contingent and personal in the experience of urban "non-places" (Augé 1995).

3. Bryan Turner understands "enclave society" as one in which "governments and other agencies seek to regulate spaces and, where necessary, to immobilize flows of people, goods and services" (Turner 2007, 290).

Clearly these identities are framed as well, enclosed as they are between socially identified spatial and temporal parentheses. This framing has something in common with the snapshot. No matter how arbitrarily framed, these pictures somehow lose their contingent character as soon as they are shown and appear as recognizable typical scenes. Family and vacation albums are full of such photographs: "In front of the Eiffel Tower," "Our baby walking," "Daddy's first fishing success," and so on. Arguably, modern urban identities are framed spatially and temporally according to practices that transpose the experience of the partitioned city into the experience of partitioned identities. Metropolitan enclaves of various kinds but are always perceived and performed as defining frames that seem to ignore the urban space that surrounds them. Actually, however, their status is founded upon their relations with the surrounding environment and these relations are regulated by concrete checkpoints.

Metropolitan enclaves are characterized by checkpoints. One must prove their innocence in advance, as Marc Augé (1995, 102) brilliantly remarks, in order to be allowed to use these enclaves. Checkpoints punctuate the city: you can see them in airports, office buildings, supermarkets and banks, clubs and theaters, and of course, in guarded public buildings.

Checkpoints are modular elements of a prevailing rhythm that produce a new dominant experience of "being in public." Checkpoints define distinct everyday routines for different categories of inhabitants of the partitioned city. Toll gates or subway turnstiles mark the everyday movements of many city dwellers. The rhythm of the supermarket cashier marks an everyday ceremony of shopping.

Collective and seemingly individualized identities are enacted in the process of participating in such rhythms. Even the temporary identities of the traveler or the purchaser are marked by the

"Advanced marginality" in Korogocho, Nairobi.

act of crossing identifying entrance points. There, one has to show his or her passport, debit or credit card in order to be allowed a seemingly liberating anonymity—"the passive joys of identity loss" (Augé 1995, 103).

We can easily discern in those new urban rhythms, regulated by checkpoints, the emergence of new linear rhythmicalities. These linear rhythms generate ceremonial practices of identity confirmation. No matter how functionally necessary those control points are, their existence requires the performance of practices devoted to ritual repetition. As in the case of "prophylactic rituals" (Turner 1977, 168–169 and 1982, 109–110), devoted to protection from unexpected natural disasters, checkpoints appear above all as self-evident protection from practices that are unpredictable, other, different—in other words, protection from "a-rhythmical" practices. Checkpoints appear to protect society from outside, foreign, and therefore hostile elements. They "normalize" rhythms.

A "state of exception" becoming the rule

Contemporary ideologies of security find fertile ground in our everyday addiction to normalizing checkpoints. What this mass obsession for security that is promoted throughout the world is adding to the status of metropolitan public space is the inauguration of a state of emergency with no apparent end. Checkpoints become metastatic, police blocks punctuate the city, public sites are heavily guarded, immigration controls are enacted everywhere. Contemporary wars, often generated by outside interventions to allegedly protect threatened populations, cause massive movements of people. Checkpoints are always there to identify, separate, and subordinate helpless people by ceaselessly searching for the "infiltrating terrorist." Security, elevated to the status of the most important goal, justifies the metastasis of control points as markers of exception. However, this situation is, in essence, a new model of governance in the making (Vecchi, 2001). The state of emergency turns out to be a test. New mutations of the partitioned city are justified by recourse to exceptional conditions that demand exceptional measures, such as those that suspend basic civil rights.

Agamben's (2005) idea of exception can be used to understand and conceptualize the contemporary city of enclaves. Central to this idea is an essentially juridico-political understanding of exception: exception must be compared to a rule. For Agamben, exception is not the opposite of the rule; it is the founding condition of the rule.

There is a historical component to this reasoning as well as a logico-mathematic component. Historically, the state of exception describes moments or periods during which law is suspended in the name of society's protection from internal or external crucial threats. During a state of exception, a sovereign authority is justified in taking such a decision to suspend the law in its promise to reinstitute law and order as soon as the threat is eliminated. This situation, Agamben argues, reveals what is essential about authority: the legitimate ability to decide when and for how long the law will be suspended. In this act, authority reveals itself to be the precondition of law and not vice versa.

During the state of exception, a very peculiar relation between law and power is revealed. It is not that naked power simply replaces the regulating force of law. Law is present in its suspension as a legitimate force, a power to impose certain actions and prohibit others, a power with the ability to punish. The force of law as a legitimate force is passed over to the executive power while law is simultaneously suspended. A kind of ambiguous zone of indeterminacy is thus created "where inside and outside do not exclude each other but rather blur with each other" (Agamben 2005, 23).

Agamben characterizes this situation as a "threshold of unde-cidability . . . at which *factum* [concrete events and acts] and *ius* [law] fade into each other" (ibid., 29). It is interesting to observe how and why Agamben employs the image and concept of the threshold here. The threshold appears as an intermediary zone where supposedly distinct areas—in spatial terms, inside and out-side; in juridical terms, law and anomie—lose their margins and "blur with each other." Had he used the image of border or limit, he would have described the state of exception as a situation of trespassing, of exceeding or crossing a limit. The exceptionality of the state of exception would have been conceived as the com-plete outside of law, the complete other of law. Agamben, how-ever, insists that the law is present in the state of exception as the legitimating element of a sovereign decision. Law is present in its suspension. In the threshold-like condition of the state of exception, opposing parts are co-present and indistinguishable (as their defining perimeters are replaced by a zone of indistinction) and thus no longer exclusive. In terms of the historical analysis of the exception, the threshold is an in-between period during which crucial differences (between law and anomie) are suspended.

There is, however, a certain inconsistency in using the image of the threshold in historical terms. If the period of threshold is an in-between period, "before" and "after" should exist as concrete and differentiated periods, their essential difference being created by the act of passage from one to the other. But the state of excep-tion is supposedly not a period that produces qualitative differenc-es and changes, rather, it is an intermediary period of difference during which a threat to the social status quo is eliminated. This period of difference mediates between two periods of order, that is, two periods that share the same defining characteristics.

We know from anthropology that the social experience of threshold crossing is an experience of change. This change does not have to be collectively created, as in an uprising or any other qualitative leap in terms of social relations. It can be a change affecting specific groups of people in specific periods of their social life. Anthropologists have provided us with many examples of spaces that periodically host ritualized transitions from one social position or condition to another. Famously, Arnold van Gennep has described "rites of passage" (van Gennep 1960) as those ritual acts connected with spaces that symbolize transitions. For example, from childhood to adolescence, from single to married life, from the status of the adolescent to that of the citizen, warrior or hunter). Ritual acts supervise the passage from one social identity to another, thus ensuring the overall stability of society and the corresponding social relations. In Agamben's threshold, however, there seems to be a kind of circular movement. The state of exception equates "before" and "after," to ensure that after this in-between period order is restored as before. The state of exception renders before and after indistinguishable.

In terms of a logico-mathematic analysis, the period of a state of exception presents itself as a logical paradox: opposing terms such as inside and outside, terms that are logically mutually exclusive as in set theory, have to be described as possibly indistinguishable. Agamben attempts to use a "complex topological figure" as the Moebius strip to represent this state "in which not only the exception and the rule but also the state of nature and law, outside and inside, pass through one another" (Agamben 1998, 37). In this image there is a slight shift towards a different understanding of this zone of indistinction. As with a Moebius strip, where one has to move (literally or speculatively) along the strip to discover that opposites "pass through one another," so in the state of exception a movement between law and lawlessness creates the dynamic situation of a temporary suspension of law. In other words, the logico-mathematical analysis of this threshold period gives to

Agamben's use of the threshold image-concept a dynamic component that is closer to the actual social experience of crossing thresholds. As we will see throughout this book, it is in the performed or virtual act of crossing that the threshold is constituted as a space of potentiality.

In Agamben's conceptualization of the state of exception this element should have been crucial, since it radically influences the understanding of a further antinomy inherent in the history of the state of exception: the exception becoming the rule. How can a temporary state, a state characterized by a temporary condition and legitimated as a critical part of the necessary rights of sovereign power, become permanent? And, since in terms of history nothing can be described as immune to change, what does it mean exactly to characterize a condition, a state, as permanent?

What Agamben probably has in mind is that in the temporary character of the state of exception, law and lawlessness must be equally present in the process of passing through one another. The zone of indistinction he describes should be understood as a mechanism rather than a state. Law and anomie are constantly compared during this period. Because the force of law is necessary for the state of exception to be imposed, the mechanism of exception has to remain at work, endlessly performing the law's suspension. In a way, law is continuously present while power suspends it. The zone of indistinction therefore is an active zone of blurring the differences. Because differences exist, differences are socially perceived and posited in order to be suspended. This mechanism's fuel, so to speak, is the legitimating temporariness. The mechanism works only because it constantly withdraws law from a situation where law is still regarded as the necessary force for ensuring social order.

Exception versus thresholds

When the state of exception becomes the rule, the mechanism turns into a "killing machine" (Agamben 2005, 86). We could say that in this case the mechanism is immobilized. The constant passing through opposing elements (spatial as well as juridical) comes to a halt. Instead of being an area of active comparisons, the zone of indistinction becomes an area where opposing elements coincide.

What Agamben wants to describe is exactly this "permanent" coincidence of law and anomie: suspension no longer needs to offer any justification. What the camp represents is the final obliteration of a crucial distinction: the distinction between exception and rule. Exception becomes normal. "The camp is the space that is opened when the state of exception begins to become the rule . . . a permanent spatial arrangement which as such nevertheless remains outside the normal order" (Agamben 1998, 169).

That the camp is a "permanent spatial arrangement" essentially means that it is no longer a zone of indistinction, given that the comparison between outside and inside (spatially as well as juridically) is no longer possible. "The camp is a hybrid of law and fact in which the two terms have become indistinguishable" (ibid., 170). There is a slight difference in expression that actually reveals a qualitative leap. If the two terms "have become indistinguishable" then the zone of indistinction as a zone where opposites pass through one another is stiffened in a state where the opposites cannot be differentiated any more. "Have become" describes a state rather than a process.

The camp is not a threshold state. Following Agamben's symbolism, the camp should not be characterized as a space of exception (as Agamben himself explicitly states) but rather as a space of normalized exception. The paradox of the camp is different from the paradox of the state of exception. The camp remains "outside normal order" (ibid., 169), but at the same time it constitutes and contains a localized "normality"; it is an exceptional law that holds only inside this gigantic enclave.

What is so terrible about the Nazi camps is that they were functionally organized as lethal machines. Administrative reason in its terrifying efficiency defined the logic of this enclave of mass murder. The Nazi camps were neither the first nor the cruelest machines of mass murder involved in civil wars, genocides or imperialist expeditions, but they can nevertheless help us to understand a specific urban-administrative mechanism through which "exception becomes normal."

When exception loses its threshold character, and becomes the rule, it also becomes a secluded enclave. For those spatiotemporally contained in the enclave, the law "outside" simply does not exist. For those outside this enclave, the enclave can be either fatal trap (if this enclave takes the form of camp) or a zone of protection (if this enclave takes the form of a secluded area of privilege).

The camp can be taken to represent the limit towards which the city evolves only if we accept as a crucial characteristic of contemporary urban life the inhabiting of disconnected and enclosed enclaves. Otherwise, the camp—considered as a model arrangement for defining and confining people without rights ("bare life")—has a concrete history that can indeed include today's detention centers for "illegal" immigrants (those treated as non-citizens). What we can gain from understanding the camp as a model is necessarily connected to our ability to distinguish between these two levels in the use of such an analytical model.

An urban enclave is a clearly defined area where general law is partially suspended and a distinct set of administrative rules apply. The force of the law is present in an enclave as a protocol of use. Experienced from the outside, i.e., experienced as an outside, every urban enclave appears as an exception. Exception is made apparent in all the forms by which access to the enclave is regulated: general rules or common rights do not apply; upon entrance one must accept specific conditions of use, specific obligations, and forms of behavior. It is as if the city, considered as the uniform locus of sovereign law, is replaced by an urban archipelago comprised of enclaves where exceptional measures define different forms of suspension of law.

Experienced from the inside, i.e., experienced as an inside, the urban enclave is a secluded world. It is defined by rules created especially for its inhabitants. Exception, to continue the comparison with the camp, is thus normalized.

An urban enclave is usually a carefully planned system of human relations regulated by protocols of use. While such protocols have the appearance of administrative or functional directions for use, they essentially constitute a localized legal system in place of a suspended general law.[4] Accordingly, urban enclaves are not simply places where general laws do not apply, but places where localized rules, having the form of functional decrees, normalize an exceptional status that becomes permanent.

Is there a specific urban order from which enclaves depart? First of all, urban order has not ceased to be a project to govern the contemporary city. Legal acts in support of zero tolerance politics are exemplary of such a project based on the reinstitution of a general law defining the status of urban citizenship. It is interesting, however, that this project is inspired by the regulating efficiency of protocols for the use of the enclaves. The city itself can thus be legally and administratively fantasized as a gigantic enclave. Order can also be projected as a system of delimiting obligations, as a

---

4. Atkinson and Blandy observe that gated communities are "characterized by legal agreements which tie the residents to a common code of conduct and (usually) collective responsibility for management" (Atkinson and Blandy 2005, 178; see also Minton 2009, 74–77).

restraint for those inhabiting privileged enclaves. Exception can be welcome to inhabitants as a defining mark of their privilege.[5]

Generally speaking, the construction of spatial as well as legal orders is always a process open to social antagonism. What seems to be a crucial characteristic of current administrative practices and logic is the acceptance of a dynamic condition of ordering. This is based on two premises: the localized order of urban-island enclaves and the regulating power of metastatic checkpoints which impose a partial and precarious order on the urban sea surrounding those enclaves.

Indeed, refugee and immigrant detention centers constitute a kind of containment that marks "a radical crisis of the concept [of human rights]" (Agamben 2000, 19). Perhaps what is more important is the fact that the camp as a model enclave of normalized exception metastasizes in every aspect of city life. We don't have to be refugees reduced to bare life to be treated as enclave-confined users. We are trained to accept as legitimate "site-specific" protocols of use without reference to general (or universal) rights. We tend to consider it normal that exception is organized in spatial terms as an area where specific rules apply.

We learn to adapt to exception without even considering what we live as exception. This is how "red zones" become normal: routine control procedures and limited access rules tend to characterize access to the city center or to specified areas guarded as potential "terrorist" (whatever the word is taken to mean) targets. Checkpoints and surveillance systems in shops have become normal. Body searches at athletic events have become normal as well. It is in this direction that the state of exception becomes a rule. It is not that we generally live in a state of emergency (even though

5. The world is a floating "residential cruise liner," the ultimate enclave of the super-rich (Atkinson and Blandy 2009, 92–110). "Moving out of public space, via gated communities and other secessionary modes of governance, has created places that are spatially embedded within, yet contractually outside many of the arrangement of state functions" (ibid., 108–109).

lots of people do, as for example the Palestinians and the Israeli people). Rather, it is that we are constantly deprived of a crucial characteristic of urban space which also happens to be a crucial characteristic of any legal culture: the ability and the opportunity to compare, to dispute by comparing, and to investigate the ways limits are imposed. Thresholds can be both spatiotemporal urban experiences and areas of actively experiencing spatial and juridico-political indistinctions alike.

If we are to investigate the liberating potential of the experience and conceptualization of thresholds, then we should clearly understand thresholds as always being crossed. A dynamic image of threshold crossing can help to locate the potential of change in the mechanism (and not in the state) of exception. If Agamben's use of the threshold image can only be taken to describe a state, then exception can only be understood as a trap. Exception, in this case, describes "a passage that cannot be completed, a distinction that can be neither maintained nor eliminated" (Norris 2005, 4).

It is important to understand the state of exception as a dynamic mechanism, which only once it's immobilized can be transformed to the setting of an exclusive inclusion (Agamben 1998, 177). In this context, Walter Benjamin's thought that "our task [is] to bring about a real state of emergency" (Benjamin 1992, 248), acquires an interesting meaning. Taken not simply as a historically specific appeal for anti-Nazi mobilization, Benjamin summarizes the task of creating thresholds in history. On those thresholds past and present are not connected in a linear way. The present is just one of the possible futures the past contained. Discovering hope in the past is the ability to locate ourselves in the past's unrealized potentialities. "Being aware of historical discontinuity is the defining characteristic of revolutionary classes in the moment of their action" (Benjamin 1980, 1236). Thresholds in history are created out of this awareness.

In this understanding of historical thresholds, the exception triggers a transformative disruption of normality. Exception, thus, can be the spatiotemporal condition of change, of difference. In place of the state of emergency's cyclical sequence of normality-exception-return to normality, in Benjamin's "real" state of emergency, normality is replaced by exception leading to possibility. Exception thus destroys normality instead of becoming its supporting mechanism.

Red zones as normalizing exceptions and the "city of thresholds"

Red zones appear to belong to these kinds of spatial formations that have nothing to do with the rhythms that organize public spaces. No cyclical rhythm seems to govern their emergence, no linearity calculates their presence in the modern city. Red zones instantiate a form of temporal conception which is not based on repetition, i.e., rhythmicality, but on exception. Red zones are erected in exceptional cases and represent the "state of emergency." Red zones though, are not as exceptional as they seem. Rather, they constitute "exceptional" cases of a whole category of urban rhythms that tend to define the characteristics of today's urban public spaces.

Red zones are only the extreme case of ubiquitous checkpoints in the city. On the occasion of a major meeting of world leaders, the city is divided into forbidden and accessible sectors. The new "forbidden city" an enclave "temporarily" marked by fences, walls, surveillance cameras, police barricades, searchlights, flying helicopters, and so on is becoming the image of a publicized utopia of complete security. On the body of the city, the mark of a new project of subordination is inscribed. All the more so, because the city is increasingly becoming ungovernable. Urban conflicts erupt in major cities and the police assumes the role of an "interior army." It used to be Beirut, Jerusalem, Belfast, Los Angeles, Paris or Rio; but now urban conflicts and riots, urban violence, and racial clashes are everywhere. As Agamben (2001) remarks, modern authorities tend to adopt the model of the infected medieval city, where zones of progressive control were erected, leaving part of the city to the plague while securing disinfected enclaves for the rich. In 2001, Genoa, with its prototypical red zone, appeared as an "infected city." The new world order, utopian and nightmarish, is based on zones of varying degrees of control, where checkpoints attempt to introduce the globalizing rhythms of neoliberalism. The utopia of absolute governance is tested at various scales in cities as well as on continents. Eventually, a partitioned globe is strategically designed to emerge.

Red zone in front of French embassy in Tunis, 2013.

Red zones are temporary constructions aimed at permanent results. As the "terrorist threat" (which, as a term, is designed to encompass any threat to the status of the new order) is constantly renewed, exception becomes the rule and emergency becomes canonic. While red zones appear as exceptional when compared to ordinary urban rhythms, they in fact inaugurate new urban rhythms in view of a heavily mythologized new metropolitan order. Exception thus becomes the model of repetition.

Jon Coaffee has revealingly shown how the economic core of London, "the City," has evolved into an enormous enclave defined by an urban "ring of steel" (Coaffee 2004, 276–296). As "counter-terrorist" urban policies have evolved from temporary responses to Provisional IRA threats and acts, to more permanent measures taken after 9/11, the City has gradually become an area "excluding itself from the rest of central London, through its territorial boundedness, surveillance and fortification strategies" (ibid., 294).[6]

Red zones deliberately dramatize threat as a recurrent exception. As with prophylactic rituals, what the red zones ceremonially act out is a demonized otherness. Those potential or actual trespassers, are described by the mere existence of the red zones as outsiders, not to be allowed in the "forbidden city." Law-abiding citizens are asked to comply with the measures, consenting in the suspension of their "right to the city." They are asked to participate in a ritualistic purification of the city, in the exorcising of the evil, which, as in most rituals, appears as both unnatural and beyond society. Red zones ceremonially describe the new citizen: just as the supermarket cashier (itself a checkpoint) defines the purchaser, the airport check-in defines the traveler, and the police blockade

6. An analogous security "enclavism" is occurring in New York, especially after 9/11. Security zones define both public and private corporate buildings in ways that destroy public space (see Nemeth and Hollander 2010).

sanctions the authorized driver or the legal immigrant, so does the red zone aim to define the new citizen. Always eager to abandon his or her rights in exchange for a feeling of security, this new citizen accepts a permanent state of emergency. The wall erected by the Israeli government in Palestine is only an extreme case of a red zone concretizing a permanent state of emergency, circumscribing through a series of checkpoints the social life of the new citizens.[7]

Red zones are purposely presented by the media as a spectacle that celebrates state violence as justified and effective.[8] The display of absolute control contradistinguishes the image of power created by the neoliberal mythology. No more leaders parading in open cars or shaking hands with common people. Modern politicians exhibit themselves mostly through the media, posing as benign, humane, but also determined. The images ceremonially reproduced by the red zones are images of exclusion and distinction constructing the profile of a quasi-feudal power that paternalistically promises to provide security above all. All those constructions of control, completely out of scale and functional only in the case of a civil war scenario, constitute a new fortress, a castle for the governing elites. This mediatized castle, however, is only the extreme case of the protected enclaves of the partitioned city (Davis 1992, 221–260).

In challenging the acceptance of red zones, the antiglobal movement has revealed the pedagogic use of these zones in forming the characteristics of urban dwellers. Their role in an emerging

---

7. The Israeli wall is indeed a "temporary" security measure that is becoming permanent. "The Occupied Territories are trapped in a time loop where temporariness becomes permanent and exception becomes the rule, where no reality is fixed, no rules are clear, and no legal definition is stable" (Weizman 2005, 241).

8. For Kurt Iveson (who uses as an example the red zone created in Sydney in September 2007 during an APEC Leaders Meeting), "physical regulatory measures . . . far from being kept secret . . . were endlessly circulated through a wide range of media interventions" (Iveson 2009, 243). The protestors also used the media to their own means, to interrupt, expose, and fight the red zones: they thus "combined actions in the street with action on the screen" (ibid.).

model of government remains to be actively shown. All of the movement's practices show explicitly enough the transformation of public space into a series of controlled enclaves culminating in the mediatized Castle of World Leaders.

To borrow a term from Edward P. Thompson, we can observe a "counter-theater" (Thompson 1993, 57, 67) created by people's symbolic acts of civil disobedience in front of red zones. Demonstrators may sometimes show, through the theatricality of a controlled clash, that red zones are actually drawing lines inside the society and not between the society and an external enemy. By doing so, they refuse to play the part of the plague in a sanitizing city and thus reveal that what presents itself as a prophylactic (protective) measure is in effect similar to those discriminating rituals of initiation that most societies use to define their members.

Citizens before the fencing politics

The identities of contemporary city dwellers are defined by frames but also act themselves as defining frames for those who have them. Identity borders are carefully defined and correspond to the defining perimeter of the spatial and temporal enclaves in which they are performed. Not only do checkpoints enforce the discriminatory effect of a fenced spatiotemporal perimeter, they also test urban identities in their recurrent performance constantly proving their efficiency in defining recognizable citizens.

Contesting contemporary identities would thus mean contesting their repeated performance enacted in framing enclaves. A different public culture, based on mutually aware and open identities, would need different spatial experiences. Public space would have to be transformed from a series of enclaves, indifferent to each other, into a network of communicating areas. A permeable membrane instead of a frame would have to indicate the perimeter of these areas. Instead of checkpoints that discriminate, passages that connect would have to ensure spatial and temporal relations as necessarily formative of interdependent identities.

Liminality, the experience of temporarily occupying an in-between territory, can provide us with an alternative image for a spatiality of emancipation. Creating in-between spaces might mean creating spaces of encounter between identities, instead of spaces that correspond to specific identities.

The act of recognizing a division only to overcome it, yet without aiming to eliminate it, might be emblematic of an attitude that gives to different identities the ground to negotiate and realize their interdependence. Emancipation may thus be conceived not as the establishing of a new collective identity but rather as the establishing of the means to negotiate between emergent identities.

From van Gennep's seminal study on the "rites of passage" (van Gennep 1960) we can borrow a revealing insight: societies have to instruct and guide their people when they change social status through crucial events in their social life. Birth, marriage, death of a relative, coming of age, entry into a professional community, army service, acquiring the status of citizen, warrior, etc., all mark specific identity transformations. As these transformations are crucial for social reproduction, and as they have to be combined with tests and the inculcation of relevant knowledge to those who are destined to change, societies devise ways to regulate those transformations and ensure that the process will always be repeated without threatening social cohesion.

Drawing from van Gennep's theory, Victor Turner has focused exactly on this threat: transformation already contains the seed of dissent, the seed of deviation. People experiencing changes connected with social identity transformation, people passing through an intermediary period during which they are being prepared for their new social duties, can possibly discover ways to challenge dominant identities. Especially in the process of abandoning former identities, often expressed by the creation of an in-between community of equals with no differentiating characteristics. In this space, *communitas* in Turner's terminology (1977, 169–170 and 1982, 26–27), there exists a threatening spark of collective rule transgression. In the experience of communitas, initiands become aware of the fact that power may suspend the rules of identity. They are not-anymore but simultaneously not-as-yet. Their social obligations and rights are suspended, but with this their awareness of the social order may arise. They will be able to see identities are social constructions and people can communicate and act together without them or by exploring ones different from those for which they are being prepared. Emergent identities are identities to be learned. That is why so often initiation through rites of passage is connected with impersonation and disguise.[9] Novices often dress as animals, wear masks, or paint their bodies to distinguish themselves from customary behavior and appearance. As they are obliged by ritual to strip themselves of any recognizable identity, they also have to prove that they are ready to attain a new identity status. Rehearsing identities is a strictly regulated procedure.

People inevitably acquire a very important social dexterity: to be able to become other, to be able to be in someone else's place. It is here that the power of inhabiting thresholds as in-between space-times lies. To be able to experience changes in identity, to be able to rehearse, test, check, and visit otherness potentially means acquiring the power to negotiate with otherness. For Turner (1982, 27), these initiating visits to otherness expose learned habits and can open identities to unexpected changes.

Recognizing, opening, creating, and inhabiting thresholds is an important characteristic of emergent emancipatory spatialities.

---

9. Specifically, Turner (1977, 95) writes about "liminal entities," "threshold people," and "liminal personae."

Opportunities for encounters with otherness—which activate comparisons, negotiations, and inventive transformations—are necessary for any attempt to go beyond existing social taxonomies and values. Throughout this book, the idea of a city of thresholds will be explored. It will be argued that we can describe a process of spatiotemporal creation through which emancipatory experiences may arise. Can we perhaps recognize glimpses of such a process in current urban mobilizations and demands? And, can we locate the potential or actual characteristics of urban movements that would support this view?

The fragmented and ambiguous experiences of protests that oppose the growing tendency to fence and control open public spaces in Athens might offer us the opportunity to answer these questions. Local authorities and the government aim to prove that Athens is safe for its inhabitants and visiting tourists. This was particularly evident in the context of preparing the city for the 2004 Olympic Games. In a localized version of an international security mania, allegedly "uncontrollable" public city parks were surrounded by tall fences, restricting access through gates that closed at night.[10] In the case of the Philopapou cliff, where some important ancient ruins are located, this was presented as an effort to protect them. The fences were mainly used to establish entrance prices to what was formerly open public space. Pedion tou Areos, a park in the center of Athens, was presented as a dangerous area needing to be controlled, while in fact it is a place where public life is rich and varied. Policing the park meant chasing stigmatized minorities, such as poor immigrants or homosexuals, out of the area.

Many local residents both in Philopapou and Pedion tou Areos demonstrated against the fences. In many cases people gathered outside parks and collectively destroyed the newly built structures. Through acts of urban civil disobedience, people joined together

10. See Samatas (2007).

to oppose the transformation of public spaces into controllable and discriminating enclaves. They equally refused to accept the privatization of parts of those public spaces (an arbitrarily growing athletic center in Pedion tou Areos or the large areas of Philopapou colonized by restaurants and coffee shops). The interesting thing about these mobilizations is not only the unpredictable acts of actually demolishing fencing constructions but also the diversity of people involved. No political party initiated these demands or acts, and neighborhood assemblies were organized with no formal or institutionalized support. In the Philopapou area, a few residents took the initiative to call for a neighborhood meeting. Five hundred people responded and in three cases (on November 3, 2002; March 10, 2003; and September 12, 2003) the assembly collectively voted to tear down the fence and promptly did so. Eventually, a loose network was formed out of various similarly mobilized groups aiming to coordinate efforts.

In these acts we see how an urban movement can form spontaneously in response to major governmental interventions in a neighborhood. An urban movement "makes urban demands which challenge existing policies and practices" (Pickvance 1995, 198). In these cases, the demands are not limited to a neighborhood enclave of outdoor public space but rather aim to ensure unrestricted public use of similar spaces all over the city. To quote from the declaration of the People's Committee for the Protection of Pedion tou Areos: "We want the park to be a free public space, accessible to all Athenians, easy to use, safe and beautiful." This statement condenses an approach to public space that does not limit itself to the protection of neighborhood green enclaves to be used by those who live nearby but invites all city-dwellers to enjoy them.

These mobilizations explicitly oppose the model of tourist-oriented public space that has already forced residents to leave gentrified areas around the city center, as with the Plaka and in Psiri.

Instead of contributing to local demands for security, policing the streets and eventually supporting homogenized collective urban identities, these movements create—consciously or not—thresholds in public space. Their forms of organization support the public coexistence of differentiated identities that aim at mutual recognition. Their action are focused on defending the essentially porous character of the perimeter of the spaces they aim to keep open to all.

From the city of enclaves to the city of thresholds

Might not we consider these anti-enclosure movements as part of a multifarious and sometimes even contradictory effort to oppose the partitioning of city space? The measures taken during the 2003 Greek Presidency of the Council of the European Union or during the 2004 Olympic Games pushed the policy of fencing and controlling public space to its limits. The city center of Athens had become a highly controlled area, with temporary fences in many cases made permanent while police blocks proliferated.

By actively refusing to accept the erection of temporary no-go zones (red zones), protesters expressed their opposition to the ongoing partitioning and surveillance of public space. These multicolored blocks of young activists of "alter-globalization" movements expressly show that public space should be where different identities are allowed to communicate, meet, exchange ideas and longings, and interact. A city of thresholds sometimes emerges when public space is occupied, organized, and made porous by all these different people. Both symbolically and practically, these groups create an open-to-all public urban space.

If a new form of governance is tested in the temporary-permanent construction of red zones, a new form of emancipating culture is spontaneously tested in public space. In the migratory and ephemeral practices of social movements oriented towards urban demands, this potentially emancipating culture is ambiguously performed. The more these acts of essentially urban protest spread in the city, the more we can hope for passages to replace metastatic checkpoints. Perhaps instead of the "bourgeois utopia" of completely secure urban enclaves (Davis 1992), or the fantasy of identity-conferring ghettoes, we can see the emergence of porous public spaces: the heterotopias. An open city is a city of thresholds (Stavrides 2002, 2007).

Perhaps, in the renewed project of social emancipation, we can replace the rhythms that define checkpoints with those that define turning points. At these thresholds a new concept of time will emerge. A new epoch is thus marked by a critical rupture in social time. Walter Benjamin calls this "messianic time." As we will see in chapter 3, Benjamin's concept of time is based on the spatiotemporal experience of thresholds. His study of urban thresholds can become part of the project of researching the liberatory potential of threshold spatialities. In this context, we can imagine that a new kind of social time awareness will emerge as the polyrhythm of collective identities secreted into spaces of encounter.

Inventing rhythms
and inhabiting exception

Inhabiting rhythms

Dominant rhythms and localized exceptions seem to prevail in contemporary big cities. Spatial discontinuities do not produce chaos or unpredictable spatial arrangements but, on the contrary, constitute a spatial order that tends to take the form of an urban archipelago. Can rhythmicality characterize forms of common life that divert from dominant habits? Can spatial exceptions create opportunities for alternative or dissident inhabiting practices?

When Walter Ruttmann released his film *Berlin: Symphony of a Great City* (1927), he could claim, in accordance with the modernist model of the "total work of art," that it was a cinematic composition of the rhythms of the city. The film attempts to capture everyday Berlin in the interwar period. He presents the different kinds of repetitive mechanical as well as human movements that characterize everyday urban life. The city appears to function as a gigantic machine with every cog and wheel having its own distinctive rhythmicality.

Ruttmann introduces into his film a very specific kind of documentary view. Putting an emphasis on movement synchronism, he not only interprets the city as a well-ordered spatiotemporal structure but also attempts to criticize certain aspects of mass behavior. A direct comparison with animal behavior is introduced in cases where mass behavior is reduced to analogous instinctual flock attitudes (passive as in cow and sheep herds or aggressive as in dog packs). Mechanic or organic, full of vitality or passive, creative or destructive, every observable urban rhythm has its role in an overarching synthesis: the city as symphony.

Even so, in Ruttmann's work there are notes of dissonance. The suicide of a young woman upsets the flow of traffic. Although it is a silent film, we can imagine certain sounds suddenly erupting: a cry, a commotion, an unexpected medley of disparate voices, a solitary splash in the river where the unfortunate girl falls to her death. From the inner workings of the repetition that defines and describes the rhythms of a large city, a temporary otherness emerges.

Is it perhaps that this unsettling symphonic reading of the city is indicative of the daily practice of living? Is it perhaps that we create this comforting feeling of repetition ourselves, reducing the unknown to what is already known, already experienced? We project continuity onto our experience of time, reinforcing our certainty about the succession of moments in time (Bachelard 2000, 19). In reality, however, succession is nothing but sheer irregularity, discontinuity. It is through our memories that we retroactively project continuity—a logical flow of succession—onto the past (ibid., 28–29).

Rhythm is a form of duration, in which the discontinuities are incorporated into a predictable sequence. In rhythm, continuity is generated because of the discontinuity that renders the sections comparable. Thus, life may appear continuous and uniform, but on the level of elementary transformations, life is wavelike.

The opening sequence of Ruttmann's film "compares" the natural rhythm of waves with the mechanic rhythm of a train arriving to the city. As Michael Cowan discusses (2007), modernist proponents of a return to organic rhythmicality (as opposed to the alienating dominant experiences of artificial "machinic" rhythms) used the image of the "undulating flow of waves" to describe natural rhythms as structured in a flow-like continuity (ibid., 231).

Rhythm, understood as undulation, is a formative element of experience. Rhythm has an impact on the manner in which the senses shape their relationship with the material world. Rhythm drives hearing, touch, and vision. The rhythmicality of breathing drives the sense of smell, as the rhythmicality of swallowing affects the sense of taste.

Rhythm is not simply repetition, it is a specific experience of repetition that is socially meaningful. For Lefebvre, "rhythms imply repetitions and can be defined as movements and differences within repetition" (Lefebvre 2004, 90). This may be interpreted as a schematization of the relationship between rhythm and time. The underlying idea is that this relationship may be represented in spatial terms. Movement combines points in space with points in time. Any sequence of movement is based on the fact that points in space as well as moments in time are distinct and unique.

When we attribute a repetitive character to movement, we consider those different points (understood as spatiotemporal unities, happenings) as similar. Nevertheless, we continue to experience them as discrete. Clearly, whatever seems to happen "again," always unavoidably and necessarily, happens, in fact, only once. Repetition as a socially meaningful diagnosis describes an inherently impossible condition. But, in its impossibility, diagnosed repetition represents a crucial human effort to understand the present and predict the future. Because the only thing that we actually know—albeit feebly—is what has already happened. Rhythm, despite the sense of similarity it conveys between what precedes and what follows, is based on the distinction between these two things, a distinction relating to their different positions in time and space.[1]

In recognizing rhythm as an active means of understanding repetition, Lefebvre points out the dialectic between sameness and otherness. Human memory enables us to recognize the rhythmical. Memory does not have a particular role to play at the extreme limits of linear, mechanical rhythm, because "mechanical repetition works by reproducing the instant that precedes it" (ibid., 79). However, when rhythm connects different time periods, memory is essential to retain the sense of repetition. In cyclical rhythms, it is memory that compares what has elapsed so as to identify the completion of a period, and therefore to identify periodicity. This ability to identify through comparison is essentially an ability to make difference the driving force of repetition.

This power of memory is what makes rhythm part of the process of creation rather than an impediment to creation. The rhythmic quality of a sound can indeed generate a sense of temporal order. In the same way, the rhythmic aspect of a texture can define spatial organization—for instance, a floor pattern. However, if the rhythm of perception is not defined in a linear way, if recognition of the periodic nature of a stimulus is already loaded with preconceived meaning, then we can discover or even invent rhythms in the process of experiencing and recognizing meaningful repetitions. We don't merely follow rhythmic instructions—rather, we are in constant need of rhythms in order to appreciate the meaning and form of social space-time.

1. In this context, Bachelard's idea of "quantum becoming" can be very helpful: "Qualitative becoming is very naturally, quantum becoming. It has to move through a dialectic, going from the same to the same via the other" (Bachelard 2000, 102).

This is the paradoxical social significance of rhythm: it incites collective behavioral patterns and simultaneously shapes specific individualizing habits. I repeat the way I light a cigarette, the way I blink when I look at you, the way I sigh or laugh. I repeat my mannerisms.

Children's relations to repetition can perhaps reveal the way in which rhythm essentially gives form to individual experiences. Children do not get tired of repetition—of repeated sounds, grimaces, and stories. But each repetition is already a variation, a discovery. Can we be mesmerized by a repetition of the same thing, as children do? Can repetition surprise us every time, like a new lease of life?

Walter Benjamin sought to recapture children's ability to see the city as a new place each time, to rediscover it by creating temporary worlds in their games (Benjamin 1985a, 315). Can rhythm offer us new opportunities to see again, to feel again, to think again about something we saw, felt, or thought? Perhaps, then, we can recognize the rhythmical quality of differentiation rather than repetition (Deleuze and Guattari 2004, 346). If our cities, our houses, the spaces where we live, do not merely exist but are different each time we experience them, then everyday life can actually be a place of potential creativity.

Comparison establishes relations intended to confirm repetition, but also relations that may seek new repetitions in place of others. How extended is the cycle of repetition? Who defines its limits? To what extent can regularity include differentiation in order to highlight that interim period when we are not sure at which point the cycle ends? And once we know the cycle has ended, which elements of what has happened before will be repeated? If we can imagine potentiality as a condition for breaking out of established habits, this is because we are trying to shatter certain expectations about repetition, not because we deny the expectation of repetition in general. Perhaps potentiality exists only as an expectation of a possible rhythm whose periodic nature is not yet apparent. Perhaps certain actions or events are experienced through the anticipation, or the hope, of their repetition. This is how we can manage our relationship with otherness. We can neither conceive nor feel absolute otherness or absolute newness. However, we can truly recreate our world by inventively recognizing its multiple periodicities.

Did Ruttman try to make a documentary film on interwar Berlin, or was his observation of city rhythms a way to reconstruct a deeper urban reality, almost in accordance with Lefebvre's rhythm-analytical project? Siegfried Kracauer, commenting on the film, believes that the contrast between natural and mechanic rhythms is limited by Ruttman's montage to a series of formal and structural correspondences devoid of any significant or revealing value (Kracauer 2004, 184–185). David Macrae, however, convincingly argues that it is the inherently filmic power to discover and read reality that is at work in the film. Thus "rhythms . . . reveal their own deeper realities" as they give shape to "the processes active throughout the broad ranging life of and lives within Berlin" (Macrae 2003, 269). This can indeed be a possible way through which the art of filmmaking can sustain a renewed awareness of the creative aspect of reading urban rhythms.

Habits, habitation, and otherness

The act of habitation seems to be constantly reaffirming a certain familiarity with the world. Recognizing a place as inhabitable, in the broadest sense of the word, means regarding it as an appropriate locus of habits. Place is therefore considered as relatively stable in its form or predictable and controllable in its changes. Habitation is indeed connected with habit. A certain kind of recurrence of practices, combined with a permanence characterizing spatial relations, appears to constitute what we can call inhabited space. Habitation appears to be sheer rhythmicality.

However, what if inhabitation practices are actually practices of appropriation in a constant confrontation with what always escapes prediction, with the spatial and temporal aspects of otherness? What if habitual practices are actually practices of accommodating to a recurrently emergent otherness? The future seems to be tamed through habit; but, is it really so? Can we expect that what we know and are familiar with will continue to be present the next day?

Our social education is not based only on establishing habits. Social reproduction would have been rather impossible if we simply had to learn and obey rules. What our education has to ensure is that we perform in different situations according to recognizable patterns. Otherness is thus a constitutive element of the process of behavior formation.

Can we then perhaps say that habitation is not only the establishing of habits, as the word etymologically suggests, but also the accommodation of what escapes habit? Accommodation is, after all, a word used to describe places that can be utilized as dwellings. An act of dwelling is an act of compromise, an act of settlement (in both meanings of the word). Specifically, it is an act resulting from a negotiation and, simultaneously, an act that creates the ground for future negotiations.

Memory seems to be a prerequisite for an act of inhabitation. But if we understand this act as inherently time-bound, a process rather than a set of habits, then memory must be much more than a sheer repertoire of prototypical acts to be repeated. Adapting oneself to varying circumstances might mean being able to compare circumstances. Rarely do similarities suffice to indicate paths of action. Analogies between circumstances are those that generate various forms of recognizable practices. Our socially inculcated ability to deal with otherness depends on these so-called "scheme transfers" from one part of our social experience to another. According to Pierre Bourdieu, "habitus, understood as a system of lasting, transposable dispositions" makes it possible for people to act in a variety of circumstances through "analogical transfers of schemes permitting the solution of similarly shaped problems" (Bourdieu 1977, 83).

Memory has more to offer these schemes than preformed molds into which polymorphous social reality can be rigidly classified. Memory provides the dwelling practices with forms of action, repertories of possible tactics actualized to deal with different circumstances. Memory develops the means for habits to be formed and transposed through analogy to different social contexts.

An "aftermath" appears to be a situation resulting from a decisive and usually disastrous blow to the flow of habits. This blow is connected to a quite literal suspension of habitation time. What we have in an aftermath is the awareness of a rupture, a stop, and at the same time, anxiety about the future. The experience of otherness seems to prevail.

Memory is strongly disconcerted when involved in a situation of aftermath. Available schemes usually get paralyzed when confronted with conditions that appear to be completely different from those already experienced by individuals or social groups. Memory, both individual and collective, has to accommodate a major traumatic trace that upsets memory routines, habits of practice based on recognizable schemes.

If, however, habitation practices are not simply the opposite of the experience of otherness, then we can discover, hidden in an aftermath, the possibility of a time-awareness already present in everyday life. The experience of time discontinuity connected with the aftermath is already part of dwelling practices. Habit is always imposed against the differentiations produced by time; it is always established in the process of defining time as rhythmically constituted. Memory, according to Lefebvre's rhythmanalysis, is essentially influenced by those diverse rhythms of social and urban life that constitute the present. "The succession of alterations, of differential repetitions, suggests that somewhere in this present is an order which comes from elsewhere and reveals itself" (Lefebvre 1996, 223).[2]

Humans weave time into a coherent medium of social reproduction. Their experience always has to deal with ruptures, turning points, and unparalleled circumstances. Let us imagine people in a situation of an aftermath, not as completely helpless in front of a totally and unbelievably new experience, but rather as suddenly confronting the social logic of time that characterizes their society. They might hurriedly attempt to bridge the gap between the past and the future that an unforeseen present has created, or they might start questioning themselves about the very foundations of their habits as practices to accommodate otherness. And this last attitude might provide them with the means to rethink how social conventions and schemes of behavior have formed dwelling practices as well as dwelling values.

What the aftermath is catalyzing is the awareness of the constructed nature of habits. The experience of one's world being disrupted or even destroyed reveals yesterday's habits as meaningless. The inherent artificiality of habits is exposed. It is not because of a generalized cynicism that prevails in human interactions today, as Paolo Virno suggests, but is due to a situation that lifts the veil of legitimacy supporting established habits. When this happens we are able to see "the naked rules which artificially structure the boundaries of action" (Virno 2004, 87).

2. Accordingly, "every rhythm implies the relation of a time with a place" (ibid., 230).

An experience of the aftermath: inhabiting a "state of exception"

The aftermath has to be a new spatial experience. For an aftermath to be experienced as a rupture in the sequencing of habits, new conditions of dwelling must emerge. Space has become other, it has become difficult to appropriate, strange. It is through space that we experience the time rupture that marks the aftermath. Spaces that used to be familiar become unhomely only to hypostasize time as other.

A certain kind of uncanny feeling might appear in the experience of an aftermath. If we are to accept Freud's hypothesis, "this uncanny is in reality nothing new or alien but something which is familiar and old established in the mind" (Freud 1975[1919], 24). The experience of the aftermath might produce a "return of the repressed" suddenly exposing the work of the unconscious, which is focused on hiding the fact that inhabitation is always a process generated by an emergent otherness. In a way, this feeling is the opposite of a generalized collective nostalgia for "home" produced, as Anthony Vilder claims, in response to the modernist campaign against the "unhealthy preoccupations" of memory (Vilder 1992, 64). Modernists tried to eliminate all those spaces and objects in the house that could potentially mediate an "unhealthy" relation with the past. Nostalgia does not reveal the existence of otherness in the center of dwelling practices. On the contrary, it fashions a mythologized essence of dwelling that only knows sameness, repetition, and safety.

We can perhaps try to understand the power that experiences of the aftermath have, their potential to upset the social regulation of space and time. We can do this by examining a specific case of aftermath that asks for new ways to deal with the spatiality of memory. Our case reveals that we need a reassessment of architectural thought and practice in the face of collectively experienced spatiotemporal ruptures. Are we to close the gap, preserve it, architecturally commemorate it or attempt to transform it by creating spatialities of a different historical awareness?

In Gyaros, a small desert island of the Cyclades, Greece, an exemplary collective experience of aftermath unfolded at the end of a devastating civil war. Starting in 1947, a huge concentration camp was constructed there, comprising five different settlements situated in neighboring bays. Barbed wire and guards separated the settlements, made of military tents and a few barracks.

Hundreds of inmates lived under extremely difficult conditions. They were forced to work on the construction of their own future prisons or simply bullied into carrying stones from the mountains to the sea as a form of torture. Having been accused of supporting the left-wing guerillas and the fighters of the National Liberation Front (EAM), these prisoners belonged in one way or another to the defeated of the civil war (Svoronos 1972).

Gyaros was conceived of as a prison-island for political prisoners. In the first period of its use (1947–1952) around 15,000 prisoners were kept in Gyaros. Most were transferred from urban prisons. Many of them were accused of participating in crimes they had never committed or were simply sentenced as "enemies of the state."

In the 1945 Treaty of Varkiza, the left-wing resistance agreed to be disarmed. However, violating the treaty, the new Greek army organized by the British explicitly supported right-wing terror. This politics culminated in the 1947 government's decision to outlaw all left-wing organizations. Martial courts passed sentences on many people in a virtual "state of exception" that remained effective at least until the end of the second phase of the civil war, when the Greek Communist Party decided to respond in arms. During this period, many were tortured and at least twenty died in Gyaros. Many others were transferred to die in prison hospitals.

Gyaros closed down in 1952 but reopened in 1955. It was shut down again in 1962 as a result of protests as well as appeals from abroad in defense of human rights mainly in Europe. During the military dictatorship (1967–1974), Gyaros was again used for political prisoners (6,000 inmates, including women) who were incarcerated there for almost a year. Once again besieged by protests, this time both in Greece and abroad, the prison and the concentration camp were shut down at the end of 1967. After briefly reopening in response to student mobilizations during the last year of the dictatorship, Gyaros ultimately closed down.

The winners of the civil war created in Gyaros a place existing beyond and outside the rest of society. Sentenced as "social enemies" and deprived of all of their fundamental rights, prisoners suffered in a "state of exception." The newly formed postwar Greek state was paradigmatically redefining the "boundaries" of legitimate action for its citizens. These "others" were to be excluded from society, therefore not protected by the laws that guaranteed their status as prisoners of war. Exception was used to illustrate and legitimate the state's exclusive right to violence. This is an exemplary case of the "voluntary creation of a permanent state of emergency" which, according to Agamben, characterizes modern "state power's immediate response to the most extreme internal conflicts" (Agamben 2005, 2).

The postwar Greek state was founded upon highly discriminatory politics that permeated public life and crippled civil society. The winners excluded anyone who dared to oppose them. The prisoners at Gyaros did not simply exist in an aftermath situation that equated to a collective "bare life," a term Agamben uses to describe the legal status of Nazi camp inhabitants, who have been "stripped of every political status" (Agamben 1998, 171).

No matter how traumatic the "exception" they were forced to inhabit, the prisoners at Gyaros secretly organized in ways that affirmed their values and dreams for a more just society.

In the everyday habits of the camp, life unfolded at two levels. Prisoners had to obey the rules imposed on them, and at the same time, they were tacitly creating their own rules and their own social bonds. If we accept James Scott's argument, dominated people invent ways of acting that have a double meaning, such as disguising "low-profile forms of resistance" behind gestures of conformity.

What Scott terms "infrapolitics of subordinate groups" can be attributed to the everyday habits of prisoners (Scott 1990, 19). A hidden solidarity produced spatialities of equality and mutual support. Collectively, prisoners were thus able to improve their dwelling environment. They even managed to build some kind of public space, such as outdoor stages on which recreation performances took place, which helped to raise prisoners' morale. These self-created spaces essentially differed from those functionally linked with the enforcement of discipline by the camp authorities.

Interviews of ex-prisoners prove that they were aware of a major rupture in their lifetime. What is interesting is that they managed to create, in a collectively written "hidden transcript" (Scott 1990), their own time of new collective habits. Their values in that situation of aftermath were tested in a new dwelling experience, in the organization of everyday life. Well aware of the exception they were living in, prisoners tried to test their own ideas about the future as different from the society that violently denied them. Their experience of rupture was projected upon a will to concretize the future as other—which means, restarting time.

The prison-island was meant to constitute a violently imposed spatiotemporal rupture in the life of the exiled. This rupture would construct a space-time of exception that could be prolonged arbitrarily. However, the exiles, projecting onto this incarcerating enclave their own vision for a liberating social rupture, have transformed it into a threshold. In their everyday hidden solidarities, they were opening holes and creating passages across every spatial and temporal perimeter that was punishingly controlling their life. While inhabiting exception, they were implicitly or explicitly fighting to make it permeable. It was a precarious and contradictory condition indeed. However, sparks of a different public culture became visible as thresholds opened the brutally imposed uniformity towards liberating otherness.[3]

Can space activate memories of discontinuity?

Recently, a research team of architects in the school of Architecture at the National Technical University of Athens became involved with the problem of finding ways to reconstruct the deserted Gyaros as a place of collective memory.[4] Interviews with survivors did not produce evidence of major heroic events. Rather, heroism was found in everyday acts of collectivity. In the various periods that Gyaros was used as a camp or secluded prison (such as during the 1967–1973 military dictatorship), people left traces of collective dwelling both in the improvised precarious constructions they used to live in at certain periods and in the buildings of the prison.

The great prison house that today looks empty and haunted, surrealistically dominating the contours of a small desert island,

3. Michel Agier has noticed similar practices in his studies on UN refugee camps in Kenya. He observes how people inhabit exception by creating new forms of sociality and by renegotiating collective identities: "The camp engenders experiences of hybrid socialization" (Agier 2002, 336). He insists, however, that there are unsurpassable limits which prevent the camp from evolving to a new form of city and which sustain in people a feeling of uselessness: "It is the liminality of all situations of exodus that gives a frustrated, unfinished character to this type of 'urbanization'" (ibid., 337).

4. In a research project financed by the Greek Ministry of the Aegean (2002–2003), information concerning the history of Gyaros camp was collected and projected onto maps, with the aim of discovering how memory refers to spatial indexes. The researchers proposed the construction of a network of "memory routes" through which visitors could "reactivate" the collective memory of the prisoners and participate in a landscape of human suffering. Members of the research team were: Annie Vrychea (project coordinator), Vica Guizeli, Vasilis Kritikos, Katerina Polichroniadi, and myself.

is just the empty cell of mundane everyday suffering. The memories that the prisoners retain are not events but rhythms of an everyday life resisting annihilation through the habits of collective dwelling. People remember how cooking was arranged by the prisoners themselves, how work was divided among them, how they secretly organized lessons of various kinds, or how they circulated information from the "outer world." Memories of a different dwelling culture mark the experience of the aftermath in Gyaros. In the paralyzing otherness of the camp, life continued in a different register. Imposed routines mingled with collectively chosen ones.

To recover the traces of collective memory, buried under a collective forgetfulness that has blurred for the younger generations the events and results of the Greek civil war, might mean trying to condense this past experience into a monument. Monuments tend to mark places by putting emphasis on events, acts, and heroic deeds. Monuments are "instruments of memory" since they constitute "rhetorical topoi," such as "calendar spaces set aside to commemorate important men and women or past heroic events" (Boyer 1994, 343).

A different perspective could be attained through emphasizing the ways events have altered the lives of people, rather than on the events themselves. If memory is to be stimulated by specific spatial arrangements, then one could search for a new spatiality that encourages the awareness of time ruptures. Pointing to the memory of discontinuity as it is experienced through a radical change in rhythms of social life, this spatiality has to "monumentalize" dwelling. Dwelling, however, cannot be monumentalized unless we completely change the content of the experience of the monumental. This would mean considering the incomplete and mundane constructions of a hard life, the traces of insignificant everyday acts, as memorable or worth preserving.

One should preserve the small low walls the prisoners have built to secure their tents from the strong winds. One should make it possible for visitors to recognize places important for the daily routines of imprisonment: the old fig tree where a prisoner was tied to be tortured; a well where one could hide for a while to rest; the remains of an electric station in which an improvised radio was hidden, providing access to hopeful news from the outer world; a series of outdoor washtubs; a detention spot where prisoners were exposed to the burning sun as a form of corporeal punishment.

Such monuments show how history becomes meaningful for people through experiences of discontinuity as well as recurrence. A possibility for temporal discontinuities to rearrange collective memory lies always dormant under experiences of extreme historic ruptures. What we need to remember from Gyaros is that people were forced to abandon the habits of their own memories. What we need to remember is that these people were forced to devise new habits for their survival and that these habits created a new collective culture. In this way, the mundane becomes monumental. Memories of discontinuity, as well as the experiences of discontinuity that characterize this period, mark a contemporary awareness. Such awareness might mean discovering in the aftermath both the devastating effects of a distinction between winners and losers, and the foundations of a conformism that marked civil society in a period that has demonized otherness. If we are to understand everyday life as flourishing in its constant negotiation with otherness, the experience of the aftermath at Gyaros can be highly instructive.

In the experience of the aftermath people are forced to suddenly become aware of time not as a flow marked by habits but as a series of turning points mediating differentiated rhythms. Every turning point, and especially the turning points that dramatically mark an aftermath situation, forces people to compare "before" and "after." If memory is fundamentally the locus of comparisons, and analogy is a form of comparison that attempts to reduce otherness to a recognizable similarity, then comparing "before" and "after" might mean understanding both past and present as open to otherness. The aftermath forces people to rework an interpretation of the past and realize that the experienced situation is not the only possible outcome of what has already happened.

Otherness is included in the past as potentially other futures that were not realized. A turning point, a crossing in time, marks potentially different future perspectives. As Benjamin urges us to think, especially in a situation of crisis as in an aftermath, a sudden "profane illumination" may reveal new meanings in the past as it is compared to the present. "To articulate the past historically . . . means to seize hold of a memory as it flashes up at a moment of danger" (Benjamin 1992, 247). The historian "grasps the constellation which his own era has formed with a definite earlier one" (ibid., 255). A constellation of past and present actually reveals a past not hitherto realized, a past full of opposing possibilities.

In order to preserve the time-awareness of thresholds that experiences of the aftermath activate, we need to develop a memory that records the aftermath as a turning point. This memory of discontinuity is "rhapsodic."[5] It unfolds in spatial practices that produce awareness of differences as well as similarities and make interdependence—however different they may be—possible. Commemorating the experience of an aftermath thus means to activate a spatial hermeneutics of time.

Instead of searching for places to commemorate, Gyaros forces us to think of routes that may offer visitors an articulated spatial

5. In Benjamin's words, "remembrance must not proceed in the manner of a narrative . . . but must . . . essay its spade in ever new places, and in the old ones delve to ever-deeper layers" (Benjamin 1985a, 314).

practice. Scattered stones, remains of barbed wire, a ruined guard-house, or a small outdoor fire stove offer the mundane spatial articulations that recite a collective experience of dwelling habits created in the face of otherness. The route is thus not conceived of as a connecting line between glorious destinations (as in a sightseeing tour), but rather as a walking experience that allows you to register the contrasting qualities of hope and terror in the landscape.

Sometimes signs are needed to suggest comparisons, but once you understand that memory has to deal with opposing possibilities, both in the past as well as in the present, you end up performing your own spatial as well as temporal experience of comparison. The simple fact that extracted stones can at the same time symbolize the agony of torture as well as the everyday resistance of collective dwelling habits reveals the power that comparisons between different interpretations of memory traces have.

Traces cannot be deciphered unless space is perceived as over-determined. Traces do not simply add up to each other, they also compete with each other. The past leaves marks that construct a multiplicity of overlapping spaces.

To activate a memory of discontinuities means to retrace rhythms that have inhabited conflictual spaces. In front of us lies not a text to be deciphered, but a multiplicity of time-spaces to be perceived in a hermeneutical constellation that reactivates possibilities. To remember means to understand and perform spatial practices as constructing and constructed. In the aftermath of a devastating past, such a creative hermeneutical constellation may resurface as a spatiotemporal experience open towards historical otherness.

In the experiences of exile, uprooting or disaster, life habits are violently suspended or destroyed. Spatial and temporal discontinuities threaten the characteristic rhythmicality of common life. Do these conditions inevitably create and legitimize forcefully defined enclaves of exception in which people are imprisoned? Is exception only and always a trap?

When people manage to inhabit exception, when people manage to perforate the defining perimeter of their enclave, they can transform exception into a potential threshold. Thresholds compare; they connect and separate. People inhabiting exception seek to activate the comparing power of thresholds in order to open the self-contained secluded and controlled locus of exception. Comparing, they can invent, improvise, and discover otherness as a relation between "inside" and "outside." An encounter with otherness emerges, different from the experience of being engulfed by otherness that happens when exception closes around you. Exception is condemnation: life is completely given over to otherness.

In the process of inhabiting exception, new rhythmicalities emerge. Rhythmicalities that deviate from imposed habits then are constituted by and through performed comparisons. Rhythms become creative responses to violent ruptures of time since they are in a constant negotiation with experiences of temporal discontinuity. Exiles, immigrants, displaced populations, victims of natural or human inflicted disasters have to live with these experiences. But they can discover in themselves the possibility to live in a continuous inventive negotiation with otherness.

We can learn from the efforts and often-contradictory behavior of people inhabiting exception. If we want to understand how thresholds, as spatiotemporal artifacts, can encourage liberating encounters with otherness then these exceptional collective experiences—or rather, these collective experiences of exception—are extremely valuable.

Trapped in exception, people devise ways to live. They open the engulfing enclosure that surrounds them. In their acts, the prospect of a city of thresholds can only be vaguely present. The city of thresholds is a precarious, uneven, and multiform process of human emancipation. Different experiences and different forms of collective action can contribute to it, as long as they create opportunities for encounter between collective identities that are open to mutual awareness and negotiations. Being able to creatively deal with otherness, as immigrants and exiles do by inhabiting exception, is a prerequisite for every attempt to imagine and pursue a liberating future.

Collective memories of discontinuity will be of great value, if we are to understand the city of thresholds not only as a future possibility but also as a latent promise already contained in the past. In the next chapter, Walter Benjamin will help us locate in modernity's betrayed liberating promise a major opportunity for the city to become a place of collective emancipation. The city of thresholds, precarious and ambiguous as it is, could have been the cultural pattern through which modern cities become performed spaces of human emancipation. As we will see, it was the modern city's spatiotemporal discontinuity that sustained not only the promise of emancipatory inhabiting practices, but also the nightmare of a new normative spatial order and the equally disenfranchising glamor of urban phantasmagoria.

Part II

Walter Benjamin's thresholds

Traces and individuality

Memory, this ability to compare past and present, can, as we have seen, create rhythmicalities; it can inhabit and divert exception. Memory gives different meanings to experienced spatiotemporal discontinuities. Benjamin's emphasis on historical discontinuity, along with his archeological search in urban modernity's recent past, gives memory a paradoxical role. It is based on memory's power to compare, to discover in the past passages to a different future. In his attempt to see modernity's break with the past as the possibility of a liberating future, we can trace the theoretical importance of thresholds: those moments in time and space when and where the promise of a future that will not repeat the past emerges.

We can understand modern city life as a multiform diversity of individualized practices, which, erupting mainly during the nineteenth century, created an impression of urban chaos and formal indeterminacy. If, however, we aim at discovering patterns in modern urban experience, as it was formed and expressed in public behavior, then we need to search for those theoretical tools that can effectively deal with the diversity of urban experiences. We can follow a well-marked path: we can utilize a bipolar analysis in order to classify forms of urban experience. Depending on the premises of each employed theory, the opposition of public versus private may become central or, alternatively, traditional versus modern, visual versus tactile, mental versus bodily and so on.

We can, however, attempt to establish distinctions that permit the surfacing of in-between elements. Similar elements can effectively present urban experience as dynamic and always in-the-process of making. Benjamin's theoretical propositions may be used in such a context, since his "dialectics at a standstill" offers us an insight into urban experience through the study of emblematic figures that not only represent antithetical attitudes towards city life, but actually live in precarious urban thresholds. Understanding modernity as promise and nightmare at the same time, Benjamin proposed that urban life cannot simply be analyzed as a coherent structure of recurrent experiences but should rather be understood as a hybrid synthesis of potentially liberating and, at the same time, "re-enchanting" experiences. Eventually, urban experience can be conceptualized through the use of terms such as "threshold," "ceasura" or "passage" that can effectively combine, as in Benjamin's thought, spatial as well as temporal aspects of those inherently dynamic elements that mold city life. Such a theoretical perspective can perhaps provide us with a method inherently influenced by its object. And this may have been one of Benjamin's main contributions to our understanding of modernity.

Metropolitan experience is a shock experience. City space-time is experienced through the traumatic mediation of shock. Already in the nineteenth century, big cities constitute an unprecedented spatiotemporal condition. Being in public space increasingly becomes an ordeal. Individuals have to cope with an accelerating tempo of fragmentary impressions that are smashing the spatial and temporal continuity of traditional collective experience. Individuals have to learn how to respond to demanding stimuli, adapting their public behavior to an emerging metropolitan experience. The result is a kind of anesthetization, according to Simmel and Benjamin, that leads people to assume a so-called "blasé attitude" in order to be able to safely absorb ever-increasing assaults on their senses (Simmel 1997a, 69–79).

Under these conditions, individual consciousness is disengaged from collective memories and common experiences. No experience is allowed to leave its mark in the depths of individual memory, no experience is compared to previous events, no experience acquires its weight and meaning in the context of shared traditions. Conveniently stored in individual memory, such "depthless" experiences are always recallable through a conscious memory able to classify and control them (Benjamin 1983, 117). Experiences thus become their own yardstick: each one self-contained and singular.

A bourgeois cult of individuality is necessarily connected to a cult of individual experience. Individuality is supposedly constructed out of an accumulation of distinct and presentable experiences. Commodities are advertised, sold, and consumed as mediators of recognizable experiences that eventually construct stereotyped life-stories (today, these are often additionally shaped in Facebook timelines). No matter how individual experiences are regulated through consumption, they function as indicators of personality in a society that makes individualism its prime legitimating ideology.

Even though experiences in metropolitan modernity are individualized, no individual marks can be traced on the body of the city. Individuality is condensed in a fleeting presentation of the self in public space, a transitory and ambiguous appearance that many times needs to be deciphered by a physiognomist's gaze.

Individuality leaves no traces in public space. It is only in the interior of the private shelter that bourgeois individuality can be lastingly presented, and for that to happen traces of individual experience need to be preserved.

As Benjamin observes, the private individual [*der Privatmann, le particulier*] "makes his entry into history" (Benjamin 1999b, 19), creating in the domestic interior a private universe. And this universe is like a shell (Benjamin 1999a, 220, compare Benjamin 1999d, 264), a cavern (Benjamin 1999a, 216), actually it is a case [*étui*] (Benjamin 1999b, 20) where an obsession with the preservation of traces prevails.[1]

What is this obsession with traces? How is it connected with the "addiction to dwelling" (Benjamin 1999, 220) that prevailed in the nineteenth century, making every private individual feel homesick even while being at home (ibid., 218)? "The collector is the true resident of the interior" (Benjamin 1999a, 9). This phrase summarizes the attitude of the nineteenth-century private individual towards his or her private shelter. Collecting is a way of attributing value to traces. Collected things are stripped from any use-value and can only convey the impression of taking hold of past experiences. Things represent those experiences through the traces they bear. In this way, "collecting is a form of practical memory" (Benjamin 1999, 205). Memory reconstructs out of an ordered series of objects a sequence of time, in a crucial way analogous to the memory that records everyday shock experiences. Both kinds of memory are inclined towards an ordering function, both "struggle against dispersion" (ibid., 211), and both protect consciousness from the traumatic experience of dismantled social time.

---

1. "Ever since the time of Louis Philippe, the bourgeois has shown a tendency to compensate for the absence of any trace of private life in the big city. . . . It is as if he had made it a point of honor not to allow the traces of his everyday objects and accessories to get lost" (ibid.).

The collector attempts to control and order the past. They thus tame past relics, neutralizing the power objects have to display history as a form of comparison between different past epochs. The collector brings together what he considers belongs together. In a somewhat futile effort, since every new acquired item may jeopardize instead of verifying the collection's order, the collector brings what is distant in time nearer to the present. They eliminate the distance that exists between his time and the object's time. And this happens because the object is petrified (ibid., 205) as the seal of possession extracts it from the flow of time. Collecting is a gesture of preservation and "of all the profane manifestations of 'nearness' it is the most binding" (ibid.).

Benjamin defines the trace as the "appearance of a nearness, however far removed the thing that left it behind may be. . . . In the trace, we gain possession of the thing" (ibid., 447). It is this power of traces that the collector activates. But he reverses the process: it is not observed traces that bring the thing which left them behind, it is objects, "things," which bring traces of the past near, into the collector's present. What is lost in this process, however, is the essentially relative character of traces. Traces don't belong to things, they are not identified by the things that bear them. We, as interpreters of the past, observe and understand as traces certain changes in objects. We have to compare different past periods in order to be able to discover, name, describe, and evaluate traces. The collector's obsession with traces and his "tactile instinct" (ibid., 206) are both expressions of a will to possess.

The collector is primarily an owner.[2] In collecting, a certain compensatory behavior unfolds, which aims at the mitigation of a feeling of loss. And this loss has to do with the elimina-

---

2. A kind of sublimated owner indeed, since his objects are detached from use, "freed from the drudgery of being useful" (Benjamin 1999b, 19). Perhaps it is the owner par excellence, since his attitude expresses not only a practice but also an ideology of possession.

tion of individual traces in the experience of urban public space. Resisting this loss, the private individual builds a shelter for his individuality. And he accumulates tokens of this individuality in the form of collected objects. These objects speak about him. Their history ends up in his acquiring them, and he represents their fate. So, these objects are not valuable because of the traces of bygone times, but because somebody, the collector, reads in these traces an origin and a fate. This makes the collector a *connoisseur*, someone who can bestow on objects a "connoisseur value" (Benjamin 1999, 9, 19). Owning things that have been collected means validating the status of a peculiar individuality that can acquire meaning only because it supports a distinctive talent of choosing. The collector not only exhibits but builds his identity out of the collected objects.

The private man as collector arranges his domestic interior as a gigantic still life. Let us remember: both everyday objects and artworks are present in the still-life paintings of seventeenth-century Dutch art. Objects are meticulously exhibited, arranged as they are in a setting that presents their characteristics through a peculiar "art of describing" (Alpers 1983). No matter how ephemeral their appearance, the depicted objects are immobilized. The flow of bourgeois domestic time is interrupted and the scenes assume an emblematic character. This is what makes still-life paintings appropriate mediators of a "tremendous pride in possessions" (ibid., 100; Berger 1972). The private man as collector performs an analogous exhibition of objects extracted from their use-context in a way that reminds us of the ethos of still life (or *nature morte* if you prefer). His canvases are in effect the cases that he obsessively uses to frame domestic objects.

"What didn't the nineteenth century invent some sort of casing for! Pocket watches, slippers, eggcups, thermometers, playing cards—and in lieu of cases, there were jackets, carpets, wrappers and covers" (Benjamin 1999, 220). Indeed, the house itself becomes an enormous case where the individual finds his place prepared, much in the same way that the outline of a pipe in a pipe's case awaits the object.

Encased in his private shelter, while he encases every object he has collected in order to present himself to his visitors, the private individual is trapped in a historically specific power of traces. True, "to dwell means to leave traces" as Benjamin proposes (Benjamin 1999a, 9). But the private individual, in an emphatic fetishization of traces, ends up being controlled by traces. Much in the same way that a pipe's contour in a pipe's case precedes the actual object, the domestic interior as case precedes and pre-orders domestic life. The individuality constructed out of a collection of objects ends up being a typified individuality much in the same way that an object's case, no matter how it appears to be specifically and distinctively prepared for it, is actually a typical case for a typical object.

The case, instead of preserving traces as markers of time and use, renders objects unapproachable, kept away, preserved. Objects attain an exhibition value, actually a "cult value" (Benjamin 1992a, 218), presenting an illusion of individuality. Objects become the markers of a mythologized individuality.[3] In a Sisyphean enterprise of seeking individuality in an alienating world, the bourgeois private individual is actually falling victim to a mythology of traces. Traces of collected objects act as markers of aura; they destroy the "appearance of nearness" in a recreated "manifestation of a distance." "The aura is appearance of a distance, however close the thing that calls it forth," to use the other half of the already mentioned passage. Traces thus become vehicles of aura, nearness is transformed into distance and a kind of re-enchantment of the

---

3. Benjamin insists: "The private individual, who in the office has to deal with reality, needs the domestic interior to sustain him in his illusions" (Benjamin 1999a, 8).

interior happens as metropolitan phantasmagoria takes possession of the domestic universe.[4]

Whereas "in the trace we gain possession of the thing: in the aura it takes possession of us" (Benjamin 1999, 447). This is not the aura of tradition. This is more an aura of an invented tradition intended to integrate the universe of bourgeois normality into the frenetic ephemerality of modernity. Indeed, in the artificially created aura of interior phantasmagorias surfaces the drama of modernity: the promise of emancipation and enlightenment is belied in the nightmare of re-enchantment. Phantasmagoria, propelling a fetishization of consumption, is restoring a magical belief in object relations that can effectively replace human relations.[5]

The bourgeois domestic interior is arranged as a domestic showcase where objects on display present their owners. Showcases and museum exhibitions share one common element: an arrangement of objects becomes meaningful because it is supposed to present the spirit of an epoch. Fashionable goods on display, thus, are taken to present a modern spirit. Showcase arrangements change often, of course. However, the logic of the arrangement remains the same, therefore always recognizable. Display always makes objects appear as unapproachable, preserved, out of the flow of time. Showcases can be described as "museums of the present" (and advertising constructions can analogously be considered as "monuments to the present"). Bourgeois domestic interiors combine the

---

4. "Phantasmagorias of the interior" become in this way the private man's "universe" (ibid., 9).

5. According to Rolf Tiedemann, "the concept of phantasmagoria that Benjamin repeatedly employs seems to be another term for what Marx called commodity fetishism" (Tiedeman 1999, 938). Benjamin, however, was more interested in "the expression of the economy in its culture" (Benjamin 1999, 460) than in the laws of capitalist economy per se. Therefore, he considers phantasmagorias of the interior as not simply the result of a bourgeois domestic economy (connected to both consumption and production) but as the product of an expressive behavior that transfigures commodities to mediators of modern myth. And this myth is creating, out of the reality of commodity fetishism, a culture that constructs individual mythologies by manipulating object relations.

ethos of museum collections and the phantasmagoria of modern showcases. Phantasmagorias of the interior are thus meaningful object arrangements which, no matter how fast they may change (due to the ever-increasing tempo of consumption), bear the aura of a "modern tradition."

In such a tradition, bourgeois hegemonic values impose themselves as the horizon of normality while subverting modernity's liberating promises of change to the ephemeral whims of fashion. Perhaps those phantasmagorias can eventually be thought of as museums of the owner's present. And they can effectively create the image of an individuality that is not constructed out of "family narratives" or memories of distinctive acts, but out of a display of possessions. Bourgeois identities are thus understood and presented more in terms of space than in terms of time.

The flâneur and urban phantasmagoria

The *flâneur* is in many ways the opposite of the private individual. The flâneur lives in public space. The streets, the boulevards and, above all, the Parisian arcades are his home.[6] In a way, the flâneur seeks and produces at the same time marks of individuality not in his private shelter but out there, in metropolitan public space. He observes and often writes about city life while being "jostled" by the crowd, inside "an immense reservoir of electric energy," as Baudelaire describes metropolitan crowds (Benjamin 1999, 443). A true physiognomist, he seeks out what is distinctive, what is particular in the everyday panoramas of city life as they unfold in front of his eyes. He attributes value to small incidents, he explores fleeting images, fleeting gestures, ephemeral and chance encoun-

6. "The walls are the desk against which he presses his notebooks; newsstands are his libraries and the terraces of cafes are the balconies from which he looks down on his household after his work is done" (Benjamin 1983, 37).

ters. The flâneur thus becomes a sublimated detective (ibid., 442). His passion for minute details revealing small dramas or well-hidden misdeeds makes him the perfect tracer. His hypersensitivity interprets everything as a trace.

Whereas the private individual collects in his private shelter traces of a studiously fabricated individuality, the flâneur searches for traces that will reveal individual trajectories in public space. The individuality that he seeks out in the streets is the very same fleeting individuality that dissatisfies the private individual who feels that there are no individual traces in public space. And whereas the private individual dedicates the phantasmagorias of interior to a "monumental" individuality that resists the transitoriness of modern life, the flâneur discovers in the depth of this transitoriness traces of an ephemeral, anonymous—if this is not a contradiction in terms—individuality. Immersed in public phantasmagorias he likes "to read from faces the profession, the ancestry, the character" (ibid., 429). The private individual as a city dweller crosses public space with his eyes "overburdened with protective functions" (Benjamin 1983, 151). Eyes that have lost the ability to meaningfully communicate and return the gaze, are eyes that are only used to inform, protect, and guide. A protective anesthetization prevails in the behavior of the city dweller.[7] Being in the street means being able to conform to rules, to adapt to typical situations with minimum involvement. In contrast, the flâneur empathizes with the crowd (ibid., 54). He feels the energy, the sparks, the dangers, the passions. And this attitude is expressed through an aestheticizing of metropolitan life. The flâneur is an aesthete. He views everything as aesthetically meaningful. That is why he presents himself in public through gestures of emphatic theatricality: taking a turtle for a walk, dressing sometimes as a dandy, appearing strange in the middle of the crowd, playing with imitative behavior, vanishing

7. "There is no daydreaming surrender to faraway things in the protective eye" (ibid.).

and surfacing again in many disguises. Zygmunt Bauman is right to suggest that "the job of the flâneur is to rehearse the world as a theatre, life as a play" (Bauman 1994, 146).

This attitude, as opposed to that of the private individual in the streets who, anaesthetized, cannot feel or recognize auratic elements in the metropolitan landscape, is an attitude of auratic appreciation. City life assumes in the eyes of the flâneur a peculiar aura. Through a daydreaming gaze that reintroduces a perspective between the flâneur and the fleeting metropolitan images "a unique manifestation of distance" is perceived. What for others is protectively presented as ordinary, for him becomes strange. Everything assumes the status of a work of art, every object becomes able to return the gaze.

Such an aestheticization of metropolitan experience makes the flâneur a possible co-producer of urban phantasmagoria. Adding through his gestures or writings to the spectacular character of a culture dedicated to "commodity worship" he may eventually become a mediating figure in the re-enchantment of public life. "The flâneur-as-idler is thus doubly phantasmagoric: in what he writes (the physiologies) and what he does (the pretense of aristocratic idleness and the reality of bourgeois commercial interest)" (Gilloch 1997, 156).

The decline of aura connected to anesthetization and alienating shock absorption is positively reserved in a constructed metropolitan mythology: The modern "transitory gods" (Buck-Morss 1991, 259) only participate in a fetishization of newness necessary for the cult of consumption. And newness "is the quintessence of that false consciousness whose indefatigable agent is fashion" (Benjamin 1999a, 11).

Public phantasmagorias are enhanced by the flâneur, this peculiar intellectual aesthete, who makes it his profession to pursue the novelties of modern life. Everything he observes is marked by a halo of originality. This turns out to be a quest for individuality and distinctive particularity, a quest for fashionable novelties in every aspect of public life (dressing, behavior, the arts, city places, views, technological gadgets, etc.).

The dialectics of disenchantment

This is not, however, the only possible role for the flâneur. He is not necessarily someone who, in a tension between an empathetic relation with the crowd and a distantiated aesthetic gaze, actually contributes to a mythologizing metropolitan aura. In Baudelaire's allegorical gaze, a new kind of aura seems to surface. The allegorist is opposed to the collector in aiming not at the construction of a signifying order but at a meaningful dislodging of acts and objects from their context (Benjamin 1999, 329). The allegorist, hollowing out objects of their mythology, exposes them. He alienates objects from their habitual use only to expose alienation as a general characteristic of city life.[8]

The flâneur-allegorist is not simply letting himself become possessed by the thing, that is, letting a phantasmagoric aura overcome him. He attributes to things an aura that exposes them, an aura that reveals the potentialities hidden beneath the mythologizing surface. The flâneur-allegorist uses the ways and language of myth in order to reveal the mythic element in the culture of modernity.

Decontextualized images of metropolitan modernity assume the status of emblematic ciphers, where meaning becomes the product of revealing correspondences. This is how the image of the prostitute can become an allegory of commodification and images of the boulevards can serve as allegories of modernity's in-

8.   He thus "loses every intimacy with things" (ibid., 336). And as a wanderer, he rediscovers the look of children always dazzled in front of the metropolitan scenes and always inventive in their appropriation of the outmoded, the discarded, the insignificant.

ner contradictions. "The setting that makes all urban humanity a great extended 'family of eyes' also brings forth the discarded stepchildren of that family. . . . The glitter lights up the rubble and illuminates the dark lives of the people at whose expense the bright lights shine" (Berman 1983, 153).

Myth appears to work in a similar way. Attributing to acts and objects the "unique manifestation of a distance," myth actually constructs "ceremonial images" out of which a uniform meaning of life is imposed (Benjamin 1983, 148). Allegory can be an antidote to myth, as Benjamin (1980, 667) proposes, by using myth's constituent elements: images. Allegory deprives images of any ceremonial value, using them instead as a means to bypass mythical obstacles. Allegory thus becomes a form of knowledge through images, which may bring to light whatever remains collectively unconscious. In order to reveal what is socially repressed, allegory has to employ images that through associations may circumscribe the meaning of collective dreams. Those dreams are not simply interpreted allegorically but read as "distorted representations" as Weigel suggests (Weigel 1996, 103).

As an unwilled collaborator to advertising spectacles, either staged in international expositions or dispersed in metropolitan landscapes, the allegorical gaze does not aestheticize. It purposefully distorts, much in the same way the meaning of a dream is concealed behind a distorting mechanism. The allegorical gaze, therefore, uses mythical elements in order to reveal the dominant myths. The auratic force discovered by the allegorical gaze is not the product of the mystifying aura of commodity fetishism. Rather, its force results from revealed correspondences, from chance encounters that illuminate new possibilities for deciphering the culture of modernity.

For the aura of the allegorical approach to surface, a very delicate treatment of experience appears necessary. Benjamin attributes this treatment to the genius of Baudelaire. Or, perhaps he is projecting his own ideas onto the work and practices of an extremely ambiguous and talented poet of the nineteenth century? In any case, this idea is revealed in a somewhat enigmatic commentary on Baudelaire's criticism of paintings: "Baudelaire insists on the magic of distance; he goes so far as to judge landscapes by the standard of paintings in the booths at fairs. Does he mean the magic of distance to be pierced, as must happen when the spectator steps too close to the depicted scene?" (Benjamin 1983, 152).

Here we find a suggestion about the ability of the allegorical gaze to destroy through aura itself the deceptive aura of metropolitan phantasmagoria. This may happen in the fleeting moment of a sudden revelation. It will have the form of a peculiar clash between absolute distance (magic distance, auratic distance) and absolute nearness. A peculiar dialectic of aura and trace is at work here. The flâneur-as-detective feels empathetically close to the crowd. "Botanizing on the asphalt" (ibid., 36), he steps too close to the scenes of urban life. He observes, touches, smells, and hears; he is immersed in the materiality of the city. This attitude exposes what is hidden, demystifies, and eventually contributes to a withering of aura, since the "appearance of nearness" prevails over the "appearance of distance." "The desire of contemporary masses to bring things closer spatially and humanly" (Benjamin 1992a, 217) is "also a stepping too close to what is depicted," whether it is reproduced works of art, architecture or, indeed, film. The public, as an "absent-minded examiner" (ibid., 234) who is not absorbed by the work of art, is correspondingly not possessed by the work's aura.

Tracing on the surface of things, experiencing closeness, is not enough to understand. Understanding means discovering the hidden potentialities of past and present. One needs, to use a Baudelaire's phrase, the "useful illusion" (Benjamin 1983, 51) of the magic of distance. The simultaneous experience of distance and nearness indicates an impossible position. Or does it indicate a precarious position where under the tension of two conflicting tendencies one can suddenly realize the ambiguous status of reality? Reality is not what remains after lifting the veil of myth because myth is a constituent element of the historically specific reality of modernity. This reality is revealed in the process of piercing the veil for just a fleeting moment. This reality is present in the act of its momentary redemption by an allegorical gaze.

A "study of thresholds"

Trace and aura oppose each other, in the same way as the experience of nearness opposes the experience of distance. In the dialectics of their simultaneous influence a third element emerges. This element is not a synthesis of opposites—rather, it constitutes a field of force activated by opposites. That is why this element can be invoked in a so-called "dialectics at a standstill." Where tension between dialectical opposites is the greatest, thinking comes to a standstill and recognizes a "dialectical image." This third element must have the revealing power of such an image (Benjamin 1999, 463 and 475).

In the middle of this force field, a precarious, dangerous, almost impossible-to-occupy place surfaces. Benjamin attributes to it the status of a "caesura" (Benjamin 1999, 475) that indicates a possible passage: a threshold. Thresholds unite what is separate and separate what is different (Simmel 1997a, 68–69). To experience the power of thresholds means to realize that nearness and distance are simultaneously activated in the dialectics of comparison: the separating action of thresholds differentiates adjacent areas. Nearness is operative in creating the distance of difference. At the same time, thresholds unite those areas that differences tend to keep apart. Thresholds create out of distances a nearness without which differences will never be able to constitute themselves as mutually "other."

Trace-aura dialectics are crystallized in the concept of threshold. This concept can express the dynamics of temporal and spatial discontinuity. Recognizing turning points in the past, where potential alternatives to past history are revealed is a crucial element in Benjamin's critique of historicism (Benjamin 1992, 254). Can't we extrapolate an analogous treatment of the mythologized metropolitan experience? Winfried Menninghaus proposes that Benjamin's work can be "construed as a multifarious 'study of thresholds'" [*Schwellenkunde*] (Menninghaus 1991, 309). This suggestion makes sense especially when we take into account the characteristics of the flâneur, the central figure of this study. The flâneur, the "connoisseur of thresholds," is himself a figure on the threshold (Benjamin 1999a, 10). Immersed in urban phantasmagoria and at the same time distanced from it, the flâneur embodies the ambiguous power of thresholds. His position, within the crowd but also observing its behavior from a distance, enables him to experience the illuminating sparks ignited exactly on this verge.

The allegorist flâneur not only appreciates the threshold character of specific urban places but actually, in the art of losing himself in the city (Benjamin 1985a, 298), decomposes the unity of urban phantasmagoria. He invents points of rupture in urban space: passages and thresholds. Deliberately destroying the continuity of any urban trajectory by refusing to accept what constitutes a trajectory's meaning (its destination), the flâneur experiences the city as fragmented and dispersed.[9]

By combining near and far, by comparing fragments of space as well as fragments of the city's history, the flâneur reads the city not as the coherent text of "progress" but as a multilayered allegory

9. Combining those fragments in unexpected ways, flânerie provides the ground for sudden revelations. This is how, "in the course of flânerie, far off times and places interpenetrate the landscape and the present moment" (Benjamin 1999, 419).

of modernity. The allegorical gaze does not discover an alternative narrative but many new constellations of meaning, each one of them pointing to the inherently ambiguous, contradictory, and potentially emancipating character of urban modernity.

Involuntary remembrances emerge in experiences of temporal discontinuity. According to Benjamin, "he who seeks to approach his own buried past must conduct himself as a man digging" (Benjamin 1985a, 314). The excavation site thus becomes a threshold to the past, and every unexpected finding mediates a re-emerging of past experiences.[10] In the experience of involuntary remembrances, a threshold opens toward the past. In a revelatory momentary flash, past becomes suddenly near while traces appear emphatically legible. No matter how forceful the experience that "calls it forth," the past remains distant, unapproachable, radiating the aura of its uniqueness.

Perhaps we can understand Benjamin's concept of actualization [*Aktualisierung*] (Benjamin 1999, 392 and 460) as the piercing of the unavoidable magic of distance that separates us from the past, by "stepping too close" to the material concreteness of the traces left by past experiences. Actualization, which aims at blasting open the continuum of history, can thus be considered as an act of creating thresholds that unite while separating past and present. Those thresholds can indeed be characterized by the "now of a particular recognizability" (ibid., 463).

It is by no chance that *The Arcades Project* focuses on a type of urban space that possesses the characteristics of a threshold. The arcades, existing between public and private space, between street and shop, are home for the flâneur and at the same time urban phantasmagorias for the private individual. Above all, however, the arcades present in a concrete form the ambiguous character of modernity as hope and hell simultaneously. According to Howard

10. In chapter 2, we encountered Benjamin's idea of rhapsodic remembrance.

Caygil, Benjamin "read this prematurely archaic form of architecture speculatively, that is, as containing latent unrealized futures" (Caygil 1998, 133).

In the dialectical image of the arcades the "tension between dialectical opposites is greatest" (Benjamin 1999, 475). And this fact makes the arcades an appropriate locus for the precarious experience of a "profane illumination" where distance is pierced by nearness and collective dreams reveal their liberating potential exactly as they are pierced at the moment of a forced awakening. Dwelling is dialectically presented in the arcades only as a possibility. On the threshold the potentiality of a modern liberating dwelling experience flashes illuminatingly.

In the essay "Experience and Poverty," Benjamin calls for a "positive concept of barbarism" that may profit from the growing "poverty of experience" in modern life in order to encourage a new, liberating start, "by clearing a tabula rasa" (Benjamin 1999c, 732). A new housing culture is needed for such a new start, a housing culture hostile to the "coziness" of bourgeois domestic interiors.[11] Glass becomes the appropriate building material for such a culture, being the enemy of secrets, the enemy of possession, the enemy of aura, the enemy of the interior-as-collection. Glass is also an enemy of traces, making it difficult for the owner to leave his mark (ibid.). Indeed, it exposes, bringing the interior very close to the exterior. Glass preserves the "useful illusion" of the "magic of distance" becoming a kind of screen on which the faraway is projected as a "view" in a panorama. The enemy of aura and trace at the same time, glass is actually at the center of their dialectical opposition.

Can we discover in these thoughts an alternative to nineteenth-century dwelling experience, one that attempts to embrace

---

11. In such bourgeois domestic interiors, the inhabitant is forced "to adopt the greatest number of habits—habits that do more justice to the interior he is living in than to himself" (ibid., 734).

the twentieth century's optimistic "transitoriness of dwelling" with its "porosity and transparency" (Benjamin 1999, 221)? This idea, clearly, should not be identified with the nightmarish reality of modernism's housing blocs, hotel rooms, or office towers. Benjamin was perhaps trying to integrate a heroic affirmation of modernist values (which capitalist modernity has twisted in order to confirm to the myth of progress) into a philosophy that focuses on revealing discontinuities.

Glass appeared to him as the element that could mediate this experience of discontinuity both in time and space. Between inner and outer space, glass forms a precarious threshold always being virtually crossed, that separates and unites public and private, nature and culture, inside and outside. Maybe for Benjamin the glass panel assumes the role of an allegorical threshold, a threshold that represents the revealing potential of the dialectics of nearness and distance. Glass could thus express as a "dialectical image" the "piercing" of "the magic of distance."

Unfortunately, the reality of the modernist "glass culture" (*Glaskultur*) did not bring forth the threshold character of this modern building material. It is more in agreement with Benjamin's ideas that "glass culture" was a potentially liberating culture, provided that society had moved towards an emancipating future. In Bloch's words: "the broad window full of nothing but outside world needs an outdoors full of attractive strangers, not full of Nazis; the glass door right down to the floor really requires sunshine to peer and break in, not the Gestapo" (quoted in Heynen 1999, 123).

Benjamin was neither simply lamenting the "decline of aura" in the modern world or condemning modern urban phantasmagorias. With his image of the piercing of distance by nearness, he was pointing to the revealing power of exposed discontinuities both in historical time and metropolitan space. He was not aiming for a redeemed aura, nor for a re-enchantment of the world by modernity's myth of "newness." Nor was he for transitoriness, either, as long as not every ephemeral present revealed a "weak, messianic power" that may open it to a possible, radically different future (Benjamin 1992, 246). In an allegorical gaze that pierces urban phantasmagoria, the experience of modern dwelling is disenchanted and the monumental order of the interior as a private collection is forever shaken.

Can we perhaps imagine that a redeemed modernity, respecting the inherent transitoriness of modern dwelling without reproducing the nonplaces of metropolitan alienation, could create a modern city of thresholds? And, can we understand this city as epitomizing an experience of discontinuities that may orient collective behavior towards an emancipating public culture?

Navigating the metropolitan space: walking as a form of negotiation with otherness

The metaphor of navigation

A metaphor is a convenient way to describe an unfamiliar experience through the use of a familiar image. This is probably why so many metaphoric terms and expressions are used for the Internet. Many of them emanate from the simple and easily graspable idea that cyberspace is like a vast sea in which every user seeks their way.

No metaphor used to describe cyberspace is innocent. As Alice Rayner suggests, the metaphor of the theater that we tend to use for describing representations of possible human actions is not valid in the case of cyberspace. Although in a video game, representations of simulated human actions may unfold, the "as if" of scenic space is replaced by the functionality of an imaginary setting meant to facilitate interactivity. The distance that supports the theatrical "as if" is collapsed and the imagined becomes virtual: a crafted reality that responds the way reality is supposed to respond. Thus, according to Rayner, the metaphor of the theater will be misleading in its use to convey the experience of interacting with cyberspace (1999, 285–290).

In a different context, Kevin Robins criticizes as "conservative and nostalgic" descriptions of the Internet that deploy the metaphor of "*agora*." According to them "the Net is seen as rekindling a sense of family—'a family of invisible friends.'" They thus present the Net as an "electronic variant of the Rousseauist dream of a transparent society" (1996, 98).

What the two examples above indicate is that metaphors do not only help us to approach the unknown as analogous to what is already known, transporting—as the etymology of the word indicates—characteristics and meanings from familiar areas of experience to unfamiliar ones. Metaphors, in a way, contaminate the experiences they mediate through an image-centered comparison.

Not that everyone on the Net imagines herself surfing the waves of a California beach. The metaphor creates a kind of understanding that constructs a whole ideology or a set of value-invested cognitive schemas. A metaphor effectively molds the way we grasp an experience as socially meaningful and therefore possessing a certain social value. Lakoff and Johnson propose, "human conceptual systems are metaphorical in nature and involve an imaginative understanding of one kind of thing in terms of another" (Lakoff and Johnson 1980, 194). Through metaphors, the Internet experience is molded.

Understood in this way, experience is actually lived differently, depending on the different meanings and values attributed to it through metaphoric descriptions. Metaphors sometimes become so powerful and so effectively integrated into an experience that they end up being considered as literal descriptions. Just think what it means to describe the mode of doing something as a kind of route: we say, forgetting the metaphor we use, "I will do it my way."

The image of a sailor riding over the waves, finding ways to discover new lands, the image of a cybernaut cruising the seas of information, is surely powerful enough to instill in the act of Net browsing the positive values of an adventurous and heroic navigating experience that promises pleasure and, most probably, profit.

Can we possibly discover a different, latent potential in the metaphor of navigation? Can we transport this potential from the virtual space of the Net to the actual urban environment, and can we imagine ourselves navigating the material world instead of the immaterial one? Is it certain that a buried collective memory of an actual sea navigation cannot be revived with new meaning in the metaphoric appreciation of the modern experience of traversing metropolitan space?

The ancient Greeks seemed to place a lot of value on the abilities of a skillful sailor to depict the general characteristics of a peculiar and distinctive wisdom, which they called "*metis.*" Different from the wisdom of philosophers, metis is an inventive competence immersed in the universe of social practices and molded though practice. Metis must guide decisions on the spot, within limited time, exactly as in the case of a sailor facing situations that mostly require fast and accurate decisions.

This intelligence must also be multifaceted, resourceful, and cunning; because situations to be confronted are multiform, versatile, and open to unexpected events, however typical their form may appear:

> there is no doubt that metis is a type of intelligence and thought . . . it implies a complex but very coherent body of mental attitudes and intellectual behavior which combine flair, wisdom, forethought, subtlety of mind, deception, resourcefulness, vigilance, opportunism, various skills, and experience acquired over the years. It is applied to situations which are transient, shifting, disconcerting and ambiguous, situations which do not lend themselves to precise measurement, exact calculation, or rigorous logic (Vernant and Detienne 1978, 3).

So, somebody equipped with metis possesses the ability to be as inventive as the circumstances demand.

The navigation metaphor instills in the practical intelligence of metis one crucial image. To be able to take advantage of an unexpected, strange situation is to be able to find a way through and perhaps out of it. Navigating thus means being able to discover the signs to guide you (as in the case of the archetypical sailor watching the stars), being able to seize the opportunity in order to profit from a situation (like the archetypical sailor swiftly rearranging the ship's sails), being able therefore to invent a passage, to establish a route in what appears as a hostile unknown environment (like the archetypical sailor governing the ship in open sea).

For the ancient Greeks, the image of an unknown sea with no recognizable points of reference, with no seashore in view, was an image of absolute alterity. That is why it used to metaphorically describe passage to the Nether World. To cross the sea, the sailor must actually invent a passage, a *poros*. Sea navigation becomes an activity that may metaphorically represent the experience of confronting an unknown otherness. Thus, it can be employed to provide a meaningful representation of habitual activities that are meant to deal in inventive ways with the unknown or the unexpected. Knowing how to behave at work, in public space, during war, in the market, at court, or in the athletic games and exercises meant for the Greeks knowing how to behave in a variety of circumstances that escape prediction.

Not only were there different persons who developed different strategies in different social circumstances but also the gods always intervened, often involving mortals in their quarrels. Navigating through the circumstances could mean creating passages of escape or approach, thus regulating a potential relationship with the surrounding otherness. And this otherness equally encompassed both the unpredictable whims of the gods and the multiform interests of mortals.

One crucial characteristic of this ancient art of navigation is that it is constantly on the move. It is a kind of mobile art. And to be mobile is being always inventively different from one's self. This is the art of changing in order to cope with change. It has nothing to do with the ability of the chameleon to adapt to the surrounding environment. Metis is a form of taking hold of the situation not because someone is powerful enough, yet equally not because someone is so hopeless as to only try to give up whatever distinguishes him or her from the surrounding social environment in order to face the alterity of others.

The ancient navigator uses the ruses of metis in order to negotiate with otherness, to create passages, often aiming to propitiate the gods and the sea alike. The ancient navigator thus provides an archetypal image of the everyday politics of social interaction. And their practical intelligence is indicative of an ancient wisdom: the wisdom that develops ways to negotiate with otherness whether it stems from human actions or from the actions of nature and those of transcendental beings.

Crossing passages to otherness

Does this mean that the navigation metaphor could lead us to a new way of understanding how to deal with the experience of otherness erupting everywhere underneath the homogenizing blanket of globalization? If every modern social encounter means not only confronting everyone as a potential enemy but also being able to negotiate, judge and estimate otherness, then metis offers a model of action rich in nuances.

"Navigating the material world" constitutes not only a convenient metaphor, with the air of heroic colonialism filling its sails but, essentially, a metaphor instilling in social interaction a new or equally quite old form and value. Is it then possible for us to conceive of navigating the metropolitan space as actively constructing a relationship to otherness? And if this activity is actually a passage-creating activity, is it perhaps at the same time an activity that is based on the ability to inventively become other in order to cope with otherness?

In ancient Greek, the word for passage is *poros*. A ship that crosses the unknown sea is called *pontos*. For example, the ship of the Argonauts is a *pontoporos* ship (a ship literally creating her own route as a fleeting passage). If one cannot find his or her way, one stands in front of what appears to be unknown or "other," being in doubt. The Greek word for doubt is *aporia*, literally "lack of passage."

Otherness therefore takes the form of a seemingly unapproachable land. Passages to otherness, however, do not tame or eliminate otherness. They may only create, with the help of a resourceful intelligence, intermediary spaces in order to approach otherness: spaces of negotiation (we must not forget that the Greeks were actually negotiating with their gods, they were not simply afraid of them).

In English, "aporia" may be described as an attitude characterized by "an awareness of opposing or incompatible views on the same matter" (Gove 1981). Can't we then perhaps say that aporia is actually a form of heterogeneity awareness? And couldn't we consider the discovery of a necessarily temporary solution to the problems posed by heterogeneity as the discovery of a precarious passage, an unsteady poros? The art of navigation is the art of transporting aporia, not the art of eliminating it. As the passage closes behind the ship, so does the passage to otherness. It's always temporary. Social artifacts are created on the move.

There is another meaning for the Greek word poros. Poros also refers to the small holes on the surface of the skin. Pores are the passages that connect our body to the surrounding environment.

Urban porosity: immigrants on the streets of Yenikapi in Istanbul.

"A grain of Sunday is hidden in each weekday." A social housing terrace in Athens.

When we describe something as porous, we consider that it is communicating with its environment. A body in aporia would thus be a body hermetically sealed.

In one of his famous "city portraits," Benjamin uses porosity to describe everyday life in Naples:

> As porous as this stone [the stone of the shore by the sea] is the architecture. Building and action interpenetrate in the court-yards, arcades, and stairways. In everything they preserve the scope to become a theatre of new unforeseen constellations. The stamp of the definitive is avoided (Benjamin 1985b, 169).

And:

> Porosity results not only from the indolence of the southern arti-
> san, but also above all, from the passion for improvisation, which
> demands that space and opportunity be at any price preserved.
> Buildings are used as a popular stage (Benjamin 1985b, 170).

In the above passages, porosity appears to describe those circumstances that bear the distinctive marks of an occasion. That is why
porosity results from the "passion of improvisation," this everyday
theatricality, this art of coping with ever differing situations, becoming inventively other without losing oneself.

In such a city as Naples, where "a grain of Sunday is hidden in
each weekday" as Benjamin observes (ibid., 172), social interaction
becomes more than a series of prefixed and schematized procedures.
Social interaction is characterized by porosity. As in the navigator's
art, porosity is the creation of passages, poroi, and "pores" through
which every social body breathes the air of inventive interaction. In
the generalized mobility of Neapolitan life as Benjamin sees it in the
twenties, a metaphor of the bodily mediated experience of the modern city emerges. Porosity is the key to this metaphor, as the quality
of both material and immaterial elements of this experience. The
buildings and people's habits are porous. The streets and everyday
encounters are porous. Porous are the omnipresent staircases, the
families, and the relationships in open-air markets.

Negotiating choreographies

When we recall that Benjamin was a theoretician of the art of wandering, we can understand why porosity and navigation coincide in
a metaphor for modernity's hidden liberating potential. As a metropolitan wanderer, an idiosyncratic pedestrian, the flâneur loses

himself in the city only to discover, hidden behind the metropolitan phantasmagoric façade, the false promises that have propelled modern civilization. The flâneur in "the chorus of [his] idle footsteps" (de Certeau 1984, 97) has a feel for passages, a feel for thresholds (Benjamin 1999, 416). He discovers and invents passages even when he recognizes them as points of rupture in the city's fabric.

The flâneur has a feel for passages because he has a feel for heterogeneity. True, he may fall victim to the deceptive heterogeneity of appearances that imitate pluralism in the modern metropolis. But while navigating the metropolis without following obligatory itineraries, one can potentially discover ruptures in the projected uniformity of modern urban phantasmagoria. The flâneur disturbs the continuum of habit as well as the fabricated coherence of the urbanistic ratio. Walking assumes the status of a paradigmatic act that reinvents discontinuity at the heart of uniformity and thus discovers otherness at the heart of homogeneity.

It is not enough to acknowledge the power of every individual spatial practice to concretize individual though anonymous "ways of use" or "styles of use" as de Certeau (1984, 100) does. We have to see in every walking act not only an idiosyncratic rhetoric but also the power to move towards otherness. To walk in the modern city, no matter how strict the rules delimiting pedestrian movement are, always contains a grain of unpredictability, a mark of individuality. The predominance of chance encounters and the complexity of contemporary city life makes it necessary for city dwellers to develop an inventive navigational intelligence. Walking—not only wandering—opens often-unnoticed potential passages towards undefined destinations that are nevertheless explicitly felt. This revealing and exploratory encounter with otherness gives to walking gestures an expressive power.

Dance theory can help us locate the modalities of such a walking expressivity. Tracing the history of modern dance's interpretation of pedestrian acts, Susan Leigh Foster distinguishes three different forms of theatricality:

The first is characterized by modern choreographies based on the "blending of pedestrian and dancerly elements" (Foster 2002, 128). This is a theatricality in which the effects of theater are transported into everyday pedestrian acts (ibid., 131). We could say in this case, walking is seen in a new way; it is appreciated as theatrical.

The second, according to Foster, is an alternative theatricality constructed together with an alternative viewing practice. Pedestrian movement in this context refers not only trivial quotidian walking gestures but also the flow of movement. It makes this flow the guiding principle for dance improvisations. "Letting the dance happen" (ibid., 132) thus extracts from walking a structural principle rather than a repertoire of formal elements.

In the third kind of theatricality, an emphasis is put on the discontinuity of movement: "choreography conducts an anatomical investigation, not of the body, but of its movement" (ibid., 140). Recognizable pedestrian gestures are reflexively presented (ibid., 142): movements are connected both with the bodies that perform them and with their own structural characteristics.

What Foster's inventive research can perhaps show is that walking, this act of artful connection of places, can be understood and employed as a form of individual presentation that goes beyond the expression of individual moods, sentiments, and orientations. Walking is a form of bodily practiced negotiation with otherness; it is a form of addressing others.

In this kind of gestural theatricality, the actor-walker not only presents him or herself but also creates a temporary stage on which the other is implicitly invited. "Acting-out" a walk can thus become a negotiating gesture towards the otherness of those who pass by.

Baudelaire, the poet-flâneur, describes *une passante* in her erotic, implicitly theatrical walking:

Tall, slender, in deep mourning, with majesty,
A woman passed, raising, with dignity
In her poised hand, the flounces of her gown;
Graceful, noble, with a statue's form.

A pedestrian spatial practice is taken to be expressive not simply because somebody chooses to address somebody else but because every gesture, no matter how trivial or functional, can be taken as demonstrative, as revealing hidden intentions, as orchestrating its own meaning. Ambiguous and elusive or powerful and demanding, this kind of meaning can only emerge in an urban setting. First, it is assumed strangers are likely to meet. Second, it is assumed or deliberately transmitted that people in such a setting do not simply walk, they navigate.

Benjamin's navigation is both similar and at the same time symmetrically opposed to the ancient Greek navigating intelligence, metis. It is similar because it creates a negotiating and inventive relationship with otherness mobilizing a multilayered time-awareness. And it is its symmetrical inverse because whereas metis navigates through otherness creating passages, Benjamin's navigation seeks to discover the otherness hidden beneath the uniformity of modern urban phantasmagoria. Benjamin seeks to open modern social life, trapped in the myth of human progress, to the otherness of human emancipation.

Navigating the metropolis may be considered in terms of a distinctive experience, but may also provide us with a metaphor to evaluate and understand such an experience. The navigating image may thus constitute a metaphor describing the creation of passages towards, in the direction of, otherness. Navigating essentially means negotiating. Or perhaps, as in the theatricality of Neapolitan life or in the resourceful ruses of an inventive sailor, navigating means attempting to approach, to discover, to face otherness. What makes walking a practice which may condense navigating act's metaphoric potential is the fact that negotiation with otherness is not the result of a carefully constructed plan. This negotiation happens as people walk, whether they improvise to face unexpected encounters, whether they decide to express an interest in somebody as they pass or whether they let their moves be expressive, purposefully or not, addressing everybody or nobody. Walking, understood as navigating, epitomizes a particular embodied wisdom, the wisdom that understands social identities and behaviors as constantly in negotiation, creating out of differences and similarities the fabric of human interaction.

Theatricality:
the art of creating thresholds

Approaching the other

Thresholds mediate a relationship with otherness by marking passages in time and space. In the inventive social interaction characterizing life in Naples between the two World Wars, thresholds appear to function as—often temporary—urban stages where encountering otherness is practiced. Is perhaps this encounter with otherness an act based on the socially acquired ability to become other; the ability to assume, check, express or even deny identities? And is it perhaps that thresholds, because of their inherently comparative and relational character, provide the ground for these gestures and acts of becoming other? Are thresholds the spaces such a negotiating encounter creates? Are thresholds those precarious stages upon which a theatricality of encounters develops?

Theatricality is connected to the temporal dimension of human interaction. It emanates its time of unfolding and, as all practice, it is defined by its rhythm. Theatricality is not ascribed to a homogeneous time; it intervenes in its flow, accelerating or decelerating it, even suspending it (at the moment of the "strike," a *coup de théâtre*) or reversing it (embedding elements of the past or the future into the present). How else could theatricality, this art of becoming other, approach otherness? How else, considering the most radical expression of otherness is its unpredictability, could theatricality help us to be in "the place with the scent of the other. . . . For a little while, at least" (Cixous 2005, 182)?

Josette Féral argues that "theatricality as alterity emerges through a cleft in quotidian space" (Féral 2002, 97). Actually, this cleft produces a meaningful interruption in the continuity of quotidian space-time. As we will see, the interruption does not simply establish an "inside" and an "outside," but an in-between space in which a comparison between in and out, identity and otherness, real and possible can take place. Theatricality emerges as a process of comparisons that reveals the inherently relational character of every identity creation.

Let us borrow from the philosopher Vladimir Jankelevitch a concept that will clarify the time dependent character of the theatrical approach of the other: the concept of modesty [*lapudeur*]. Approaching the other requires a certain restraint. "Intimacy at first sight is like a premature child: it is quickly weakened, as it has not entered, in order to acquire depth, in the purificatory zone of trials and disappointments" (Jankelevitch 1996, 166). Modesty, therefore, is a sense of postponement and, at the same time, a postponing sense which delays and approaches its target indirectly. This dilatoriness is not a product of hesitation or fear; it is a product of circumspection: "modesty is the circumspection of the soul which regulates transitions and classifies targets" (ibid., 75).

The other is not transparent. The language and gestures we address to the other are not transparent either and, consequently, not unequivocal. It is the continuous postponement, the periphrastic and tentative reference to the other, that activates the field of the encounter. One hides in order to reveal, disguises one's self in order to unveil.

Communication is made up not only of what we wish to say but also of what we wish to hide. As we administer what we show, as we disguise ourselves to reveal a self that seems to rise to the occasion, we necessarily obscure or illuminate. All this procedure does nothing but highlight communication as a field of action. As action always addresses others, it is always assessed in the course of its development, continuously being modified according to the reactions of those others.

A relation is indeed a temporally structured exchange, as it unfolds in a time that is controlled differently by those who shape it. Modesty, this postponing circumspection, handles a meaning that can reach the other only through obstacles. Obstacles force one to attempt to unlock meaning, attribute it to the otherness of the other and, as such, accept it as something not already familiar. In a relation between different instances of otherness, meaning can circulate only under disguise. A lot of effort is needed and continuous comparisons and transfers are necessary in order for meaning to reach the other side, in order for it to bridge the distance with an always precarious construction. Meaning hovers in midair, for the visiting of otherness is always accompanied by the danger of error. Visiting otherness is the very matrix of the conceptualization of time, and it possibly constitutes the essence of the event as a foundation of temporality. That is why it is only as a practice which creates time and is defined by it that theatricality can be compared to a periphrastic modesty which conducts the disguises while shaping its path through the obstacles (Jankelevitch 1996, 45).

The postponing disposition creates a temporal distance that offers itself as the field for the realization of the encounter, as the field for the establishment of communication considered as an action of approaching otherness. Temporal distance appears as a precondition for the approach. As Jankelevitch points out, the outright encounter is necessarily temporary and superficial. Could it be then that distance is itself the condition for the encounter? Could it be that the encounter requires distance, spatially as well as temporally?

Distance and democracy

The fact of difference is already considered in terms of distance. The other belongs, or is taken to belong, elsewhere. To put it in other words, it is only because of distance that we can describe the other as other. Absolute proximity, i.e., intimacy, turns the other familiar, recognizable, the same as us. So, if we wish to accept someone in his or her otherness, we must not eliminate the distance that separates us.

The wager of the encounter is played precisely on this distance. If the distance is big, it becomes obvious that the encounter is rendered impossible (we will see that the encounter is also rendered impossible when the distance is marked by boundaries-barriers). But if the distance disappears, the relation is short-circuited. What is different becomes identical; the difference, which cannot be reduced to the same, disappears. Only if the distance between these two limits continues to exist, can the encounter possibly take place. Only then, as a spark between two poles, can the sparkle of approach be born.

It is obvious that the definition of such a distance does not correspond to any measurement; it rather corresponds to a sense, to a socially inculcated intuition. The necessary distance is rendered sufficient to the extent that it defines a field of exchange, a field of interaction.

Massimo Cacciari describes this distance through an image: the instances of otherness are islands floating in an archipelago. Each island is defined as a dominion and its relation with the surrounding islands is mediated by the sea. However, the sense of participating in a greater whole, what is called "archipelago," transforms the islands into instances of otherness oriented towards one another. Here, the sufficient distance describes a condition of vicinity: "the idea of vicinity encloses a necessary distinction of places" (Cacciari 1999, 47).

Cacciari considers the abolition of distance a characteristic obsession of the figure he calls *homo democraticus*. He essentially describes what Sennett refers to as the "tyranny of intimacy" (1993, 337–340). However, he also believes this obsession destroys all vicinity. Vicinity is born by distances capable of creating relationships. With his omnipresence, the *homo democraticus* renders the existence of the stranger not only intolerable, but also inconceivable (Cacciari 1999, 160). Indeed, it is the certainty that anything can be reduced to a common norm in a common matrix which stigmatizes the other as a deviation.

In the equalizing discourse of mass democracy lurks a homogenizing discourse. Whatever is beyond homogenization, whatever is rendered non-recognizable, simply does not exist. So we have either absolute proximity or absolute remoteness (such that the other is permanently located somewhere else). The distance of vicinity, which renders entities distinct and differences as distinguishable, is crushed between these two poles. The stranger is either assimilated—i.e., turned into the same—or becomes a stranger to the extent of becoming inconceivable. Augé describes this condition as a crisis of otherness, as an inability to symbolize the other, as a crisis of meaning, in the sense that the other is inconceivable. As we have seen, meaning is the product of negotiation (Augé 1999, 132).

So what is the possible answer to such a threat? Maintain distances? Keep the others at a distance, thus ensuring the impossibility of expropriating their otherness? Could it be that this attitude conceals a danger inverse to the one caused by the global expansion of mass "democracy" and globalized cultural uniformity?

Distance, difference, and racism

Deeply inscribed in the cultural subconscious of the West is the feeling of difference from the people it studies. In Western civilization ethnological interest walks hand in hand with the approaching of others as different from "us." Exploring its foundations, ethnology inevitably faces the problem of distance. Is distance necessary for the other to be understood as another? Could it be that the other is a product of this distance? And what happens when distances are lessened or eliminated?

Claude Lévi-Strauss sensitized ethnology towards the search for unified structures in human thinking. The anthropologist recognized in "savage thought" values equivalent to the scientific thought, attributing to people once considered barbarians, savages, or primitive, virtues equivalent to those of the Western people. And he established, in his late work, the anthropological view as a "view from afar."

In the name of cultural difference and its usefulness for the evolution of culture, Lévi-Strauss argued these distances should be kept. In his own words: "All true creation implies a certain deafness to the appeal of other values, even going so far as to reject them if not denying them altogether. For one cannot fully enjoy the other, identify with him, and yet at the same time remain different. When integral communication with the other is achieved completely, it sooner or later spells doom for both his and my creativity" (Lévi-Strauss 1985, 24).

It is obvious that such an opinion defends identity—cultural identity to be more precise—as a clearly defined field and as capable of distinguishing human groups. According to Lévi-Strauss, vicinity, in a way, neutralizes differences. However, the relations between instances of cultural otherness are never relations moved by the content of otherness itself. No civilization is imposed due to one of its values nor is any cultural synthesis only a product of cultural exchanges.

Civilization is a field of antagonisms that refract or transform competitions of economic and political power, just as relations between civilizations are hierarchical. So, in order for someone to conclude that distance preserves particularities, one needs to perform an abstraction. One must forget the powers of imposition that can operate from a distance, overlook the contests of hegemony in which, by choice or not, any cultural entity is involved. The problem of distance is a problem of power and of identity administration.

For places of encounter to be created at sufficient intermediate distances, one must renounce two pretensions that prevent negotiating encounters between different people: the pretension of predominance and the pretension of having a definite, closed, and invariable identity. The distance of encounter presupposes conditions for the opening of the identities and for the elimination or questioning of the power relations between different identities.[1]

The distance of vicinity, as a distance for visiting others, brings dominions in touch—dominions which define identities by their boundaries. Sufficient distance allows for the breaking of these boundaries without causing a diffusion of dominions. It is, ultimately, a distance where sheer power negotiation (a relation between unequal instances of otherness) is transformed into a negotiating encounter (a relation between instances of otherness communicating on equal terms).

Oddly enough, Lévi-Strauss's line of thinking offers arguments to combat contemporary racism, a *racisme différentialiste*, as Balibar calls it (Balibar and Wallerstein 1991, 36). According to

1. We will see in chapter 6 how Foucault describes disciplinary power as a process of classification and control of identities. In this inherently spatial model of power relations, distances between identities create social taxonomies and regulate hierarchies.

such logic, it is not biological heredity which justifies the boundaries between social entities, but irreducible cultural differences. In the name of such irreducible differences—that is, differences which cannot be negotiated and blended or cannot coexist—this new differentialist racism searches for the isolation and purity of those it considers culturally superior. The others have the right to difference, they have their particularities, as long as they stay where they belong (immigrants, refugees, all those who are permanently driven away as others).

Four steps towards the different

It is obvious that neither the sole invocation of difference nor the concern for its preservation can guarantee communication amongst different instances of otherness, necessarily leaving negotiation at the mercy of open confrontation which is often—if not always—waged between unequal parts. Strangely enough, the conservation of otherness can be imagined only as the horizon of a relation between different instances of otherness. Otherwise, confrontation—for, naturally, there are no safe distances, neither metaphorically nor literally—will always reduce all particularities to those of the most powerful.[2]

The search for a sufficient distance must come to terms with the idea that it will be a distance which not only defines a safety zone, a no man's land, but a distance which is crossed again and again. This distance is a field of coming and going, a locus of trial, a field of visiting. This continuous movement between self and other is described by Tzvetan Todorov as a "universalism of

---

2. Iveson argues for "a critical politics of difference," which will have to support "oppressed groups who seek to have their values and needs included in public space" (Iveson 2000, 234) not simply by equating differences but by creating the ground for negotiation and communication while protecting the most vulnerable from an all-pervasive cultural imperialism.

itinerary" (Todorov 1993, 74). Let us look more in detail at his reasoning regarding the distribution of such reciprosity from self to other. The experience of anthropologists studying a society different from their own offers the pattern for the description of an encounter-relation with otherness. And, according to Todorov, the development of such a relation is marked by four steps (ibid., 83–84).

The first step towards the different cannot help but lie in one's tendency to distance oneself from society and the self. According to Todorov, this is the motive of departure. Without this first feeling of distantiation, there can be no movement.

The second step refers to the first approach to the other society. One dives into it trying to understand, communicate, etc. However, one carries one's own ways of acting and thinking, one's own categories of conceptualization. They will be deployed in the first place, for they are the only ones available.

On the third step, one goes back to one's own place. Even if the return is only mental, this movement defines a reversal of the course of approaching. However, this return inaugurates the process of a second distantiation. The emigrant observer sees his own society—and the identity given to him by the latter—through the eyes of a stranger. If he does not give in to the schizophrenia that possibly arises from such an experience, then this new distantiation will offer the opportunity for the conciliation of these two apparently incompatible aspects of his experience and, at the same time, their ways of conceptualization.

The fourth and final step refers to a new approaching of otherness, enriched, one could say, by the evaluation of the first visit, whereby the others are neither a deviation from the ecumenical values that he considers his culture represents, nor an exotic model of a new set of values. Then, without losing from sight the horizon of universalism (that is, the horizon which renders communication and meeting in advance necessary and legitimate but also feasible) this person will be able to study the society of others as well as his own and compare. So, Todorov concludes, "Knowledge of the others is not simply one possible path towards self-knowledge: it is the only path" (ibid., 84).[3]

Thus, the visiting of otherness constitutes an action which not only preserves a distance; it also weaves a relation on this distance, a relation which opens up the particularity of the visitor itself, leaving it exposed before the other. And if we also imagine that the other might begin his own reciprocal course towards the otherness of the visitor, then this reasoning has the possibility of describing the relation towards otherness as a symmetrical departure of the one towards the other. The distantiation from oneself and the return to a self that is not the same anymore will be the horizon of such a departure.[4]

Theatrical distance

The opening of identities and the effort to approach the identity of others is, as a social practice, inherently theatrical. Departing towards a different self, one offers a field of encounter.[5] Crafting a

3. Starting from Benjamin's notion of historical discontinuity, Susan Buck-Morss sees the horizon of "human universality" as being explicitly verified when people have to face ruptures in their culture: "It is in the discontinuities of history that people whose culture has been strained to the breaking point give expression to a humanity that goes beyond cultural limits" (Buck-Morss 2009, 133). This enforced visit to otherness makes the inhabiting of exception, aftermath or uprooting, as we have seen, an inventive practice open to new forms of solidarity.

4. According to Richard Schechner, "Acting, in most cases, is the art of temporary transformation—not only the journey out but also the return" (Schechner 1985, 125). There are however culturally important forms of acting which are explicitly focused on transforming the actor. Schechner refers to initiation rites as "transformation performances" (ibid., 127). The idea of visiting otherness, as explored in this chapter, offers a unifying formulation for the understanding of various degrees of transformation connected with acting. It is the social context that gives meaning to acting as a form of negotiation with otherness and therefore creates the ground for meaningful deviations, transformations, and "returns."

5. Schechner's performer learns "to act in between identities; in this sense performing is a paradigm

self to facilitate the encounter means departing from an assumed rigid identity without however losing oneself by assuming the identity of those participating in the encounter. The meeting is carried out through tentative disguises provided that the particular terms for the meeting parts are preserved. Particularity thus can be understood as an identity in constant movement.

We can consider that the theatrical skill that processes approaching disguises practically defines a first distantiation from one's self (understood as a fixed identity). This distantiation corresponds to what, in Todorov's reasoning, constitutes the driving force of departure. The approaching attempts dictate movements, invented behavior, and gestural experiments that construct aspects of a self that is capable of creating the field of communication. These attempts have a disguising theatrical character, since they construct features of a devised self, performing them in view of the encounter. This approaching theatricality tries to turn distance into its stage. However, theatrical action itself, when not trapped in the equating illusion that conceals the profound power of comparison that feeds it, emphasizes its theatricality in a theatrical way. Such theatricality keeps the founding comparison—which forms the disguising activity—operative, when not only does it establish itself on stage but it also points beyond the stage.[6]

In such an inventive approach of the other, the theatrical disguise is not only a gesture of concealment or misleading information. It is also a gesture of pointing out the activity itself, revealing the distance that is turned into a stage. In a way that

of liminality" (Schechner 1985, 123).

6. Tracy C. Davis provides an extended discussion linking Carlyle's use of the term "theatricality" with Brecht's and Boal's ideas of a critical theater. In this discussion, theatricality is not synonymous with mimesis but involves "an alienation from character and circumstances" (Davis 2003, 153) which effects "a critical stance in the public sphere, including but not limited to the theatre." Davis sees theatricality's self-reflexive power not in the actor's performance but in the spectator's "active dissociation" from what he or she witnesses (ibid., 145).

reveals the constructed character of the enacted self (something that is essential in any theatrical performance) this gesture tries to underline the effort needed to create a common ground without reducing one identity to the other. It emphasizes comparison; it points out the very distance that separates instances of otherness and distinguishes them. The distantiation that inaugurates a doubled theatricality, i.e., the movements which display the theatrical character of the approaching action, annuls the closed nature of any misleading disguise.

Theatrical approaching behaviors take the form of constructions, inventions, and disguises which do not intend to deceive, but to explore ways of acting in the direction of otherness suggested by the other, patterns of action which "stage" encounters. Theatrical actions can show that the reality of the encounter is not separated from the operations that form it. The encounter does not "happen" after some first inventive theatrical gestures have produced, in one way or another, results. The encounter—on the whole and in all its aspects—is a field of operations, if it wishes to conserve the force of comparison that moves it, if it wishes to preserve the otherness of the meeting parts. The skill of approaching disguises is not only a convenient tool for the encounter, but also its necessary horizon. The whole field of approach between instances of otherness is a mosaic made from theatrical micro-movements, which are movements of negotiation. Meaning is woven in without necessarily being expressed and constitutes the constructed and constructing horizon of the encounter.

The doubled theatricality of the encounter corresponds, in essence, to the doubled distantiation Todorov identifies in the form of the reciprocal approach of otherness. The second distantiation—that occurs when one sees one's own society through the eyes of a stranger—reveals the relative character of any role and therefore, its essentially constructed nature. Through the eyes of a

Immigrants inventing their own ad-hoc public stage (Athens).

Beauty salon or urban threshold? (São Salvador de Bahia, Brazil)?

stranger, what was until recently familiar and evident is rendered strange and unjustified.

However, he who returns does not simply adopt the identity of a stranger and its perspective. Visiting otherness does not amount to assimilation with otherness. It is the dynamics of comparison that activates a new behavior, one that tries to handle the distance between two cultural systems of reference on stage. Thus, he who returns does not behave as an "other," but as someone who knows other people exist, as someone who knows his identity is formed solely in relation to others. And so, in his behavior, he points out the theatricality of the approach as a double theatricality. For the second distantiation, the distantiation of awareness and not of loss in an unbridgeable division, shows in a theatrical way, inside the game of negotiation, that the others exist and that they have an influence on behavior through the constant interweaving of intermediate instances of otherness which are under constant negotiation.[7]

Thus, this reasoning neither discharges in an absolute denial of difference (which aims at submitting the instances of otherness to a normative ecumenism) nor an absolute affirmation of difference (which leads to the relativism of coexistence but also to *racisme différentialiste*). It is important to understand the relation with otherness as a relation of acceptance that can exist only to the extent that the encounter is attempted. The outcome of the encounter, either in the form of synthesis or in the form of new antagonisms or new balances, is not predetermined. However, in order to explore a relation with otherness, otherness must be accepted as such. And this can be the underlying effort of an approaching theatricality.

7. For Féral, "Initially, theatricality . . . is a performative act creating the virtual space of the other, the transitional space discussed by Winnicot, the threshold [*limen*] discussed by Turner, or Goffman's "framing." It clears a passage, allowing both the performing subject as well as the spectator to pass from 'here' to 'elsewhere'" (Féral 2002, 98). Intermediate instances of otherness, created in and for the encounter, employ the power to create "virtual spaces of the other" in order to establish relations with actual, experienced forms of social otherness.

Todorov claims that such a constant movement between two poles of otherness creates people who feel constantly exiled, "uprooted" (Todorov 1993, 74). They belong to neither the country they visit, nor the one from which they departed. He is right, but only if we accept that such an attitude, in producing open non-recognizable identities, leads to a temporary exile, an estrangement from those who insist on safeguarding boundaries of a common self-sufficient and non-negotiable identity. Such a temporary exile corresponds to the experience of the encounter; however, it does not predetermine the future of a relation that could result from such an encounter. This encounter can lead to compositions and mutations, as well as displaced antagonisms. Temporary exile, then, will describe the sense of adventure of an approaching theatricality.

Proximate otherness

The symbolic handling of distance defines the relations between people and groups. It is a way of telling apart the familiar, the friendly, the remote, and the hostile. All norms of behavior, be they manifest or only hinted at, define distances. The wisdom of "propriety" in a relatively closed system of reference, such as the traditional neighborhood, is epitomized, according to de Certeau and colleagues (de Certeau et al 1998, 21), in a shared feeling of "social distance" that shows "how far is not going too far" (until what point is one allowed to go without "going too far," as we would say).

Social distances always end up describing distances in space: how often one is supposed to approach a stranger in the street, how one hugs a friend or one's wife, how close to the salesperson one gets or from what distance someone greets another person, etc. Distances are "kept" according to the commonly used expression, in keeping with the directions that mark the expressivity of the body itself. Distances are essentially established as bodily relations. At the same time, however, they exist to be crossed. A "praxeomorphic" measuring system (Bauman 1998, 28) holds a special significance for the concept of near and far. And it can, proportionally, recognize the degree of kinship as well as the differentiation of the surrounding space in a graded relation between more private or more public spaces. Such a system, which emerges in practice and offers it a necessary provision, practically measures the distances to be crossed. We cannot thus interpret distances without implicitly or explicitly considering human actions meant to employ them for some purpose. "[T]he only void space that exists exists by nature of the action undertaken in order to cross it" (Virilio 1997, 59).

The perceptive, empirical sense of distance in the practices of inhabiting space supports an awareness of symbolic potential: it creates interpretations of crossing actions. The effort needed to cross the distance is itself turned into the measure of this distance. Therefore perceptively and empirically, distance corresponds to different forms of body-environment relations. These different relations are recorded by the body's senses in their effort to estimate, cross, and use space. Bodily experience renders the distinction between here and there acceptable as an evaluative distinction, thus offering an empirical basis to the symbolization of near and far, close and beyond.

At a time when the perceptive distinction is affected by the "pollution of distances" which renders intermediate space indifferent, the symbolization of otherness as a condition of distantiation or graded nearness undergoes a crisis (Virilio 1997, 58). The crisis of otherness understood by Augé as a crisis of symbolization of the "other" (Augé 1999, 132) has definitely been affected by the crisis the blurring of distinction between "far" and "near" introduces into the symbolic mechanism. Even more, the crisis of otherness as borne of the difficulty in approaching the other is closely related to the incapability of symbolizing distance as a field that is crossed and exists to be crossed. Instant proximity destroys the encounter with the other just as excessive distantiation creates impassable boundaries. Maybe we should consider that a skill corresponding to a dilatory circumspection is needed for the processing of distance as a necessary condition for the encounter. Such a skill would support a space-creating circumspection; one that not only handles distances but also constructs distances capable of hosting the relation with otherness. Without such intermediate spaces, without the skill of differentiating them or creating them, it seems that we are losing the capacity of communicating with difference, with what is other in others. If the visit to otherness is a voyage that has its own time and space, which defines a field of maneuvering and consecutive approaches, then to cancel this field renders the visit problematic if not unfeasible.

Baudelaire and the clown

Theatrical behavior offers the social individual dexterity with regards to distantiation. Theatricality—depending on one's awareness of distance between the self and the presented self—needs this particular distance between two selves, or two behaviors or two expressions, which render the comparison active. Without the catalytic presence of comparison, the theatrical "as if" collapses into a mimetic act that destroys the boundary between the actor and the role, between the self and the other.[8]

In an actor's body, on the scale of micro-movements, "a continuous pulse abstracts the body from a hypothetical meaning and sends it back, from this meaning back to the literally physical

---

8. In a much discussed formulation, Schechner observes: "Olivier is not Hamlet, but he is not not Hamlet: his performance is between a denial of being another (= I am me) and a denial of not being another (= I am Hamlet)" (Schechner 1985, 123).

presence" (Starobinski 1970, 58). We know she is not the one she pretends to be. So does the actor herself. In the distance between the body that already exists on stage and the body that the role constructs, the field of impersonation emerges. What is impersonation, if not a visiting of otherness?

Baudelaire tells us the story of Fanfarlo, a radiant stage dancer with whom the story's hero falls in love. But whom exactly does he fall in love with? The dancer or the roles that she so brilliantly impersonates on stage? From what it seems, neither her true self nor the roles she impersonates are what makes him feel attracted to her. When she gives in to his love and he gets to know her outside the magic of the stage, when she is proven incapable of recovering the magical properties conveyed to her by the characteristics of the Shakespearean heroes or the characters of the Italian *commedia dell'arte*, then he pushes her away contemptuously. She seems "incapable of prolonging the retraction between the true presence and the symbolically revoked meaning" (ibid., 61–62).

So Baudelaire's hero had fallen in love with a body on the threshold. It is not only love inspired by a symbol, it is one that falls apart when the symbol is demythologized. It is love focused on a face-body that is capable of bridging over and over again the distance between here and there, the tangible and the dream. The driving force of such a love does not lie in the illusion of the image but on the intensity that emerges from the distance between the self and the role. The visiting of the role's otherness, the poetic dimension of the distance crossed again and again by the body of Fanfarlo, is what renders her an object of desire.

The power of theatrical distance—as the distance between two selves or bodies—is represented in a particularly vivid way by the traditional figure of the circus clown. The clown is a disguised person, his behavior is theatrical, but what role is he impersonating? Is it the role of an unreal personality, completely alien to others?

This is made obvious by his extravagant costume and excessive makeup. But it is also the role of a familiar personality. A clown is prone to clumsy errors, just as we all are. He is an eternal blunderer but also a crafty mischief-maker, a kind and emotional fool, both young and old. We know that whoever impersonates him is not simply pretending to be something he isn't. He is putting part of his soul into it, part of his inventiveness and mischievousness. Not everybody becomes a clown. It seems then that, here, Diderot's *paradoxe sur le comédien* (translated in English as "the paradox of acting" or "the paradox of the actor") does not apply.[9]

The clown is a role at the borderline of theater; a role of improvisation and the constant irresolution between the impersonator and his appearance. The clown is literally born and lives in the distance that separates the two bodies. On the one hand, he is the limit of a theatrical distantiation that dissolves the boundaries between theater and the world. So, the clown is an acrobat of impersonation. He knows how to balance in the void between theatricality and life. Maybe that is why he points out the theatricality of life by driving it to its extremes? If everything is theater and everything is, at the same time, familiar as life, the clown reveals life as a fleeting pretext: nothing has the stability of an unequivocal meaning. Thus, the clown becomes an objector without a place for his objection to turn into a stance.

Due to this, the clown invades the stage in a particular way. He comes from elsewhere; his entrance must be planned with great care. A trick, a gesture, a noisy event marks the passing of the stage itself into another world. Starobinski writes, "His entrance must depict the overcoming of the boundaries of reality" (ibid., 139). Could it be that the importance of the clown's entrance is another

9. "They say an actor is all the better for being excited, for being angry. I deny it. He is best when he imitates anger. Actors impress the public not when they are furious but when they play fury well" (Diderot 1957, 71).

way of underlining the critical hovering above the threshold that constitutes his "theatrical" identity? Could it be that this odd mischief-maker—so mischievous that he is never totally entrapped by the role's clichés even though his patterns of behavior must be recognizable—by linking the worlds of paradox and intimacy offers us a model for the self-other relation? With his entrance on stage, the clown crosses the threshold space that separates us, the public, from a different, disparate world, a world of happiness that is at the same time fantastic and mundane.[10] In the end, the clown can cause an interior resonation of our memories of liberating oddity, of the liberating laughter of carnival as a collective reversal and overcoming of roles (Bakhtin 1984, 217–220).

The theatrical city

If we accept the opinion of architectural historian Manfredo Tafuri, twentieth-century theater took special care to call attention to the relation between what is happening on stage and in life in a modern megalopolis. The stage of modern theater was taken as a "virtual city" (Tafuri 1990, 95–112) that tried to depict the intensity of the metropolitan experience with the avalanche of stimuli it transmits to the human body, either by adopting an affirmative attitude towards metropolitan life or criticizing it in many different ways.

The interventionism of early twentieth-century vanguards is marked by the presence of bodies that transmit the feeling of a new life rhythm to their movements and forms. From the nervous, frantic grimaces of dadaist performance to the monumental human puppets of Bauhaus theater, the body is no longer the field

---

10. Exploring Shakespeare's theater in search of a general theory of human action, Kirsten Hastrup interprets the stage as a "site of passage," "a passage between separate worlds and viewpoints, between then and now, between this world and another." "Social agents," she points out, "in general inhabit a comparable site of passage, a momentously unknown present" (2004, 111).

for the expressive search of a particular psyche which corresponds to the content of a role; rather, it gives form to common sensations. These common sensations represent, reform or even prefigure the metropolitan experience in its development.

Why does the body acquire such a role? Why does the experience of the megalopolis become immediately—and often painfully—perceptible in the body of the inhabitant? The contemporary experience of the crowd which floods the streets, subway stations, department stores and public buildings, this experience which defines the personal relation to the city, is an experience of body relations. The rhythm of the movement of masses, the forced proximity and random path-crossings make up the field of a reflexive behavior of the body that is often expressed in an almost hypnotic compliance with traffic rules. If one is to analyze the experience of the crowd as a new social convention of handling the distance between two bodies, one will see that this convention is taking the form of a particular expressivity of the bodies. It is precisely the theatricality of this new convention regulating encounters between city dwellers that the theatrical avant-garde of the beginning of the century seems to explore, either explicitly or implicitly.

Let us consider the Italian Futurists, for example. In his *Variety Theatre Manifesto*, Marinetti exalts the shock technique, which is capable of destroying the spatial and temporal unity of the stage (Tafuri 1990, 98). The reality of the metropolis, as a welcomed experience of excitement and intense rhythm, is called upon to flow into the theatrical space as an explosion. Chaos is but a polymorphic blend of life fragments. So, a "body madness" [*fisicofollia*] (ibid., 99) is channeled into the physical action on stage, capable of turning the "madness" of metropolitan life into a principle of un-founding all value systems. In the name of an aesthetic affirmation of the new world, an affirmation which embraces the praise of the futurists for the industrial landscape and their conception

resonance of the concept of vicinity. That is, of the sensation of proximity which gives birth to encounters.

In the neighborhood, the presence of the other resides in the boundaries of a manageable proximity. The other is not necessarily an acquaintance, but there are many possibilities of him or her becoming one through the intersection of movements that organize everyday life in space. The other is not necessarily a stranger either. Participation in the world of the neighborhood turns someone into a potential other in a relation that could be transient, accidental, or even regular (as in the repeated accidental encounters at the bus stop, the bakery, the park, etc.). So, the neighborhood is not the locus of mimetic "tribalism" (Maffesoli 1996)—as the homogenizing gated communities are[11]—but a web of spaces created by the multiform tactics of habitation.

The accidental structure of encounters results from intersecting personal routes which organize a personal and, simultaneously, collective inhabitation of the space. "The neighborhood is thus defined as a collective organization of individual trajectories" (de Certeau et al 1998, 15). One learns to live in the neighborhood by developing and sharpening the capacity to handle the spatial relations defined by these paths: one must always find "an equilibrium between the proximity imposed by the public configuration of places and the distance necessary to safeguard one's private life"(ibid.).

This "dexterity," this capacity of finding the point of balance, is a skill of appropriation of public space of the neighborhood, in which personal paths are embedded in their singularity. Residents must behave in ways which make them recognizable. That will place them in a web of exchange-relations with neighbors, where different degrees of intimacy are developed. The awareness and resourceful administration of this graded intimacy is based on the control of a graded proximity with others.

11. See chapter 1.

Theatricality of encounter (Havana, Cuba).

Creating an everyday public stage (Niscosia, Cyprus).

In his study of the art of coexisting in the neighborhood, Mayol suggests that the weaving of this sense of acknowledgement by others is based on the ritual confirmation of the rules of "propriety." Specifically, he writes, "Propriety is the rite of the neighborhood" (ibid., 19). Propriety defines the stage on which everyone's manners, expressions, and body movements will present an acceptable self. In this sense, as in all ritual theatricality, the neighborhood normalizes behavior. "However, in the ritualized confirmation of a sense of participating in the neighborhood's universe, specific, individually chosen tactics, which support the presentation of the self, reveal all their diversity.[12] Propriety defines a theatricality of behavior that is not oriented towards the confirmation of roles and hierarchies, but towards the indirect, sometimes, according to Bourdieu (1977, 171), misrecognized or, according to Vernant, pretentiously calculating, but always oblique and periphrastic negotiation with the small and large differences that characterize others as other (in Vernant and Detienne 1978).

In this sense, the theatricality of propriety has the particularity of "regulated improvisations" (Bourdieu 1977, 78). Desires are disguised but also secretly subjected to the implicit, inexpressible rules of propriety. Bodies learn to appreciate distances. Greeting the neighborhood's shop owner has its own small theatricality of encounter, as does the encounter with the hurried neighbor whom we come face to face with every morning, at the same time, on our way to work.

All the multifarious negotiations of distances, which give birth to varied relations, define the neighborhood as a threshold space between the city space and domestic space. As a field of encounters, the neighborhood is a space where one learns how to transform distances into controlled bridges towards others and how to administrate relations with others as relations of vicinity. In con-

12. See chapter 1.

trast to the forced proximity of the metropolitan crowd, the neighborhood creates conditions of encounter out of vicinity, making distance a prerequisite for relation building.

The neighborhood does not offer this wisdom of inhabitation—which administrates the intermediate distances of vicinity—only to reproduce a closed world where nothing happens.

The neighborhood constitutes a birthplace of events big and small. It has its history. The ritual theatricality of propriety does not coincide with the stereotypical structure of mass culture. De Certeau insists on this. However, he reflects, this resourceful, poetic culture of everyday life is not only a culture of the habitual that "hides a fundamental diversity of situations, interests, and contexts under the apparent repetition of objects that it uses" (de Certeau et al 1998, 256). The fundamental variety of inhabitation practices that approach the other with the periphrastic and distance-creating wisdom of theatricality are dependent on the birth of events irreducible to norms of social reproduction. What is recognizable is compared with what seems unfamiliar.

The neighborhood is potentially open to social change; it is always the stage of minor or major transformations. If the power of "approaching theatricality" can remain an element of its culture, then the neighborhood can remain a field of synthesis as well as a field of differentiating relations. Thus, the much-discussed unraveling of the contemporary city's social fabric does not amount to the dismantling of a real or fantasized community of people knowing each other. It marks something more serious: the short-circuiting of the capacity to approach others as others. Beyond exoticism and hostility, and against assimilating mimetic practices, the theatricality of propriety reveals to us an art of supporting differences through practices that continuously weave the fabric of common life.

Part III

Celebrating heterotopia at the end of a large antigentrification demonstration (Berlin).

06

Heterotopias:
appropriating Foucault's geography of otherness

Power, order, and places

The concept of order is deeply involved with the experience of space. When we speak of order, we refer to there being a place for each thing. Perhaps one of our most immediate experiences is of space as a sum of places. The concept of order contains a latent image of a tidy space, the image of an arrangement of places.

The notion of order [*ordre*] runs throughout Michel Foucault's analysis of power. He is not particularly concerned with an ontology of power, i.e., with the essence of power, as if power were a condition that transcends history and society (Foucault 1983, 217). How power is exercised and how relations of power are created are questions at the center of Foucault's interest. However, if power manifests itself only when it is exercised and it is ascertained in the historical relations that constitute social subjects, then how are these relations assembled? What defines them in a historically determined society? The concept of order can come in handy here. In a relational model that does not wish to be perverted towards the ascertainment—completely devoid of prospects for knowledge—that everything is connected with everything in ways that do not obey any kind of normality, it is important to know whether or not relations construct forms of order. That is, in what ways—or not—are relations connected? What links them as unities, coordinates them, arranges them or lines them up?

In his research on the birth of prisons, clinics, and psychiatric hospitals, Foucault seeks the historical particularity of a "chaining" of relations of power that corresponds to a "disciplinary society" whose characteristics are crystallized in the eighteenth-century Western world. However, this systematic subordination of power relations to order does not correspond to an order of places that can be defined as power centers. "Power is not something that is acquired, seized or shared" (Foucault 1990, 94). That is why it cannot be accumulated in places and it cannot be found in places. Order corresponds to the layout of the field of actions that constitute the exercise of power. In essence, this field constitutes "the system of differentiations which permits one to act upon the action of others" (Foucault 1983, 223).

The historical particularity of disciplinary society lies in the fact that the system of differentiations on which power relations are articulated reaches the borderline "molecularity" of individuation. Discipline classifies and defines the action of people to the point that it separates them. Discipline as a power relation guarantees action will be imposed on the action of people, defining them as subjects—bodies on which a "microphysics of power" (Foucault 1995, 26) is exercised. So, instead of centers of power, order refers to places of exercise. In their molecular differentiation, these places are the bodies themselves of the individuals who form the society. Thus, order, as a condition of relations between places, is a condition of relations between places that define subjects,[1]

1. As Andrea Mubi Brighenti observes, "In order to work properly, government needs to territorialize a given population within its own framework of sovereignty. In Foucault's account, this

with the double meaning that Foucault rediscovers in the term "subject": an active subject as well as someone subjected to some kind of power differential.

The spatial image that underlies the concept of order does not become a vehicle for Foucault to describe power as the distribution of specific social forces in certain places. It assists in the formulation of a very important view: in disciplinary society, power classifies, distributes, defines, demarcates, and controls the compliance of people as an active acceptance of the defining elements that society attributes to them. It is in this sense that power is exercised as a process that constructs the field of possible action for disciplined subjects.

The spatialization of knowledge

The notion of order and the spatial image that goes with it help Foucault define—on the same level and with the same means—the logic of the distribution of power relations in the social body and the logic of the materialization-perpetration of those relations in specific material environments. Here we can find one of the most interesting ways to develop Foucault's work. The author himself admits he didn't follow that path, although he believes it would have been quite fruitful: "space is fundamental in any exercise of power" (Foucault 1984, 252). It is possible to interpret this claim somewhat differently: in the organizing logic of space we can discover not only the results of power relations but also the preconditions of their articulation. In *Discipline and Punish* (1995), Foucault identifies the Panopticon as the model of disciplinary society's spatial organization.

is precisely the aim that disciplines help to achieve. What counts is not space per se, but the relationships among people that are built through space and inscribed in it in the effort to sustain the triangle sovereignty-discipline-government" (Brighenti 2010, 55).

Observing the birth of the prison in Western history, he detects a series of detention practices and seeks the common precondition for their emergence. It is not about tracing a common ideology or looking for a center of regulation that programs and acts, but rather about trying to find a common matrix (in the sense of a mold); a model which could highlight the common elements of all power relations that sustain a disciplinary society as well as the articulation of those relations. Foucault discovered this model in a spatial arrangement, an imaginary architectural creation, a system of spatial relations envisioned by Jeremy Bentham as the perfect system of supervision.[2] The importance of this spatial organization, which has inspired a great variety of task-specific buildings such as prisons and asylums, lies in the fact that the person is forced to comply and adjust his or her behavior because of the feeling that he or she can be observed from the tower at any time, without ever knowing when this is indeed happening. Surveillance becomes an interior norm of the observed; it becomes inscribed in the body. "Visibility is a trap" (ibid., 200).

The Panopticon "is the diagram of a mechanism of power reduced to its ideal form . . . it is in fact a figure of political technology" (ibid., 205). By placing bodies in space, it affects their behavior through its architecture and geometry, virtually classifying the behavior of the enclosed. It is the precondition for the exercise of power upon them.

For Foucault, discipline is above all an art of distribution. That is why "discipline proceeds from the distribution of individuals in space" (ibid., 141). So, it is a specific order in space, in the sense of

2. "At the periphery, an annular building; at the center, a tower; this tower is pierced with wide windows that open onto the inner side of the ring" (Foucault 1995, 200). The building is divided into cells, each of which extends the whole of its width. Each cell has two windows, one on the inside and the other on the outside. In essence, an observer from the central tower can watch the interior of every cell without himself being visible. All one has to do is place "a madman, a patient, a condemned man, a worker or a schoolboy" in the cell, and their activities become exposed to whoever is in the tower (ibid.).

an active interference in the spatial distribution of people, which gives disciplinary supervision a material form. Foucault finds this power that controls and supervises as well as strictly defines the obligations of the inhabitants in the image of a plague-stricken town. In order to record and control the spreading of the disease, all persons must be in their place, their condition must be reported, and their controlled access to the means of subsistence guaranteed. "The plague is met by order" (ibid., 197). So, the "plague-stricken town . . . is the utopia of the perfectly governed city" (ibid., 198).

The Panopticon transforms a condition whose legitimation and efficiency was linked with an "emergency situation" into a permanent state, a model articulation of techniques of surveillance with an exercise of controlling power (ibid.).

The model of panopticism is not a spatial condition that is reducible to the geometry of relations between positions. The Panopticon, Foucault insists, is an ideal social machine. It must be in operation for disciplinary power to function. The spatiality of the model is a performed spatiality, a realization of specific spatial relations by specific subjects that are found in places of power precisely because they "inhabit" these spatial relations. In his writings on Foucault, Deleuze claims that in the mapping of disciplinary power, the notion of a "diagram" as a "space-time multiplicity" is activated. "The diagram . . . is a cartography which is coextensive with the whole social field" (Deleuze 1988, 34). For Foucault, the concept of diagram stresses the potential, process-oriented character of spatial association. Thus, the diagram could offer the image of a spatial order that is in process. Stuart Elden makes a similar comment on Foucault's idea of spatial ordering: "Foucault's mappings are far from totalizing, perhaps best seen as sketchmaps, approximations toward, signposts" (Elden 2001, 115).

Spatiality thus emerges as a determining factor in understanding the disciplinary surveillance that characterizes a particular articulation of power relations in a specific society, but also, in the development and realization of those practices in a given social arrangement. The specific architecture of prisons, asylums, factories or schools in this society is not an epiphenomenon of power relations but simultaneously a term, precondition, and result of their deployment.

If power relations in the disciplinary society are integrated in the model of panopticism, their role in the conservation of this social regime depends on their efficiency in detecting and classifying individuals and guiding their actions. This way, power relations produce knowledge which is not only useful for their enforcement but also results from it.[3]

"[I]n the eighteenth century, the table was both a technique of power and a procedure of knowledge. It was a question of organizing the multiple . . . of imposing upon it an 'order'" (Foucault 1973, 148). In this operation, knowledge and power provide the foundation for each other; it is not a relation of base and superstructure. Discipline is, above all, an art of distribution. Ultimately, the logic of classification for the organization of human behavior—of people but also of objects and of a city in one order—is both an act of power (of controlling reality) and one of knowledge (of reality). In the same period when classificatory knowledge (the detection of the particularities of behavioral types) is brought forward as an issue, natural history is also constituted through the classification of beings (ibid., 128–132). In both ventures, vision plays a crucial role. What is visible is collected and classified, and at the same time, rendered the object of observation and supervision.[4]

3. "There is no power relation without the correlative constitution of a field of knowledge, nor any knowledge that does not presuppose and constitute at the same time power relations" (Foucault 1995, 27).

4. "To observe, then, is to be content with seeing—with seeing a few things systematically" (Foucault 1973, 134).

Natural history constitutes a true "spatialization of knowledge" (Foucault and Rabinow 1984): herbariums, collections, and gardens are the material forms the "non-temporal rectangle" assumes, in which "creatures present themselves one beside another, their surfaces visible, grouped according to their common features" (Foucault 1973, 131). The timeless rectangle is yet another version of the table, of the tables constructed by panopticism: it orders space so as to control and come to know at the same time. And this spatialization of relations is the necessary precondition for the consolidation of identities and characteristics of beings as "characters" (ibid., 140).[5]

Spaces of otherness?

In the experience of relations defined by spaces materialized as places, as well as in the constitution of the way we think and talk about things presupposing a certain order that defines them, space appears as a condition of association, and simultaneously, as a condition of discrimination and comparison. According to Foucault, space as an experience and as a concept that nurtures Western thought, has its own history. In a short text presented in 1967 before a group of architects and published in 1984, shortly before his death, Foucault attempts a rough periodization of this history. In the Middle Ages, the hierarchization and blending of spaces according to their sacred or cosmic significance gave birth to medieval space as "the space of localization." In the seventeenth century, Galileo confirms the existence of an "infinite and infinitely open space," introducing an understanding of space as extension. In our time, the uniform space-extension is substituted by space-loca-

5. "Natural history in the Classical Age . . . constitutes a whole domain of empiricism as at the same time describable and orderable" (Foucault 1973, 158). "The structure selected to be the locus of pertinent identities and differences is what is termed the character" (ibid., 140).

tions (emplacement). "We are in an epoch in which space is given to us in the form of relations between emplacements" (Foucault 2008, 15). These locations are perfectly distinguishable and ir-reducible to each other. Thus, a fundamental heterogeneity runs through the space of modern life.

In this scheme—which Foucault left unfinished—there is an emphasis on how space as a social condition constitutes a system of discrimination and differentiation. The way in which relations of power are articulated in such a system is not clearly described. However, what is particularly interesting in this text is a category of spaces that apparently constitute a crucial field of articulation of power relations, a crucial field in which the relation between clas-sificatory identification and heterogeneity is regulated. Foucault calls these spaces heterotopias and defines them as the "real [*réel*] places—effective places [*effectifs*] that are written into the institu-tion of society itself, and that are a sort of counter-emplacement, a sort of effectively realized utopia in which the real emplacements, all the other real emplacements, that can be found in a culture, are simultaneously represented [*representés*], contested [*contestés*], and inverted [*inverses*]" (ibid., 17).

Foucault distinguishes these spaces from those described as utopias, ascribing them with a specific, real existence inside so-ciety. These spaces are absolutely distinguishable from all other spaces in which the life of a society unravels. What is less clear, is the place of heterotopias in the intertwining of power and space constituted by disciplinary order—the squaring of the social field and the space of common life. Are heterotopias strictly delimited and stigmatized in this order or do they constitute another version of the articulation of power and space, different from and antago-nistic to the order of disciplinary society?

At the beginning of the Classical Age, in the seventeenth cen-tury, Foucault detects a turning point in Western society: the birth of the institution of confinement.[6] As he tries to show with his historically focused research, commitment gives birth to a new relation of society with what it defines as normal and abnormal, natural and unnatural in human life. By banishing what it considers unnatural, unsocial—madness being the emblematic threat in this equation—society delimits in its interior an area under surveillance, in which "dangerous others" are enclosed.[7] The confinement of madmen estranged from society, or of those who are generally considered antisocial, constitutes a spatial determination of radical otherness. If the model of the supervised, plague-stricken town could impose a generalized classification and control of inhabitants, the asylum constitutes a model in which the other is exiled, just as it occurred with lepers, but in the interior of a society that strictly delimits the perimeter of a malignant "abscess." The classification of social subjects, of which panopticism constitutes the clearest example, seems to presuppose a different register and at the same time a register elsewhere, where the otherness that escapes classification can be found. So, one could identify heterotopias as the places of the other, outside the generalized disciplinary order, where differences do not describe different characters but the boundaries of the social.[8]

If one wishes to consistently observe the logic of the intertwining of space and power pointed out by Foucault, one must promptly place the asylum and the prison not only outside order

6. The institution of confinement is not only defined by the fencing of a space but also by the distribution of people. "Each individual in its place and a place for each individual. . . .Discipline organizes an analytical space" (Foucault 2006, 102). It is the coding of a structural organization, as Dreyfus and Rabinow (1983, 155) observe.

7. Such a gesture "did not isolate strangers who had previously remained invisible, who until then had been ignored by force of habit. It altered the familiar cityscape by giving them new faces, strange, bizarre silhouettes that nobody recognized" (Foucault 2006, 80).

8. Madmen "upset the order [*ordonnance*] of the social space," as appears in the first French edition of *The History of Madness* (1961), quoted in Elden (2001, 126).

but also inside it, within a dynamic system that regulates deviation through the process of therapy and disciplining. It is a necessary outside, in which the findings of an unceasing panoptic observation are constantly analyzed and classified.

According to Foucault's definition, prisons and asylums are heterotopias. He distinguishes a special category of heterotopias of deviation, in which he includes such institutions (Foucault 2008, 18). The absolute otherness of these institutions does not, however, simply give them a distinct position in an established order of space. It renders them an active factor in the definition of this order. Precisely because they can "reverse" other places, heterotopias do not transgress order but rather reproduce it. The distinction normal/abnormal as a counterpart of the distinction acceptable/unacceptable and social/antisocial is the motor of classification. These distinctions and the safeguarding of their validity and effectiveness are the object of disciplinary power.

However, Foucault detects the following principle in the prospect of the exploration of a possible "heterotopology": "The heterotopia has the power to juxtapose in a single real place several spaces, several emplacements that are in themselves incompatible" (ibid., 19). Here he seems to allow for the formation of a different horizon for the role of heterotopias in the articulation of power and space. It is as if heterotopias were not approached from the outside, considered according to their relation with an outside that distinguishes and separates them, but from the inside, as worlds with their own logic of organization. From such a perspective, heterotopias appear as complex worlds, not only as statutorily external to the ruling order but also as fields of emergence of an "anti-order." What examples does Foucault appeal to in order to show this power of heterotopia? The theater in whose stages we see the alternation of different spaces, the cinema with the singular superposition of the two-dimensional space of the screen and the three-dimensional space of projection and, finally, the garden, the oldest example of a space where distinct and different locations coexist.[9]

Constitution in turmoil

One can single out the particularity of a displaced perspective in the analysis of heterotopias. They fundamentally involve interior incompatibilities and tensions. The fact that many places coexist in one place throws the exercise of classification into a crisis.

Foucault singles out the zoo as a contemporary heterotopia. He probably refers specifically not to these zoological gardens which present the species of animals for educational purposes, defining relatives and similar environments, but rather to those which seek to stimulate surprise and satisfaction by placing the most disparate animals, exhibits of the exotic and the unexpected, side by side. Animals from different parts of the world, each one in a miniature version of their environment, participate in a collage of places and images and compose a heterotopian superimposition of locations.

When, in the preface to *The Order of Things*, Foucault comments on the famous Chinese Encyclopedia described by Borges in one of his stories, he observes that it is a kind of "disorder" in which "fragments of a large number of possible orders glitter separately in the dimension, without law or geometry, of the heteroclite" (Foucault 1973, xvii). He also calls this condition a heterotopia and detects in it the absence of a "friendly space" where a common place could be defined through differences between things. That is why heterotopias destroy the syntax of the word

9. "The garden is the smallest parcel of the world and then it is the totality of the world."
    According to Foucault, the modern zoo develops from this heterotopian dimension of the
    garden (ibid., 20).

and above all the syntax that makes words and things stand together (ibid., xviii).

Although Foucault's point of view in the above references is oriented towards an archaeology of Western knowledge, one can observe an interesting analogy between this understanding of heterotopias and the one inferred so far. A peculiar and disturbing ambiguity defines heterotopias: they are characterized by the coexistence of fragments belonging to differing taxonomies. Beyond the dilemma of order-disorder, there is the "incongruous" and "the impossibility to define a common locus" (ibid., xviii). At the limits of an impossible knowledge, i.e., at the limits of a disorder which is filled with potential order, a heterotopia becomes place that can perhaps only be defined as pure unrest, a parallel birth and mutual refutation of orders.

Maybe the importance of the reversal that heterotopias entail in their comparison to other real "locations" could become visible here. Insofar as they are locations of otherness in relation to what surrounds them, heterotopias become places that bring relations between instances of otherness to prominence. They not only project their difference, but also render otherness an internal condition of their constant rebirth.

The many divergent critical readings of Foucault's heterotopias place emphasis on the dynamic character of the heterotopian condition. Geographer Edward Soja does not consider heterotopias as yet another kind of space that can be added to "geographic imagination," but insists that they make us think of spatiality in a different way, different from the current geographic discourse (Soja 1996, 163). For him Foucault's "heterotopology" is in many ways compatible with Lefebvre's readings of urban space as full of potentialities that challenge established spatial and social order.

Sociologist Kevin Hetherington considers heterotopias "alternate orderings," in the sense that—historically—they challenge existing forms of social order by inducing unexpected comparisons and combinations of elements (Hetherington 1997, 8–9). To illustrate his approach to the dynamics of heterotopian ordering he analyzes the factory as one of the most important heterotopian sites of modernity. In it "an alternate mode of ordering production" (ibid., 137) developed in a dynamic and conflicting coexistence with established work places.

Benjamin Genocchio wonders whether heterotopias point out the limits of the impossibility of a completely "other" place (Genocchio 1995, 42). Drawing on Foucault's definition of heterotopias in the preface of *The Order of Things*, he shows how discourse—as a system of systems; a field of order that renders possible all other forms of order in knowledge and action—cannot represent or describe heterotopias. Thus, for him heterotopia "comes to designate not so much an absolutely differentiated space as the site of that very limit, tension, impossibility" (ibid.).

Tafuri suggests that Foucault's definition of heterotopia in the preface to *The Order of Things* may apply to Piranesi's "obsessive technique of assemblage" (1990, 40). Piranesi's "hermetic fragmentation of architectural *ordo*" in his famous plates *Campo Marzio* and *Le Carceri* (ibid., 27) is indicative of a heterotopian reading of space that challenges urban syntax. Heterotopian dynamics are activated in this case through images that introduce a feeling of otherness into unexpected arrangements of recognizable architectural elements.

In all these interpretations, perhaps the internal tension detected in heterotopias does not characterize locational relations but rather space-time conditions in which the emergence of otherness intertwines with and confronts similarity. Could it be that inside the heterotopian condition the same and the different (inherently relational terms) are combined in multiple relations, which by constantly suspending the order that defines them, become exposed to the tensions that simultaneously confirm this order and deny it? Faced with classification that identifies and detects, the heterotopian disorder, as a multiplicity of possible orders, continues to produce differences. Heterotopias emerge as suspended spaces of otherness.[10]

According to Hetherington, heterotopias are born when a dominant desire for order that is characteristic of modern society has to confront the ambiguities created by the practices that materialize it. The utopian reformative logic of society itself, which imagines governance in the form of a perfect city where everything has its place, contains an inherent contradiction: "the utopian ideal that lay behind the desire for order was not necessarily ordered in itself" (Hetherington 1997, 67). Hetherington recognizes heterotopias as the intersection of alternative strategies for the creation of order. This differentiates them internally just as it differentiates the subjects that operate in their dominion. Heterotopias are thus composed of the contradictions that characterize them but also the confrontations that undermine any clarity in their objectives (ibid., 69).

Such an interpretation of heterotopia's dynamics tends to exaggerate the aiming for order, to the detriment of the recognition of practices imbued with the denial of order. If we define these practices as resistance, what role do they play in the creation of heterotopian conditions?

Heterotopias as spaces in suspense

Foucault puts it clearly: "Where there is power, there is resistance" (Foucault 1990, 95). The relation between power and resistance is mutually constitutive. Power relations involve a multiplicity of

10. One can find simulations of heterotopias in modern consumerism. The city of Las Vegas has been considered emblematic of this: "New York, Paris and Venice are shrunk down, remixed and repackaged for the consumer of mediated otherness in a space of convenience" (Chaplin 2000, 216).

resistances, and it is because of resistances that the exercise of power is historically differentiated. The incorporation of resistances in the "strategic field of power relations" (ibid., 95–96) is consistent with the logic of the necessary intertwining of the opposite poles normal/abnormal in the organization of the social order.

However, in the history of social confrontations, of rebellions large and small, it is precisely this fundamental distinction between normal and abnormal that is a *de facto* judgment, and not necessarily because some choose to do so. Resistances should not only be understood as denials or obstacles to power, they also delegitimize the practices of classification through which power relations are articulated. Resistance is not external to power. Because power and resistance are mutually constitutive, the field of power is created through processes that can be destroyed, reversed or become exposed to the possibilities of confrontation.

In one of his last texts, Foucault suggests that "[r]ather than analyzing power from the point of view of its internal rationality" we can "go further towards a new economy of power relations" by "analyzing power relations through the antagonism of strategies" (Foucault 1983, 211). With this, he highlights resistance as a field characteristic of the type of power they oppose. Against the "objectifying power" that Foucault establishes as the modern form of disciplinary power, against the power that attaches subjects to forced identities (ibid., 213), appear struggles that precisely deny such forms of definition. These struggles "for a new subjectivity," according to Foucault, have also existed in other times. What renders them particularly important in modern societies is the fact that they question the most fundamental element of disciplinary society: the classification-surveillance nexus.

Should we reserve the term "heterotopia" for the description of power-space relations in emergent struggles and resistances? Could it be that, precisely when the order that expresses a specific articulation of power and space is threatened by a "disorder" in which "fragments of a large number of possible orders glitter," heterotopic conditions are born? And, if these struggles upset the order of space as well as social order, it is not necessary to assume that they do this in order to foretell a new order, unless we consider that the social condition is always ordered. In that case, any practice that causes the emergence of new relations between people would by definition involve a new order. However, it is likely that the acts and practices of resistance create possibilities for new social relations that are not necessarily part of a new social order. Ernesto Laclau convincingly claims that "any representation [of society] is an attempt to constitute society, not to state what it is" (Laclau 1990, 82). When society is represented as an ordered totality, what is left out is the dynamic of change that essentially makes domination (or hegemony) a process open to history. Thus, order is more like a hegemonic stake than a fact.

Heterotopian conditions emerge when heterogenesis intertwines with reproduction. In this context social individualization takes place on precarious ground. Heterotopias are thus born as places of discontinuity, cracks in the molding, classifications of space and time. In them heteroclite fragments of space and time come together in processes that provide a place to emergent social relations.

We can consider heterotopias not as places of otherness but as passages towards otherness.[11] The spatial image of the passage does not present a space through its characteristics only, but rather through its relation to others, to such an extent that it becomes identified with this relation. All passages are "passage-towards." Heterotopias as passages are moving places, places

---

11. "Heterotopias thus mark an osmosis between situated identities and experiences that can effectively destroy those strict taxonomies that ensure social reproduction" (Stavrides 2007, 178).

Heterotopias of dignity. The construction of a self-managed childcare center by the Movimiento Popular La Dignidad in Villa 21, a Buenos Aires slum.

in which whatever is happening has departed from the previous order without a given destination.

Every society protects its passages. As we have seen, through rites of passage societies control and ensure the passage from one identity to another without the order of social reproduction being threatened. However, there are dangers of disorder and infringement lurking in passages. There, control could always fail.[12]

Heterotopias have some of the attributes of places of transition, where those who undergo rites of passage temporarily remain. In these places, as Turner pointed out, there is a hovering between an identity that has already been abandoned and an identity for which the initiated has not yet been considered worthy (Turner 1977, 102–106). The trials that accompany this in-between phase, which happen in places symbolically and often materially outside any place, are exercises in how to assume an imposed social identity. In heterotopias, these experiences of initiation to otherness of an impending identity are not strictly predetermined but rather assume the form of a visit to otherness (Stavrides 2002, 391); the form of a visit to a world that does not yet exist. It is a trial departure from what is characteristic of oneself without a given destination. In these trials of otherness, identities might shimmer, simultaneously appear and disappear, be expressed and refuted.

That is why it is reasonable to consider that heterotopias essentially host instances of theatricality. There is a trying on of new masks and roles without a definite access to another identity. The art of becoming someone else, not as an art of deception but as an art of searching for new forms of subjectivity, wells up in heterotopias. Heterotopian conditions harbor theatricality as a means to approach otherness (ibid., 233–241), a theatricality that does not give birth to identifications but rather to trials,

12. For a well-documented anthropological presentation of this argument, see Turner (1982, 45).

denials rather than assertions of roles, hybrid compositions and unfinished subjectifying practices.

The art of becoming someone else can also be an art of survival.[13] Those who find themselves in strategically disadvantageous positions due to the dominant power relations often invent ways to protect themselves from the consequences of control by pretending they don't stand out or pretending they comply with normalizing classifications. Disciplinary power and the classificatory knowledge that corresponds with it could be falling into a trap by mistaking signs of compliance with compliance itself. The dependence of disciplinary power on panoptic surveillance exposes it to the danger of identifying what is visible with what exists. Control through classification can possibly lose its target, failing to produce reality as it produces knowledge.

In heterotopias, the art of adopting another face or look—an art that is nurtured by the resourcefulness of the weak in the everyday game of survival[14]—becomes the motor of a socially critical visit to otherness: as a strategy of protection, pretending becomes an inventive questioning of the rules of identification, an ad hoc synthesis of incomplete and hybrid identities, identities under construction.

In the Parisian arcades of the nineteenth century, heterogenesis gave birth to collective and personal identities that evaded normalizing codifications: the flâneur, the bohemian, the intellectual, the dandy, the prostitute, are all figures whose presence turned the arcades into heterotopias of modernity.[15] In the collective ex-

13. It can become a form of the inventive arts of the weak, as de Certeau mentions. See de Certeau (1984, 24–28 and 40) for the tactics of deception used by workers pretending to be at work in order to temporarily escape from exhausting working conditions.

14. James Scott (1990) offers a systematic analysis of this inventiveness and the "arts of disguise" that distinguish it. See also his direct reference to Foucault, who underlines the theatricality of exaggeration found in the demands of the royal subjects in their complimentary formulation before the king (ibid., 93).

15. In respect of this, Walter Benjamin's (1999) analysis of the Parisian Arcades is essential.

Heterotopias of struggle. Teachers on strike occupy the central square of Oaxaca, Mexico (2016).

perience of an occupied factory in present-day Argentina, where the collective control of production and the new relations born through an antihierarchical logic are being tried, modern heterotopian conditions emerge. Maybe young skateboarders create their own heterotopias at night on the stairs outside of a bank, on a monument or in a square (Borden 2001, 182). Those who protest by blocking roads experience at the same moment this heterogenesis in their extraordinary relation with the city, just as the unemployed *piqueteros* in Argentina, the homeless in Brazil, the French students in the days of May '68, and the rebellious outcasts of the European suburbs and the U.S. ghettos experienced it. And, of course, whenever movements have tried to locate the

Heterotopias of struggle. Teachers on strike block the highway outside San Cristóbal de las Casas, Mexico (2016).

face of the future in heterotopian conditions, they have discovered the creative power of this trial visit to the "not-yet." These types of experiences were born and continue to be born in the demonstrations of the multiform movement against neoliberal globalization, just as they are born in the Lacandon jungle, in the autonomous municipalities of the Zapatista Indigenous rebels.

In his tenacious research on the connections between power and knowledge, Foucault pointed out the importance of space, not as a field of expression of social relations but as a factor in the articulation of power relations as well as the knowledge that corresponds to them. Space has history as concrete experience but also as a concept we use to think of society as a field of interdependent relations. It is important for the archaeology of knowledge as well as for the genealogy of modern power. Foucault did not follow a focused analysis of space in his research; his work, however, sheds light on the importance of such a perspective. As a geographer of otherness, and as an analyst of the relations of power that "subjectify" and "situate," he has made normalizing classifications problematic. Spatial and social orders both support and express the exercise of classificatory power in surveillance societies. Foucault has also shown that the field of control is discontinuous, that there are no centers of power but only relations and conditions of exercise that produce subjects.

The limited and historically confined effectiveness of normalizing power renders a microphysics of power necessary. A microphysics of resistance is likewise necessary,[16] insofar as it reshapes the rules of the exercise of power. Heterotopian conditions that go beyond the symmetrical involvement of power and resistance create new possibilities. "The ship," Foucault says, "is the heterotopia par excellence. In civilizations without boats, dreams dry up, espionage takes the place of adventure, and the police take the place of the pirates" (Foucault 2008, 22). When the Zapatistas organized the First Encounter for Humanity against Neoliberalism in the Lacandon Jungle, they too imagined their heterotopia as a ship. "The awning [of the convention in the jungle] is in reality a sail, the benches oars, the hill the hull of a mighty vessel, while the stage becomes the bridge. . . . Now I am a pirate. A pirate is tenderness that explodes in fury, is justice that has not yet been understood . . . is an eternal navigating toward no port" (Taussig 1999, 257).

---

16. "If it is true that the grid of 'discipline' is everywhere becoming clearer and more extensive, it is all the more urgent to discover how an entire society resists being reduced to it" (de Certeau 1984, xiv). De Certeau also speaks of "the network of an antidiscipline" where molecular actions are articulated.

The Zapatistas did not wish to protect their ship in the safety of a secret anchorage. They did not wish to entrench it in the arrogance of a well-planned utopia, and rather sent it everywhere, into the dirty waters of the social archipelago (Stavrides 2004), so that it might come across all kinds of vessels of resistance. Sometimes, in these often-crude vessels, the future sails, full of hopes and ambiguities, simultaneously here and elsewhere, today but also tomorrow and yesterday. A future that is unknown yet familiar as it is being created with materials taken from the present.

07

Identities and rebellion in Zapatista heterotopias

Thinking of how individual and collective identities define the members of a society does not amount to thinking of society as a classification of groups of named and invariable entities. Identities appear and disappear, they are projected in social antagonism, expressing it, diffracting it or concealing it. We must imagine identities as the product of social relations rather than as their precondition, and therefore consider their construction as an ongoing process that is open to changes and confrontations.

Precisely because it is the duration, confirmation or even overthrowing of social relations that are at stake in the creation or annulment of identities, it is not possible to imagine insurgent policies that pay no attention to the social conditions surrounding the birth of specific identities. If an individual or group recognizes itself in features that define the horizon of a promised continuity, then the conservation of this continuity calls for acts of assertion and reproduction. It is through attacking continuity and challenging its self-evident reproduction that dissident politics can set the field for the negation of the established identities.

The manifestation and reassertion of identity occurs through actions that are socially meaningful. An identity has consequences and it is produced as a consequence. In this sense, identities exist by being performed and thus constitute active elements of the social condition. They interact with social relations and literally happen in the deployment of these relations.

This doesn't mean that identities are born and lost at any moment. Nor does it mean that, today, in a society where social relations are expressed with tremendous complexity, each one of us is no more than an amorphous entity that molds its characteristics according to the different social environments one can temporarily be in. Mechanisms of domination continue to impose recognizable and enduring identities, they continue to classify, prejudge, and hierarchize. Nevertheless, the reassertion of these discriminations is not automatic but active. It is produced through actions and through practices that "perform" social relations.

Such a perspective in the discussion of identities cannot easily embrace the enduring certainty that, in the past, defined the politics of denial for a specific society: the certainty that the dominated must react in the name of their own collective identity. If social identities are born and live under conditions of unequal confrontation and are imposed as the result of the domination of one group of people over another group of people, then it is baffling—to say the least—that those who react should appeal to all that is attributed to them in a condition that defines them as subdued. Identities would be "neutral"—that is, outside the field of domination—if they described individuals and groups on "instrumental" terms. For example, workers are the people who work, women have specific biological characteristics, immigrants are those who were forced to leave their land, etc. However, a historically specific structure of domination names some people workers and sets conditions for their activities, their characteristics, rights, appearance, discourse, dreams, or ways of life. The identity of a woman, as any gendered identity, has a social signification, it is defined by performances that describe and normalize it, and it imposes obligations and shapes behaviors.

So, going against what exists, or—even better—appealing to a dream of emancipation and self-determination, amounts to not only distrusting established identities but also recognizing the necessary connection between the production of identities and social reproduction. Such awareness seems to run through the discourse and actions of a contemporary movement that opposes the "monetary society" (Lascano 2002, 13).

The Zapatistas, the rebels of modern-day Mexico, stormed on the horizon of the international capitalist order, not in the name of a collective identity which sought its reassertion, but in the name of the emancipation of all those who are denied the right to self-determination. Many were quick to classify this movement as part of the struggles for the establishment and defense of a repressed Indigenous identity. Since the days of classic colonialism up to the conditions of colonialism under globalization as we experience it today, liberation movements of all kinds have brought and continue to bring to the fore such collective identities as claimed forms of determination. However, the Zapatistas do not demand the reassertion of the identity of the contemporary Mayas. On the contrary, they consider that the contemporary Mayas will encounter their modern face in a Mexico that will include many others, in a world where "those below" will exchange experiences and dreams of equality and justice.

Those without a face

The discourse and political practices of the Zapatistas were born in a time and space that was marked by the encounter of at least two worlds. In the Mexican state of Chiapas, a small group of Marxist rebels, with more or less the characteristics and way of thinking of the armed guerrilla fighters of Latin America, encountered the Indigenous communities of that area, mostly made up of people who had abandoned their villages, fleeing from the corrupt local authorities (Gossen 1999, 262). The rebels thus came across a structure of communal life that resembled their vision of democracy and emancipation. However, it disturbed their certainties of the roles of the vanguard, the revolution, and the social subjects. The Indigenous forms of collective resistance, the principled internal organization of communities based on "rule by obeying," their conception of time which bridges enormous distances between the past and the future at a pace that refers to generations and not to personal trajectories, all these elements modified the Zapatista's way of thinking and their political projects. Above all, they learned how to listen, how to wait, and how to respect the particularities of the oppressed drawing from the everydayness of their resistance. For their part, the Indigenous were imbued with ideas of human emancipation on a global level and began to comprehend the powers that shape the world of capitalist globalization.

The communities themselves decided upon the Zapatista insurrection. Not by a liberating army acting on their behalf, but by an army that they manned and which guaranteed their defense. It was their "Enough is enough!" that the EZLN [*Ejército Zapatista de Liberación Nacional* or Zapatista Army of National Liberation] turned into action, under their word of command and in the name of a common goal.

The Zapatista insurrection condenses the particularity of their politics. It is a politics shaped through asking; through asking those who support it and essentially produce it in the big and small moments of the struggle. It is a politics that seeks to fight this unjust society without reproducing similar forms of injustice.

It refuses to be carried away by the logics of violence, discipline, and hierarchy that defines all armed groups and weaponized ventures. Constantly stressing that they are armed against their will, they destroy all perspective of the army becoming the means or the model for the birth of another society. At the same time, because their politics is not based on the idea of a vanguard or paradigm that must be followed, it draws its force from the everydayness of resistance which is resumed in the goal of "dignity," both on individual and collective levels.[1] The particularities of their politics do not shape a specific type of person that they defend. Perhaps they shape the features of a field where different figures can emerge as subjectivities of a new world.

How can the Zapatista uprising, founded upon the Indigenous communities of Chiapas, be differentiated from an insurrection for the rights of the Indigenous? Indeed, since the beginning of the rebellion, the rights of the Indigenous people of Mexico have been amongst the central demands. The prospect of the abolition of the constitutionally recognized right to collective ownership of communal land [*ejidos*], under the logic of ratifying the NAFTA agreements, was the spark that set off their explosion of their "Enough is enough!" However, in defending the Indigenous populations of Mexico, the Zapatistas defend the rights of all the oppressed. In the ignored, silenced, and often violated difference of the Indigenous, they saw the epitome of every difference that those in power destroy if it does not serve the universal terms of "monetary society" (Lascano 2002, 13). The Indigenous particularities, in terms of language, civilization, history, political culture and values, thus became material not for the fencing of a closed universe but necessary elements of a rich world that is being destroyed by capitalism.

1. "We will resist! We have dignity! If the dignity of the Mexican people has no price, then what good is the power of the powerful?" (Marcos 2002, 50).

"All rebellious movements are movements against invisibility," John Holloway writes (Holloway 2002, 156). And it is this general characteristic of such movements that the Zapatistas stressed in their defense of all those "without face." The Indigenous communities literally did not exist for the Mexican State. They were unseen, condemned to invisibility and the impossibility of expressing that which constitutes them and making demands that go beyond the values and priorities of the society that negates them. The Indigenous "without face" are, in a way, the faceless oppressed par excellence. Monads only when devoid of characteristics, they compose the masses that make society's mechanism operate, offering their forces in workplaces and battlefields alike.

Subcomandante Marcos summed it up in an exemplary way in one of his most famous postscripts to an EZLN communiqué:

> "Majority disguised as an oppressed minority: Marcos is gay in San Francisco, Black in South Africa, Asian in Europe . . . Palestinian in Israel, Indigenous in the streets of San Cristóbal . . . a rocker in the University Campus, a Jew in Nazi Germany . . . an artist with no gallery or portfolio, a housewife alone on a Saturday night in any neighborhood . . . a landless peasant, a marginal publisher, an unemployed worker. . . . To sum it up, Marcos is any given human being of this world, Marcos is all the untolerated, oppressed minorities that resist, explode, saying 'Enough is enough!' All the minorities, when it comes to talking, and all the majorities, when it comes to shutting up and taking it. All the untolerated seeking their voice, something that will give back the majority to the eternally fragmented, us."[2]

In modern discussions on the value of difference and particularity that cannot be reduced to a general norm the tendency is to describe society as a complex field of differentiations. However,

2. Marcos communiqué, May 28, 1994. Partial translation provided by Taussig (1999, 264).

the Zapatistas do not only confirm the differences, the ones that exist and the ones that are crushed, they also ask for differences to meet.[3] That is why the Indigenous demands were never condensed in a slogan such as "Let's fight for a modern Mayan state" but rather "Never again a Mexico without us" (which was also central in the great march towards Mexico City, in February 2001). Before the Zapatistas, it seemed that the Indigenous agrarian movement could completely identify with the defense of a common and distinctive Indigenous identity. Marcos describes the *Union of Ejidos Kiptik*, created in 1975 during the Indigenous Congress, as "fundamentalists" wanting to articulate an Indigenous identity closed to internal differences and up against all others.[4]

The postmodern critique of grand narratives does not necessarily crush the collective dream of a just society. However, in Zapatista discourse and praxis, such a critique can liberate from the extortive adjustment of the action of "those below" to a hierarchical and transhistorical model. Instead of turning into a hymn of consumption in the name of the reassertion of individuality, the appeal to difference becomes both a measure for the dream of emancipation and also the means to approach it. If liberated humanity is defined as a world which can fit many worlds, then the fight for that future will be a struggle which can fit many different struggles.

In the Sixth Declaration of the Lacandon Jungle, the Zapatistas take on a public initiative for the meeting of all resistances and struggles against the neoliberal horror. Their proposal for a "national program of struggle" wishes to be a "left-wing alternative proposition" which will be constructed "from below

3. "We are the revolt of heterogeneity against homogenization, the revolt of difference against contradiction," says Holloway in his support for a multiform movement that produces "cracks" in capitalist dominance (Holloway 2010, 220).

4. For more about the Union of Ejidos, see Cal and Mayor (2002, 162 and 216).

and for those who are below." The declaration states: "We will ask them about their life, about their struggle, about their opinion on what is happening in our country and how to manage not getting defeated." It asserts the political ethos characteristic of the Zapatistas, who deny the role of a vanguard or a leadership of such multifarious movements.[5]

The mask

"We hid our faces in order to be seen." This enigmatic phrase sums up the politics of the Zapatistas as a politics for the defense and discovery of those "who have no face" in this society. Assuming the place of the invisible that are deprived, along with their visibility, of their role in public life, the masked rebels consciously hide their faces. As many have already observed, the need to protect themselves from their persecutors, official or paramilitary, is not enough to explain the Zapatista fixation with the famous *pasamontañas*, the balaclava. Zapata and his fellow revolutionaries wore no masks, neither did Che Guevara and his fellow fighters. Beyond the protection of the EZLN outlaw fighters and their leadership, the use of masks has acquired a symbolic force that is completely compatible with their political particularity. Marcos points towards such a symbolic intention: "The mask is a symbol which does not result from planning, it rather constitutes a product of the struggle. . . .Nobody looked at us while our faces were uncovered, now they do because our faces are covered" (Montalban 1999, 144, author's translation). The Zapatista mask does not disguise, nor does it conceal. It essentially emblemizes the unity of "those below" of all those who, in their differences, are "everyday, ordinary people, that

5. The Declaration can be found in English at http://enlacezapatista.ezln.org.mx/sdsl-en/

is rebels." Through the mask that depersonifies them, the oppressed project their invisible faces. They appear at history's fore, not as distinct persons with distinct characteristics, but as persons—simultaneously visible and invisible—who are present in struggles that give them the only identity that can include them without wiping out their differences. This is the identity of the rebel. "We, the forgotten, have a name. We still hope that now that we have a name, our brothers, you, will tomorrow also give us a face." With these words the Clandestine Revolutionary Indigenous Committee—General Command (CCRI-CG) of the EZLN addresses the "brothers and sisters," the people of the world.[6]

The depersonification of the mask, which does not homogenize but rather gives birth to places of encounter, has a ritual essence. Marcos is constantly sarcastic regarding all those who wonder about his true identity, saying that he fears he might lose his allure. It is a tendency to style that makes him wear the mask, he says, and for him and his fellow *comandantes* to hide their ugliness. With his sarcastic disposition, Marcos seems to invert the dominant adoration of the face. It is as though he is turning the Western ritual projection of the face as the center of personal identity against itself.

Behind Marcos' words, a world with profound roots in the Indigenous past endows the mask with magic power. It is not that the Zapatistas adopted ancient Indigenous visions of the world and their symbols so as to entice them into supporting the movement. It is rather the inhabitants themselves of the communities in Chiapas, those who make up the Clandestine Revolutionary Indigenous Committee, the EZLN command, and every aspect of the Zapatista movement, who brought their culture to the crossroads of their encounter with the Western emancipating dis-

6. CCRI-CG of EZLN communiqué, March 12, 1995.

course. Their collective wisdom corresponded to a relationship with the world which is open to difference, open to the awareness that identities are born in their relation with others, they join people and groups in their long journey around the world and are exposed to constant trial.

The Indigenous culture, exiled by the conquerors from their religious as well as secular affairs, was forced to hide in invisible practices which, however, weaved the thread of collective resistance. For the Indigenous descendants of the conquered Mayas, each person has outside her a powerful, consubstantial soul that accompanies her. This soul usually corresponds to an animal into which one can transform due to absolute kinship, winning over its power and support (Gossen 1999, 228 and Taussig 1999, 247). One's relation with the animal-soul [*tonalli*] greatly determines one's identity, and it is a relation that can interfere in the bonds that exist between the different individuals of a society. *Tonalliismo* is essentially a system of relations that regulates the social reproduction and control of the community. This is why it interfered and secretly conserved its continuity during the years of silent resistance against the conquerors (Gossen 1999).[7] The conquerors did not have the power to harm the Indigenous identities, insofar as their birth and reproduction occurred in terms of a faith that remained unseen.

It is interesting to note that this necessary ingredient of identity that is outside the individual, the consubstantial soul-animal, in fact inscribes a destination. It is not a teleological metaphysics that operates by normalizing the behavior of the Indigenous Maya, but

7. This resistance has sustained an explicit reference to a common cultural identity while incorporating elements of the dominant culture of the colonizers by turning them against suppression, as happened with the Christian religion. As June Nash observes, "The dialectic of continuity related to the ability to adopt changes that allows Mayans to remain themselves is a departure from the discourse of *Indigenistas*, which assumes a merging of Indigenous and *ladino* cultures that will allow the former to assimilate to the more advanced, or modern, culture of the West, but offers no entry for indigenous traits into modernization" (Nash 2001, 236).

rather a concern to adapt to the outside—which along with the self conforms an entity—that produces a modest behavior.

Unlike the Western adoration of the face, the Indigenous face is not glorified as a personality. The face carefully expresses the person it characterizes, without revealing its secret relation with the outside that constitutes it. Thus, society is above individuals not because it homogenizes them but because it offers the safety of their difference. It's maintained as a secret difference—fragile, however, for it is vulnerable to external forces—that articulates the personal destinations each person must find without considering them superior to the others. Here lies the root of the moderate expression of the Indigenous, the careful "depersonification" in their public demonstrations and, likewise, the protection of the community notables from the hubris of a self-projected exception. Indeed, we may consider the mask that depersonifies the Zapatista leadership as a direct result of this Indigenous conception of face. Exposed to the ill-intentioned intervention of their enemies, the Indigenous leaders must reject all personifying features so as to rule by obeying: not the leaders but the mediating servants of a community (ibid., 261).

The ritual force of the mask that depersonifies is deeply rooted in a collective attitude of the Indigenous people that also mediates their relationship with others and their relation to their community. Insofar as this relation expressed resistance but also a political culture which impeded discrimination between the rulers and the ruled, it has managed to find its place in an emancipating communal vision. The corrupt *caciques*, the potentates who collaborated with the State and sold off the rights of their people, were considered guilty of precisely such hubris where the personal—as in personal interest—replaced the impersonal role of a ruler who governs by obeying.

An element that distinctly reveals the ritual force of the use of the mask is the act of unmasking; its removal. The official Mexican

State, in an effort to strike the movement and harm the local and international prestige of its leadership, presented photos of what they considered to be the true identity of Marcos. Without his mask, the legendary *Sub* was but the son of a humble furniture salesman. How confident the State was about the effectiveness of revealing, and therefore demystifying, the alleged "leader" of the rebels! Not one week had gone by from that day in 1995, when thousands of people took to the streets of Mexico City and Chiapas, shouting "We are all Marcos!" Nobody was concerned about the face behind the mask except those who wanted to crush the movement it represented. As Marcos himself stated: "At stake is *what* Subcomandante Marcos is, not *who* he *was*" (Mertes 2004, 15). He limits his role to that of a mediator. "Marcos as a mediator, as a translator, is a window that allows you to bend over and look at the internal world or look from the inside out to the exterior. Only the windows are dirty. . . .The people see their own reflection on the glass and that is when Marcos turns into a symbol, he becomes what the people wish to see" (Le Bot 1998, 190).

The removal of the mask does not reveal a person, as those in power would believe. Behind the mask there is an open space for the rebels to see themselves. The mask displays the collective face of those below. Thus, the mask as the negation of the face acquires a multiplying force. The transformation of the rebels depends on their capacity to win the faces that the powerful have deprived them of. Faces which are not mirrors of a true interior—such as the Western mythology of the face as the mirror of the soul wants it—but mirror the outside. Faces which are born according to the *nahualic* belief in the interference of a consubstantial entity in combination with an active longing for a just world.

This revelation provided an unexpected stage to the theatricality of a politics that intends to demolish the foundations of the essentialist prejudice with which modern society has suffocated the imaginary of many of those who have turned against it. "The collective manipulation of symbols, either from one side or the other, entails a theatrical representation," says Marcos (Montalban 2001, 133). The unmasked himself turned into the unexpected director of the scene of the unmasking: it was the state that was revealed in its gesture, proving that it is "those without face" who are behind a collective mask, and not any specific Mexican "conspirator." Once again, Marcos reveals the theatricality of the mask with an allegory. It is staged at the National Democratic Meeting organized by the Zapatistas in August 1994, in the Lacandon Jungle, the area which is under their control: "When they are alone, the Sup [Marcos] makes a sign. . . .Everyone, including the Sup, tear off their ski masks and their faces. A multitude of fierce-looking sailors appears, the Sup has a patch on his right eye and begins to limp ostentatiously on his wooden leg." The mentioned communiqué is signed: "Pirate without bearings, professional of hope, transgressor of injustice . . .man without face and with no tomorrow" (Taussig 1999, 256–257).

The face which is torn along with the mask is a face and, at the same time, a passage that shows the way to an uncertain destination. The theatricality of the unmasking proves that what is unveiled is elsewhere. The essence of the depersonification through the mask appears at the moment of the unmasking which, instead of identifying, sums up differences (ibid., 263). The mask did not conceal an identity; it rather unveiled a collective reference of many different people. The mask pointed beyond the face of its bearer. It aimed at the emergence of the faces of all those who demand their emancipation from a society which struggles to identify, to control through classification, to define.

The unveiling leads to a revelation. A discovery. That is why the mask remains active as a symbol even after its symbolic removal. Is it a discovery or a disguise that shows the way towards the birth of a new world? Unlike the identity of the oppressed, looked upon as humble or even as unimportant (such as with the identity of a son of a furniture salesman), here it is about the birth of an identity of the rebels, humble but also infinitely rich. The mask renders the identity possible, but does not conceal it, for behind it there is not a face that represents an identity, but many faces that give birth to identities.[8]

In the antipode of the mask that depersonifies so as to show those who have no face are the masks worn by the state. In 1998, after a long period of silence from the Zapatistas, in the text "Above and Below: Masks and Silences," the rulers are portrayed with the masks that conceal the brutality of their politics behind misleading disguises (Marcos 2004). The nation's political life "has turned into a volatile masquerade." "The primary peddler of National Sovereignty" bearing "the mask of chauvinism" (Marcos 2004, 325) has set out to pursue foreigners, says Marcos as he describes the country's president. "Behind the macro-economic mask, is hidden an economic model" (ibid.) which conceals the face of an economy that renders the already poor even poorer.

The state and its staff, those whose faces appear on the news, wear masks that present them as faces. The disguises of the state mislead; they try to fool the dominated. The distorting mirrors of power stage personalities that claim they care about the people. The counterpart of the personifying mask of the rebels that reveals and discovers, the masks of the rulers literally conceal. And when the government's show window is taken over by the bureaucrat-politicians, their faces freeze in the same homogenizing facade. When the government's negotiators initially refused to talk to people wearing masks, the Zapatistas answered: but it

8. "Marcos has inaugurated a space of intersubjectivity, of intercultural relations between a multiplicity of selves and others that is uniting peoples from all over the world in an unprecedented 'postmodern' revolutionary movement" (Garcia 2001, 172).

is the state that always bears the mask (Taussig 1999, 134). "The culture of resistance is an answer to the conspiracy of the masks," says Montalban (2001, 32), commenting on this text. "Silently, these indigenous see and are seen," the text goes on. "After such a silence, these indigenous speak a ship, a Noah's ark, a navigable Tower of Babel, an absurd and irreverent challenge to who crews and directs it, a figurehead on the prow lights a ski mask! Yes, a ski mask which reveals, the silence that speaks" (Marcos 2004, 240).

So this is how the mask of the impersonal appearance, the mask of the "ritual leveling" of the rebels can become the new face that unveils, which renders possible the existence of new identities for "those below."

Any face

"The face," Agamben says, "is the only location of community, the only possible city" (Agamben 2000, 91). The myth of the dominant Western civilization considers the face to be the bastion of subjectivity. In a world where individualized destinies lead the many to humbling defeats and disappointment and the very few to the acquisition of power and wealth, the face appears as the emblem of a promise. An advertisement says, "Become yourself," meaning "become what we would want you to be in order for you to buy what is in our interest." In the absurdity of a personification which categorizes, in the delusion of the possession of personal and particularizing characteristics which conceal subjectification as a productive dimension of power, the face remains the most obvious part of individual identity.

With the political magic of the Indigenous rebels, the Zapatistas showed how the face can become the emblem of a collective resistance which allows space for difference. In this sense, we can bring about an explosive encounter of their political culture with the restless and militant thought of Agamben. In his argument, the place of politics is a position of exposure. However, not the exposure by which famous men present paradigmatic personalities in public acts. The "whatever singularity" that Agamben mentions is this new figure of politics that represents the perspective of a "coming community" (Agamben 1993). Its emancipating dimension will lie in the fact that, in this community, there is an action and a union of individuals whose difference does not personify them as individuals in the sense of the dominant culture, nor it reduces them to the homogenizing anonymity of a community that does not tolerate differentiations and particularities. In a world where it is meaningless to continue looking for "appropriate identities" as individuality is already an empty shell, Agamben asks us to imagine "uniqueness without an identity."[9] He says: "If humans could . . . not be-thus in this or that particular biography but be only the thus, their singular exteriority and their face, then they would for the first time enter into a community without presuppositions and without subjects, into a communication without the incommunicable" (ibid., 65).

It is not sure that the coming community will be distinguished by the fact of belonging, without its reduction to certain preconditions which characterize its members. Resistance against the essentializing identification of social individuals should not ignore the historicity of each struggle against the identities in which the

9. Hardt and Negri propose the term "singularity" in order to deal with the inadequacies of the term "identity." For them, singularity is defined by and oriented towards multiplicity and is "always engaged in a process of becoming different" (Hardt and Negri 2009, 338–339). Hardt and Negri share with Agamben a will to conceptualize "cobelonging" by departing from the dominant understanding of community as identity. Whereas, however, Agamben sees "whatever singularities" communicate on the level of a common humanity, a "community of being" (Mills 2008, 133), Hardt and Negri believe in the power of institutions to create a context for [singularities] to manage their encounters" (ibid., 357). Institutions are thus open to conflict and do not impose collective identities while, at the same time, they provide the ground for the creation and collective appropriation of the "common" (understood both in terms of common wealth and as shared forms of democratic managing this wealth).

rulers want to trap the ruled. Only the policies of the insurrect can produce the different paths that the formation of collective identities will follow, beyond the specifications of any power.

In their multilateral confrontation with globalized capitalist domination, with the "monetary world" as they call it, perhaps the Zapatistas are outlining the profile of a coming community. Through the rich experience of the insurgent communities, they constituted a form for autonomy that does not fall into the trap of setting the boundaries of an inside and an outside.

The Autonomous Rebel Municipalities were born through the practical materialization of the defense and protection of the Indigenous grounds, of the culture, rights and natural wealth of the Indigenous people.[10] Their organization is based on direct democracy and the participation of all. It is worth noting that women, unlike what occurs in the tradition of the communities, take on an active role in the autonomous councils and, with their own initiative, form a judicial system based on gender equity. Presenting a model of a coming community based on the value of each person, the Autonomous Rebel Municipalities have forbidden, since their constitution, the creation of permanent poles of power. Authorities are elected and revocable. Decisions are made as unanimously as possible, without forcing choices for which not everybody is ready. And minorities, whenever they arise, are treated with respect.

In 2003, a new self-governing model was applied in the autonomous areas and from this the Councils of Good Government are created. Their members come from the corresponding Autonomous Municipalities of the areas that have their own centers, the *caracoles*.

---

10. "Zapatistas and their supporters in civil society are enacting the foundation for a pluricultural coexistence based on their experience as distinct indigenous entities within regions characterized by a multiplicity of languages and customs. . . .The cry for autonomy as distinct self-governing entities is correlated with a mode of socialization in their families and communities where respect for the will of others, including that of children, still promotes an awareness of what autonomy may mean in a collective setting" (Nash 2001, 244).

Not only do the Councils of Good Government "rule by obeying," the delegates of the Municipalities also change quite often (in some cases every fifteen days), so that the people can be trained in the social justice that must serve the insurgent community.

The organization of production, of autonomous education, health services or justice, is based on the participation and the particularity of each area. Instead of elaborating a singular pattern of administration, what is brought forward is a set of principles that run through the Zapatista ethics of rebellion. Thus, a mosaic of practices is born, all of them converging in the defense of the dignity of all and of each man and woman separately. Their own version of the particularity of each person considers autonomy as a collective experience in which the oppressed create their own bonds of solidarity. And if the defense of individual and collective dignity emerges as a goal in all the communiqués and actions of the rebels, it is because each moment of the struggle depends on all, men and women, living in equality and solidarity. "In the world of the powerful there is no space for anyone but themselves and their servants. In the world we want everyone fits" (Marcos 2002, 80); "We don't need to conquer the world. Creating it from the beginning will do. Us. Today."[11]

Heterotopian experiences

This politics inspired many around the world. In Greece, an initiative of practical solidarity towards the Zapatistas resulted in the creation of various collective experiences that can possibly represent aspects of a coming emancipated community.

The "School for Chiapas" initiative was not only a campaign of solidarity. It aimed at collecting money for the construction of

11. CCRI-CG of EZLN communiqué, January 1, 1996.

a Learning Center for Educators, but also at contributing with on-site labor for the construction of the buildings. The Center for the Training of Teachers of the Autonomous Rebel Municipality Ricardo Flores Magón was built with the help of the Greek solidarity group (called "A School for Chiapas") in 2004. In a symbolic act of opposition to the Athens 2004 Olympic Games, the school's inauguration took place on the 5th and 6th of August, in the community La Culebra, in Montes Azules, Chiapas.

A school in the heart of the jungle, where it is not the civilization of the conquerors that is taught to the oppressed, but the civilization and cultures of freedom of the insurrect Indigenous, is a school-heterotopia. The school buildings, constructed with great effort and endless deprivations, are a place of reunion for all those who will learn in order to teach others, who, in turn, will teach yet others. It is not a knowledge which is based on power, but rather knowledge and questions based on hope. There is a predominance of the plural form in the Zapatista education syllabus: we must learn about histories, not history, about geographies, not geography, about civilizations and not civilization. It is this plural form that also fuels the heterotopian experience.

If their dream was of an absolute outside, this school would have the shape of an introvert arc. It would hide, in its protected holds, the seed for the future, waiting for the waters of the capitalistic flood to dry up. However, this school, with its oblique rooftops and its airy, open walls, is above all a passage, a porous membrane, a crossroads of hope. It is imbued with the anxiety for the creation of another world, disrupted by the contradictions and discontinuities of such a struggle. In it, knowledge is interwoven with the joy of a collective festivity, dispute meets the detailed study of the Indigenous traditions, and the usefulness of practical knowledge runs into the force of creative imagination.

The account of the celebration of the school's inauguration given by the Mexican author Bellinghausen, published in *La Jornada Semanal* on August 22, 2004 as "Homer shouldn't have died," is quite revealing about the heterotopian dynamics of this venture, and deserves extensive quotation:

> Let us imagine a group of dissident Athenians who will not put up with the militarization of their private lives under security pretexts that reach the limits of paranoia. Who, instead of devoting themselves to constructing palaces, gigantic stadiums and roads . . . for the merchants of the Olympic Games, decide they will come together with some improbable indigenous rebels located thousands of miles away, at the very belly of the tropical jungle, and together build a modern and exemplary school for the boys and girls of the Tzeltal and Chol people. They, in turn, devote themselves to "promoting education," that is to educating the children of the autonomous municipality Ricardo Flores Magón, which is made up of communities supporting the Zapatista Army of National Liberation.
>
> Two Greek architects think up a school made out of wood and iron sheets and give it wings. That is, they create an architectural project with the materials that can be found in the jungle. They do it for free and hand it over to a collectivity of Greek citizens committed to the original idea of supporting some Zapatistas who live beyond the Mediterranean and the Atlantic Ocean, in a place which, from the Parthenon, must seem like the end of the world. A very well-known end of the world, however, after a decade of uprising and public struggle.
>
> With no money (well, the inevitable minimum), out of fraternity and gratitude rather than mere generosity, the brave Athenians handed over plans, materials, and labor power to the Indigenous Mexicans, and for more than three years they built together the Companero Manuel School at La Culebra. It is not a place for reading. Let us not idealize. Not in Tzeltal and Chol,

Celebrating the inaugural opening of a Zapatista School in Culebra, Chiapas, Mexico.

the area's native languages which aren't usually written, but neither in Mexico's national language. However, big photocopies of odes to Ulysses and Achilles, in ancient Greek and Spanish, are displayed as soon as one walks through the door of the library (of the building that will be housing it). As if the long voyage of this school from a drawing table in Athens were a sort of return journey home for Homer . . . home being wherever words, struggle, and history are cultivated.

And if the Homeric wanderings through the Mayan jungles encountered an impoverished and rotten world, full of war, epidemic and the rapacity of the rulers, it also showed that underlying solidarities and brotherhoods flow together into open seas and reach jungles that do not know the sea. For the second time (the first was in August 1994, in Aguascalientes of Guadalupe Tepeyac) I heard of the ship *Fitzcarraldo* in the Lacandon jungle. But this time she was not washed away by a tropical storm.

The Tzeltal and Chol people have been rebelling against the Mexican government for eleven years and, although they seem so far away, they are in the first row of the global struggle against totalizing neoliberalism. In their encounters with the brigades of Greeks-turned constructor workers (because that was what was needed), the Indigenous Mexicans became brothers and sisters without using false Olympic metaphors, realizing that things can be done well in more than one way. That another world is possible, cheaper, and even better.

And, well, if on arriving at his new and poor home in the Lacandon Jungle, three thousand years later, the blind poet finds it poor and peasant-like but inspired by struggle and joy, he will discover that nothing has been in vain and, as the modern poet of Alexandria would have said, he will have lived the journey. Together with the sons and daughters of maize, he will finally know the meaning of the Ithacas and Las Culebras.

These crossroads are an ingredient of heterotopia. In a sense, heterotopia is an expanded threshold. Temporal and spatial at the same time, it is a transitional space in which the birth of new social experiences occurs in all its contradictions. If the Zapatistas "walk asking," it is because the future is not a faraway elsewhere, in an unattainable horizon. In their political thought and action, deeply marked by the wisdom of Indigenous civilizations, the path is made as we walk. The communities not only correct the reality of the struggle with the criterion of utopia, they learn from their mistakes. And if, in the 1994 uprising or the "March of Dignity," the Zapatistas did not talk on behalf of others but rather gave the floor and the space to "all those suppressed minorities who are a majority" it is because their political culture considers the birth of spaces of freedom and action fundamental. The Zapatista heterotopias were born in villages and cities along the big march. In the central square of Mexico City, the people created their own—

however temporary—heterotopia of solidarity. And each act of rebellion, big and small, creates today its own heterotopia of dignity in a world of horror, no matter how little it may last.

Could it be that a network of such heterotopian collective experiences leads to the materialization of the dream of a liberated world in which many worlds will fit? And is it possible that a school deep in the jungle can signify and materialize, fearless of problems, such a perspective of collective emancipation? It is no coincidence that the construction of this school-passage, of this school-threshold, brought together so many people from countries, cultures, habits, and histories that are so far away from each other. If hope brought them together, it is because in the Zapatista communities' everyday action is, above all, the most tangible sign of the birth of a culture of emancipation, one that constructs bridges rather than drawing boundaries.

A visionary dream and a lot of work in Greece and Mexico gave birth to yet another material symbol of the emancipating perspective. All this effort fueled heterotopian experiences at every step. The processes of planning and building the school constantly bridged distances—between cultures, on the map in the jungle that some had to cover in order to reach the school and work there, between the dream and the available means. The school is not actually a heterotopia, if this term is used to indicate a definitive demarcation of "otherness." The school exists in the practices that keep on developing its heterotopic characteristics. It is a heterotopia in the making. And if there is something that the celebration of its inauguration—with its discussions on the education of resistance and the expressions of joy that accompanied it—represented above all, it is that heterotopia is a path and not a fortress, perhaps a ship but not an ark.

Contrary to Marcos' metaphor, Zapatistas never really imagined their meetings or communities in the form of an "absurd ark of Noah." Such a metaphoric ark could only be understood as a stronghold or a "vivarium" of a precious but secluded otherness. Theirs was not a struggle to preserve a liberated perimeter. Autonomous areas are simultaneously inside Mexico and outside of Mexico's power institutions. In their communities, people of different political beliefs are included: they only have to accept the rules of collective self-management and direct democracy. In the many faces of struggles inspired by the Zapatista rebellion, in the many faces of people fighting for a new world, passages to otherness rather than strongholds of otherness are created. There are many ships on many ventures into unknown seas without an established itinerary.[12] Beyond fixed and dominating classifications, inventing the future now by using materials collected from the fragments of today's struggles.

12. As the Zapatistas say: "*Preguntando caminamos*" [Asking we walk]. The paths towards human emancipation are many and they are created by movements in the process of their struggle (see also Holloway 2010, 45).

08

The December 2008 youth uprising in Athens:

glimpses of a possible city of thresholds

"We haven't experienced the dictatorship but neither have we experienced freedom. Christmas is cancelled. There is a rebellion going on."

—Anonymous street leaflet, December 2008

The term "urban conflict" can be taken to include all forms of social antagonism when the resulting struggles happen in an urban spatial context. However, is the city simply a container of these struggles or does urban spatiality actually mold social conflicts, giving them form, affecting their meaning and their relations with specific urban rights and demands?

In this chapter, I will attempt to trace the history of a specific and very recent period of urban struggles in Athens, Greece, where a highly significant series of phenomena seems to have taken place. As it becomes more evident in the chapters of Part IV written after the book was initially published, this series of urban struggles has been extended to today including the Syntagma Square occupation (part of the Movements of the Squares), the dispersed urban struggles and solidarity initiatives that emerged during the socio-economic crisis, and the mobilizations in support of the refugees and immigrants arriving in large numbers (including mutual aid structures and several self-managed occupied centers in Athens).

What started as a generalized expression of youth rage, triggered by the assassination of a young boy by a policeman, has evolved into an inventive reclaiming of public space in the city. As is characteristic in most urban conflicts, the city was not simply involved as the setting of actions, urban space and its uses became one of the stakes of the conflict. Either explicitly or implicitly connected with demands related to urban living conditions, these conflicts actively transform the city. The question is: does the city, in these temporary or more permanent transformations, represent the stakes of the conflict along with the conflicting values of the social groups (or actors) involved in the conflict? Does the city become the mirror and not simply the locus of the conflict?

A spontaneous uprising

In the case of the Athens December youth uprising, we may trace the possibility to answer these questions. During the uprising, the city has temporarily become the place where new forms of spatiality have emerged. Spatiality, as a concept, is meant to describe conditions, qualities and, characteristics of space in general, not specific spaces. Even though we can locate specific forms of spatiality in concrete places, spatiality describes ways to perform space rather than spaces as concrete arrangements of physical elements. Therefore, to speak about the different spatialities of urban conflicts means to consider space as both the result and the precondition of social action. Space happens.

In order to focus on the spatiality of this urban conflict, let us recollect what happened in December 2008 in Athens. Located near the city center, the Exarchia neighborhood has, since the seventies, become identified with youth culture of protest and alternative entertainment. Connected symbolically with the November 1973 student uprising, which culminated in the bloody ending of the National Technical University occupation that took place in the University's main building, Exarchia has become a kind of antisystemic youth stronghold.

Today's picture differs, of course, from November 1973's antidictatorship action which marked the beginning of the end of the seven-year military junta. Gentrification initiatives mingle with alternative culture and commodification of both entertainment and public space tends to prevail. However, there are still many outbursts of symbolic action as well as many organized demonstrations that still begin from or end in Exarchia.

On December 6, 2008, a police car was passing in front of one the coffee shops where young people meet. Police tactics are generally focused on guarding specific "possible targets" in the area (main political party offices, banks, government buildings, etc.) with heavily equipped groups of police Special Forces (MAT). Occasionally, police raids sweep the center of the neighborhood, either in pursuit of "illegal immigrants" or drug dealers. Most of the time, police raids are meant to impose order after a violent demonstration (even though a demonstration often becomes violent because it is attacked by the police). So the passing of this police car was something irregular, something noticed. What a few boys did was to yell some obviously unflattering remarks at these policemen. The policemen in the car then did something so disastrous that it immediately triggered a huge youth outburst. They parked their car and returned armed to respond to the insult. One of the officers took out his gun, aimed at one of the fifteen-year-old students and shot him. The boy died on the pavement.

It took just a few hours for people to spontaneously organize various forms of protest and action. At night many fancy shops on the most expensive commercial street in Athens were attacked and completely destroyed. Symbols of consumption became targets all over the city. From the beginning, collective rage was directed against symbols of the affluent society.

The next morning, all the schools in Athens and many cities in Greece were closed by students (a result of coordination through "rhizomatic" communications such as email and SMS). Spontaneous demonstrations of students in all neighborhoods (even in rich suburbs) performed either peaceful or violent sieges of police stations the days that followed. Police cars were overturned, policemen chased, expensive cars were burned.

What was highly characteristic of this spontaneous uprising was that there were no guiding centers or organizations, although

"We choose colors," a poster by the Coordination of Occupied Schools, December 2008 uprising.

anarchists and leftists were directly involved in most of the actions. Every local initiative had its own means to organize and express a common rage. It wasn't, however, that every action was simply expressing this rage. It wasn't that everybody who participated was only angry and sad for the brutal killing of a young boy. A common effort to actively express a different public culture was becoming apparent, and this culture contained forms of collectively reclaiming the city.

How could this have happened? The key element seems to have been a shared idea of justice, which is felt to be absent from the acts of the state, as emblematically demonstrated by the shooting policeman. No policeman had ever been punished in the past for their brutality. Young people were asking for justice but they knew the police would not be punished.

In their everyday experience of precariousness in this society, young people feel that justice is fleeting. "If we rise up, if our acts criticize the police, the banks, the department stores, it is because all these stand as obstacles between us and real life. We therefore struggle against total injustice" (Declaration of the Open Assembly of the occupied Municipal Building, Peristeri Municipality, Athens, February 2, 2009).

It is as if every aspect of their life experience were somehow condensed in this unjust death. In a period of economic crisis, combined with major cases of government corruption revealed by the press, in a period when no true alternatives to the political situation were visible, a claim for justice by young people materialized as demand: "We want to live. This society literally or symbolically does not allow us to live."

After the first wave of demonstrations, a second wave of actions involved various forms of occupation of public buildings. Municipal buildings in various municipalities of Athens (as in Nea Smyrni, Ag. Dimitiros, Halandri, etc.) were temporarily trans-

Hooded ballerinas dance in front of the occupied Opera building during the December 2008 uprising. (Unknown photographer.)

formed into community centers. Squatters attempted to create neighborhood meeting areas, where the community's self-organized cultural events took place.

The National Opera building, for example, became a place of collective experimentation in the performing arts as well as an information center. This initiative took form as the culmination of a series of acts by a group of young performance artists. What they did is enter almost every theater of the city demanding that a sharply written antipolice manifesto be read before the show.

The occupation of the General Confederation of Workers building was a gesture of protest against the official bureaucrats of the often-paralyzed workers' syndicates. Of course, there were the occupations of university and school buildings with differing forms of participation and differing problems of coordination as communication between sometimes rivaling anarchist and leftist sects was difficult.

The quest for urban justice

Out of these experiences, the collective demand for justice in its expansive and diverse ways, has taken the form of actively pursuing a distinctively urban justice. The city was not simply the setting of collective actions and initiatives but became, more and more, a potential collective claim. In all these fragmentary, ambiguous, and diffuse initiatives, explicitly or implicitly expressed was the collective will of young people to take their lives in their hands. Urban justice had thus effectively taken the form of Lefebvre's idea of the right to the city (Lefebvre 1996). Let us just recall that, for Lefebvre, the right to the city is not simply one kind of rights among others. On the contrary, the totality of civic rights is condensed into this form of right.

It is very important that, as Lefebvre insists, this right presupposes collective action in pursuing it. The city is understood as the "perpetual oeuvre of the inhabitants, themselves mobile and mobilized for and by this oeuvre" (ibid., 173). The right to the city involves people in pursuit of a collective project: to transform the city into a collective work of art. The city thus does not simply become an aggregate of services and goods with the corresponding collective demands for democratic access. Beyond this quantitative understanding of the urban condition is a qualitative critique of the contemporary city culture. Here is where urban conflicts, such as the Athens December youth uprising, can contribute to a different understanding of the urban world, giving form to new, emergent spatialities.

When, during an urban conflict, people collectively seek to reappropriate public space, they are not simply using the city as it is; they are transforming it. Their actions do not only search for space, they invent space. These performed spaces, these practiced spaces, as they happen in the process of the conflict, acquire distinctive characteristics that tend to influence the outcome and the form of the conflict.

Emergent spatialities thus represent the ways participants imagine spaces that will house the life they fight for. At the same time, those spatialities reflect the ways in which collective action attempts to create its own space. The spatialities of urban conflicts are thus both imagined and real. It is very important, therefore, to understand how images and representations of space actively participate in forming the qualities of the spaces created, as urban conflicts transform the city.

One of the dominant modern images of a longed-for emancipated community presents it as barricaded in a liberated stronghold: a defined territorial enclave always ready to defend itself. This image, embedded in the collective imaginary of the oppressed, tends to construct a geography of emancipation in the form of a map clearly depicting free areas as defined by a recognizable perimeter. Either as islands, surrounded by a hostile sea, or as continents facing other hostile continents, these areas appear as spatially circumscribed and bounded. This image is dominant in the history of Athens' youth movements: Exarchia has often been fantasized as an alternative liberated stronghold.

As already mentioned, Exarchia is connected with a very important incident in recent Greek history. In November 1973, the central building of National Technical University was occupied by students protesting against the ongoing military dictatorship. What started as a student strike culminated as a major anti-junta resistance event. Marked by the brutal suppression of the occupation, which eventually led to the fall of the dictatorship the next year, the building and surrounding area became symbolic of youth insubordination. Exarchia's mythology as an autonomous area and youth stronghold is connected to this symbolism, and many acts of protest and disobedience have been substantiating the neighborhood's fame ever since.

Interestingly, during December 2008, a BBC News commentator referred to the November 1973 student uprising and the occupied "Athens Polytechnic" as "the symbol of modern rebellion." Linking a "latent Greek contempt for the police," with the role of the police during the dictatorship, he attempted to explain the December 2008 uprising as an event fueled by a kind of gained tolerance for young protestors. He described universities as "springboards of violence" explaining that, because of the bloody invasion of military junta's tanks in the occupied NTUA area, the post-junta constitution "drafted the right to asylum, which bans the authorities from entering the grounds of schools and universities." It is true that this right to asylum is still effective (schools were never included, though) but there is a recurrent dispute sustained by the media and most government officials on whether this is simply a way of encouraging the production of "lawless" zones, i.e., zones of anomy.

Although the NTUA building was also occupied in December 2008, the idea of an untouchable stronghold was not crucial in igniting demonstrators' confrontations with the police. Both the government and the police, along with reporters such as the one already mentioned, tried in many cases to interpret street violence as the result of the university asylum. However—peaceful or not, whether forced to react to police violence or expressing their anger in symbolic violence—demonstrators did not limit themselves to asylum buildings.

Most of December's collective acts have escaped the asylum enclosure characteristic of many previous student struggles and have spread all over the city. Students, instead of being under siege by the police in their university-asylum enclaves, have reclaimed the streets and the city as spaces of collective action. And in many cases, it was the police stations that were under siege by students and school children.

The December uprising had no center, neither a political center, nor a center in terms of urban space. In direct contrast to the situated struggle of November 1973, which has turned the image of NTUA building to a national symbol of resistance, the December actions were everywhere unexpected, metastatic, unpredictable, and multiform. During the December uprising, the fantasy of a liberated enclave, which dominated and still dominates many urban struggles, lost most of its power. What kind of motivating image has replaced that fantasy?

Emancipation is a process, not an accomplished state. It is important to differentiate it from the religious image of a happy afterlife. Emancipation is the ambiguous actuality of spatially as well as historically dispersed struggles. There may be potentially liberating practices but there can be no fixed areas of freedom.

Could we perhaps visualize spatialities of emancipation by interpreting those appeals for social justice that focus on the unobstructed use of space? Spatial justice, in this context, could indicate a distribution principle that tends to present space as a good to be enjoyed by all. Accessibility can become one of the most important attributes of spatial justice. Any division, separation or partitioning of space thus appears as preventing this kind of justice.

True, an emphasis on spatial justice may establish the importance collective decision-making has for the social as well as for the physical definition of space. A corresponding imaginary geography of emancipation, however, has to understand space as a uniform continuum to be regulated by common will rather than as an inherently discontinuous and differentiated medium that gives form to social practices. In a somewhat crude form, this imaginary could end up reducing space to a quantity to be equally distributed. And accessibility might end up being some kind of distributing mechanism. We can actually connect this way of understanding spatialities of emancipation with contemporary discourses on human rights or human communicability (Habermasian ideal speech situation included). More often than not, these discourses presuppose some kind of transhistorical and transgeographical human figure. The same figure becomes the subject of spatial justice, except this time such a figure is not viewed as the inhabitant of an ideal city but rather as the free-moving occupant of a homogeneous space.

A third kind of geographical imaginary emerges out of a criticism of this idealized view for a just city (or a city of justice). Sometimes drawing images from contemporary city life, this imaginary focuses on multiplicity and diversity, as well as on possible polymorphous and mutating spaces, in order to describe a spatiality of emancipation. This view has strong roots. The critique of everyday life put forward during the sixties provided us with new ways of dealing with the social experience of space. If everyday life is not only the locus of social reproduction but also contains practices of self-differentiation or personal and collective resistance, molecular spatialities of otherness can be found scattered through the city. As de Certeau put it, "a migrational, or metaphorical, city slips into the clear text of the planned and readable city" (de Certeau 1984, 93).

This image contains a view of inhabited space as a process rather than a fixed condition. Spaces of otherness proliferate in the city due to diversifying or deviating practices. Spatialities of otherness, in such a view, are considered inherently time-bound. Space is neither reduced to a container of otherness (idealized in utopian cities) nor to a contestable and distributable good. Space is actually conceptualized as a formative element of human social interaction. Space thus becomes expressive through use, or rather, because use—the "style of use," as de Certeau specifies—defines users. If an idealized version of spatial justice tends to invoke common rights in order to define space as common good, an emphasis on spatialized molecular otherness tends to posit space as dispersed and diversified, and therefore, not common.

According to this view, emancipating spatialities can be considered dispersed spatialities of otherness. Discontinuous and inherently differentiated space gives ground to differing social identities to express themselves. Essentially connected with identity politics, this geographical imaginary "tends to emphasize situatedness" (Harvey 1996, 363) as a prerequisite of identity formation. Identities, however, may also entail discrimination. A social inculcation of human interaction patterns is always the scope of social reproduction. Inhabited space, in societies that lack "the symbolic-product-conserving techniques associated with literacy," is, according to Bourdieu, the principal locus of this inculcation of dispositions (Bourdieu 1977, 89). Inhabited space, however, seems to have resumed this role in postindustrial societies, not because people have become less dependent on formalized education but because city life has become the educational system par excellence. A wide variety of embodied reactions are learnt through the use of urban space. Everybody has to be able to deal expressively with the risks and opportunities of city life. Where someone is allowed to be and how they conform to spatial instructions of use is indicative of their social identity. Space identifies and is identified through use.

Urban conflicts and urban struggles can become focused on the protection of specific places that contain and represent specific situated collective identities. A working-class neighborhood threatened by gentrification or an ethnic minority meeting spot threatened by racist neighbors can become at stake in an urban conflict involving different groups of citizens and different authorities. The December 2008 youth uprising in Greece went one step further: reclaiming space was not connected to the preservation of established situated identities. Collective identities, as we will see, were implicitly criticized.

Identities in crisis and the experience of urban porosity

A contemporary liberating effort may, indeed, seek "not to emancipate an oppressed identity but [rather] to emancipate an oppressed non-identity" (Holloway 2002, 156). Holloway's reasoning connects the process of social identity formation with the continuous effort of the dominating social reproduction mechanisms to ensure that identities remain distinct and distinguishable. No matter how different historical contingencies affect the resulting identity taxonomies, this effort remains a crucial characteristic of any form of governance. People have to be recognizable, classifiable, and therefore predictable in order to be governed.[1]

There is an underlying logic in this construction of social identities. People are grouped and defined in terms of what they are and not in terms of what they might become or are becoming. Identity thus has to be considered as fixed in time. But it is not the duration of time during which the identity is fixed that is crucial: what is crucial is that the rigid definition of an identity allows for no inherent dynamics to emerge. No inherent contradictions can be allowed. One cannot "be" and "not be" at the same time.

In periods of collective struggle, periods during which people seem to question part of the defining characteristics of their lives, some identities, as fixed roles, undergo a crisis. Groups of people may indeed discover during such a struggle that their collective being should not and cannot be described by the identity attributed to them. And they might seek to create a different collective identity. Or they might seek to get included in a different already existing collective identity.[2]

---

1. As we have seen in chapter 7, this is a tenet of Foucault's analysis of power.
2. All these possibilities can be contained in radical identity politics as the striving "for the freedom of identity, the freedom to be who you really are" (Hardt and Negri 2009, 331).

Emancipating struggles can open the way to even more profound identity crisis. They may delegitimize the very effort to produce and control closed identities. In the process of an emancipating struggle, people may become aware of the possibility of creating their own life as a process of mutual respect between differing individual histories and life trajectories. If some kind of identity is where they start from, if this identity just identifies them so far, then what they face is an open process in which their dreams and actions overspill from the boundaries of this identity.[3]

This has happened for at least some of the collective or individual subjects who took part in the December uprising. An "identity crisis" was an effect of their actions, their words, their new ways of seeing their defining environment (school, workplace, places of leisure, home, etc.). The power of an oppressed non-identity is this power of becoming different without yet entering the perimeter of a new enclosure. Non-identity is an identity in crisis: an open identity unfolding as an uncertain and ambiguous project.[4] Non-identity is a departure from a given identity and not an arrival to a different one. More than that, non-identity is the experience of becoming which includes interactive exchanges with others.

Spaces of emancipation should differ from identity-imposing and identity-reproducing spaces. Space as identity (and identity as space) presupposes a clearly demarcated domain. Space as the locus of non-identity, as the locus of relational,

3. For Holloway this makes people realize that they may "exist in-against-and-beyond" a specific collective identity (Holloway 2010, 112).

4. Hardt and Negri believe that identity politics can reach a revolutionary dimension when collective identities are self-abolished (Hardt and Negri 2009, 332). Identities in crisis can be the first signal indicating such a possibility. Holloway also emphasizes the importance of anti-identification struggles in the process of fighting capitalism: "Identity is the reproduction of capital within anticapitalist struggle" (Holloway 2010, 113).

multifarious and open identities, has to be, on the contrary, loosely determined space.[5]

It is people who create loose spaces, either by actively realizing some inherent possibilities in certain areas or by creating themselves those possibilities, sometimes in direct confrontation with the habitual use and regulations that define certain spaces (Franck and Stevens 2007). Collectively appropriating a street or a schoolyard by transforming it into an area of unauthorized action and creative encounters, is already a "loosening" of those spaces. And whereas "tight" determinations of use presuppose inhabitant-users with specific characteristics, the process of loosening spatial boundaries and rules of use involves a corresponding loosening of user identities.

Loose spaces do not define but rather permit. Loose spaces provide a ground for collective inventiveness. Rules are suspended or defied. If, however, space is disconnected temporarily from the set of rules that defines it, then space cannot be taken as the locus of a collective identity that describes its users. And if a specific space can no longer determine its actual or potential users, this space cannot literally or symbolically belong to anybody or any group.

It is this process of suspending spatial definition and belonging that gives to inhabited loose space an inherently relational character. Such spaces can become the locus of comparisons, the locus of communication and mutual awareness, the always in the making, always in-between, always in transition locus of identities in crisis.

Loose spaces become in-between spaces as they are used. Their existence as thresholds depends upon their being actually or vir-

5. Ritual acts aim, above all, to ensure that an intermediary experience of non-identity (Turner 1977), necessary for the passage from one social identity to another, will not threaten social reproduction. Through the mediation of purification rites or guardian gods, societies supervise spaces of transition, because those spaces symbolically mark the possibility of deviation or transgression.

tually crossed. However, it is not crossings as guarded passages to well-defined areas that may be taken to represent an alternative spatiality of emancipation. It is more about thresholds connecting separate potential destinations. The spatiality of the threshold represents a spatiotemporal experience that can be constitutive of the spaces of urban conflicts, such as the December 2008 youth uprising temporarily created.

A "city of thresholds" may be constituted as a spatial pattern that gives form to in-between spaces of encounter, exchange, and mutual recognition.[6] Those spaces, once performed, offer an alternative to a culture of barriers, a culture that defines the city as an agglomeration of identity enclaves (Marcuse and van Kempen 2002). Replacing the checkpoints that control access through interdictions or everyday discriminatory practices, thresholds provide the ground for a possible solidarity between different people to regain control over their lives. We can therefore understand the spatiality of the threshold as a possible characteristic of transformed urban space. Urban conflicts that create this kind of performed urban space actually transform the city, no matter how temporary this transformation might be.

Urban porosity redefines the city as a network of thresholds to be crossed, thresholds that mediate between differing yet mutually recognizing urban cultures. It can thus be the spatiotemporal form that an emancipating urban culture may take (Stavrides 2007),

6. The idea of a "city of thresholds" attempts to describe an array of spatial practices that may potentially destroy the enclave culture/reality of contemporary cities. In a different context, Hardt and Negri, see "the defining characteristics of metropolis degenerate when it becomes no longer a space of the common and the encounter with the other" (Hardt and Negri 2009, 255). For them "the politics of the metropolis is the organization of encounters" which requires an "openness to alterity" and a capacity to make encounters "joyful and productive" (ibid.). The "city of thresholds" as a liberating project, intersects with such a prospect, putting an emphasis on the spatiotemporal characteristics of such negotiating encounters.

and it can be approached both as a potential characteristic of spatial arrangements and as a corresponding characteristic of the spatial practices that constitute the inhabiting experience. Urban porosity may also become a prerequisite of a "relational politics of place" as proposed by Massey (2005, 181), as well as a form of experience that activates relationality rather than separation, considered in terms of space as well as in terms of time. In urban pores different spaces as well as different times become related and thus compared.

Urban porosity can describe a possible alternative to the dilemma present in various urban struggles. This dilemma can be formulated as: are we to defend a right that establishes redistribution demands of space-bound goods and services (e.g., transport, health facilities, job opportunities, etc.) or are we to defend the right to hold to or develop situated collective identities? However, "distributional issues colour the politics within explicitly identity-based movements" (Ballard, Habib, and Valodia 2006, 409), as the case of the identity-based gay movement in South Africa proves. The latter cannot but deal with "the distributional questions raised by the poverty of a significant proportion of their members" (ibid., 411).

Urban porosity can extend or enhance access rights, developing possibilities of urban-spatial justice or "regional democracy" to use one of Soja's (2000) terms. Urban pores in principle connect, establish chances of exchange and communication, and eliminate space-bound privileges. At the same time, urban porosity can provide the means of acquiring relational identity awareness transforming the city to a network of performed thresholds.

Choosing to create spaces of encounter rather than defend strongholds, the December youth uprising has transcended the limits of a specific struggle in the name of a specific group. Exarchia has ceased to be a fantasized liberated enclave. Demonstrations and occupied sites were scattered throughout Athens and all over Greece. Solidarity acts appeared in as many as 150 different places all over the world.

In all its differentiated modes of collective expression, the December youth uprising tried many forms of collective action and experienced many forms of solidarity. That is why young immigrants found ways to connect with the struggle and participate in their own manner in the conflict. That is why young and older precarious workers recognized themselves in this conflict.

It is not by chance that a few hundred Romas, those second-class citizens who often have a taste of injustice and police brutality, attacked a police station in one of their areas. The December uprising gave them the opportunity to express their anger, reclaim their own space, and even better, their own distinctive spatiality. Spatiality involves creating, understanding, and inhabiting space.

During the December uprising, osmotic relations between spaces of collective action were expressing and producing at the same time osmotic relations between identities. Students were not simply students, workers not simply workers, immigrants not simply immigrants.[7] People participating in different collective actions were finding ways to meet and communicate without simply expressing their imposed social identities, without necessarily adhering to closed political, ideological or cultural identities. In open assemblies organized in all occupied places, people tended to describe proposals for action, to describe dreams and values rather than passively describe disempowering situations or criticize others just for being others.

7. "The shout heard all over Athens is for those 18 years of violence, suppression, exploitation, humiliation. These days are ours too. . . .These days belong to all marginalized and excluded people, those with difficult names and unknown stories." In this excerpt from an Albanian immigrants' collective communiqué, the effort to transcend a stigmatized identity is expressed as an appeal to solidarity combined with a cry for recognition, a cry against invisibility.

The media presentation of the December events was almost entirely obsessed with recurrent and paralyzing questions: "Who did all these things?" and "Who is behind all that?" And the answers were more and more focused on separating the good from the bad demonstrations, the truly disappointed and angry kids from those "others" waiting to destroy the legitimate order.

The problem was that school kids were everywhere but, apart from their rage, there was no way to group them in a collective identity. Not even as people belonging to a definable age group. Their actions were mixing mature organizing abilities with actions of collective joy.[8] To further complicate things, immigrants participating in violent actions or demonstrations were transcending the limits of their imposed identity as stigmatized outsiders by expressing their anger for the burdens of work precariousness they shared with other young people and their dreams of a more just world. In the name of which of their distinctive or common characteristics were all those people taking part in the December uprising?

Well, the media and the government had finally found it: all this was done by people hiding behind hoods. People with erased characteristics, indefinable and unclassifiable, they were simply outside the legitimate and legitimizing social taxonomy: outsiders, enemies of the society, hooded and faceless.[9] What started

8. Hate and anger, characteristic of excluded people, were combined with love-and-hate appeals to their parents: "Please don't get angry with me. You taught me what to do. You taught me that revolt means disorder and destruction. Now that I rise up, it is disorder and destruction that you get. . . .I love you. In my own way, but I love you. I have to make my own world, however, I have to live my own life in freedom. And to do that I have to destroy your world" (School Coordinating Alliance Alexandros Grigoropoulos, *A leaflet to my parents*, December 2008).

9. Demonstrators with improvised tear-gas masks were demonized as masked criminals. We have already seen in chapter 7 how important it is for power to present those who fight against it as outsiders, as dangerous others. Could it be that any fantasized unmasking of those "others" carries the same power of Marcos' alleged unmasking by the Mexican state? Behind the masks were Greek society's kids, ignored by their own society as were the "invisible" natives by Mexican society.

as a panic, because everyday people, next-door youngsters, did things they were not supposed to do—they defied and mocked power and expressed a complete lack of trust for justice and government—was channeled by the official rhetoric into a reassuring interpretation of the events: it is only a matter of crushing those "outsiders" and order will be restored.

It might be a distinctive characteristic of such urban struggles that they create both for their participants, as well as those who watch and wonder, a kind of "taxonomy crisis." "Who are these people?" is a question that, in spite of media mythologies, cannot easily be answered unambiguously or reassuringly.

Is there life after December?

December's ephemeral city of thresholds left its mark in various urban struggles that followed the riots. One of them, the most characteristic one, is the struggle to transform a large parking lot in Exarchia into an ad-hoc urban park. People from the neighborhood as well as activists and environmentalists from other neighborhoods (not all of them directly involved in the December uprising, but all deeply influenced by it) decided to reclaim this site and managed to create a truly alternative public space, open to all. Everyone can participate in the open meetings where the layout of the park is designed, the rules of the park's use are decided, problems are discussed, and different views find ways to negotiate with each other.

This initiative is still flourishing while managing to keep the threshold character of the place. As no one or no group is expected to be the owner or the sole user of the area, the rules of coexistence and mutual respect have to be collectively invented. These

Walking as invention—occupied Navarinou Park, Athens. (Photo by Ioannis Papagiannakis.)

The December 2008 youth uprising in Athens: glimpses of a possible city of thresholds   205 rules are put to test every day. Identities have to be negotiated too. What does it mean to be a user of the park? Whose needs should be satisfied and how? Whose rights should prevail? Who becomes a subject of urban rights, especially in the case of a collectively self-governed outdoor public space? How can these alternative rights be expressed? Isn't this, after all, an experiment concerning the right to the city?[10]

The December spirit is a force of resistance inspiring people to see and act beyond the closed horizons of mainstream politics, transcending sometimes even the certainties of existing anticapitalist movements. Navarinou Park was only one among many similar initiatives that have proven people can demand and create new public spaces. People in the Zografou area (near the center of Athens but a separate municipality), for example, have successfully obstructed the local mayor's decision to construct multistory parking buildings in five of the neighborhood's squares. Although municipal authorities have described them as "minority vandals," young people have managed to destroy this stigmatizing identity perimeter and inspire many of the Zografou inhabitants to join this struggle. Others have occupied an abandoned botanical garden in Petroupoli, reclaiming it as a public space, and have successfully defended various areas of public use targeted by gentrification and development mechanisms.

The December uprising seems to have triggered urban struggles characterized by stakes closely connected to a collective reclaiming of public spaces. The cry for justice during the uprisings was heard in public spaces transformed or even invented by collective actions. A demand for urban justice is just one form this cry has taken during the post-December era. This probably happens

10. More details about this collective experience as well as thoughts on the problems encountered can be found in the journal *An Architektur* no. 23 (2010), special issue on the commons, with an insert on Navarinou Park.

because in struggles for the defense and corroboration of public space, people can grasp what it means to take their life in their hands. Participation in such struggles is not a matter of expressing an opinion or aligning with others who share similar political projects. It is a matter of helping to produce both the spaces for public use and a new culture of public use that goes beyond the logic of consumption and the priorities of urban "development."

December's legacy also includes forms of struggle that directly translate political aims to practices of public space transformation. During and after the December uprising another figure was to emblematize the struggles of an emergent movement. Trade unionist Kostantina Kuneva, a Bulgarian immigrant, office cleaner, and secretary of the Cleaners Syndicate (PEKOP) was violently attacked with sulfuric acid. Kuneva soon become a symbol as she belongs to all those categories of people attacked by neoliberalism: woman, immigrant, activist, precarious worker. Many initiatives supporting her right to live, work, and obtain full citizenship in Greece, along with a demand for punishing all those who profit from the exploitation of precarious workers, bore the mark of December's spirit.

For example, in four different metro stations, groups of people blocked the ticket machines, explaining to metro users that the metro corporation actually uses underpaid cleaners exploited by ruthless contractors. Isn't this a form of temporarily imposing a threshold character to the privatized and controlled public space of everyday transportation?

Solidarity with immigrants is generally high on the agenda of the Greek left and anarchist movement. After December, solidarity was even more strongly expressed as more people got involved in specific acts aiming to protect and support threatened immigrant communities. In the Athenian neighborhood of Agios Panteleimon, antiracist activists had to fight against fascist groups and xenophobic residents who wanted to expel "non-Greeks" from the neighborhood. A huge mobilization was also able to protect a large immigrant squat in central Athens that was being attacked by the same fascist groups with the not-so-hidden support of the police.

In both cases, a political struggle was also an urban struggle, as the stake was explicitly urban. Supporting immigrants' rights is directly connected to the effort to support their right to the city as the right that epitomizes all other rights. And these struggles actively attempt to convert the city to an inclusive, multiform environment: a city of thresholds.

The December uprising has shown that a collective demand for justice can create new forms of active urban justice. Is the prospect of the city of thresholds an adequate description of this potentially emancipating quest? It is really too early to know. After all, writing on an Exarchia wall justly states: "December was not an answer. December was a question."

Throughout this book an effort has been made to explore the emancipating potentialities generated by the creation, experience, and appreciation of the symbolic power of thresholds. We have encountered the concrete spatiotemporal presence of thresholds in everyday attempts made by displaced and disempowered people to breach the enclosing perimeter of their life. And we have observed how people on the threshold imagine and act explicitly or implicitly opposing the dominant taxonomies of identity that engulf their aspirations. Threshold awareness seems to encourage resistance and perhaps can help people in questioning their habits, values, life goals, and behavior. Thresholds can be those relational and transitional spaces in which encounters with a different future may happen.

In a possible city of thresholds, heterotopic moments emerge as part of a process of collective invention. The city can be a collective work of art—to recall Lefebvre's famous phrase—in which the future itself can be created as a collective work of art too. Common dreams of justice, equality and fraternity can inspire and sustain this process. And it is in everyday major and minor struggles that passages towards an emancipatory future are opened and explored. We have to discover such passages, study them, sustain their creation, and experience the hopes and nightmares that haunt them. Because, as the "threshold politics" of the Zapatistas continue to show us, "we don't need to conquer the world. Creating it from the beginning will do. Us. Today."

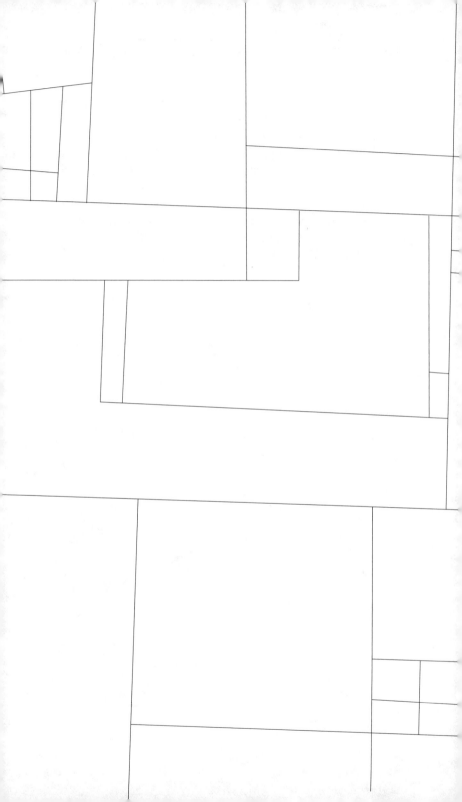

Part IV

09

Squares in movement

*Legitimacy crisis and the role of
contemporary communication practices*

Not long ago, governing elites seemed to believe they had at
last reached the absolute capitalist utopia: money begets money without any interference from disobedient and unpredictable
real people as well as always-problematic production procedures.
This euphoric optimism of the governing elites is, however, fading
quickly as the supposedly flawless machine of profit got stuck in
a socioeconomic crisis much more severe than the periodic ones.

Those real people who necessarily make this machine work are
again visible. The crisis of loans has to do with real populations
and their behavior, collective and individual. It directly affects
economic processes, disturbing plans and falsifying future pro-
jections. In a period of a supposedly absolute predominance of
the laws of the market, when politics is replaced by management,
problems of governability arise. Those below have to be reinte-
grated into a system that, caught in its own paroxysmal utopia,
thought it could function without them. As so many social erup-

tions and statistics show, people are losing their faith in a system that presents itself as a mechanism of potential wealth distribution to which they expect to have access.

It is too early to say that the policies of the governing elites have entered into a crisis of no return, but we can observe in various parts of the world two interconnected series of phenomena that deeply affect what we could diagnose as a "crisis of legitimacy." The first involves the role of information and communication in destabilizing collective faith in the system. From the Latin American movements and uprisings (as the *Argentinazo*, or the people's anticoup mobilizations in Venezuela) to the Arab revolutions (especially those in Tunisia and Egypt), including the "indignant" square occupations in European cities, communication and information exchanges through social media and interactive communication devices have played a key role in shaping collective action. The second series includes community-oriented or community-inspired actions that—quite distinct from neo-communitarian, neoconservative ideologies—create or even reinvent communities in the making. These are often unstable but always-expandable communities in movement.

Both series of phenomena converge in practices of redefining and reappropriating public space. Practices primarily connected to new forms of communication create, use, and disseminate information through new and old communicative media. But these are not practices of information exchange only: they "mark" the city through the information exchange they make possible. It is a process of marking specific places with inscriptions that not only disseminate information (as in the case of wall writings or graffiti), but also connect places and create shared points of reference for specific emerging collectivities that recognize them. This happened, for example, during the December 2008 youth uprising in Athens,[1]

1. Stavros Stavrides, "The December 2008 Youth Uprising in Athens: Spatial Justice in an

when a "migrational" stencil art spread all over the city center and condensed the uprising's messages into emblematic images. Some of these markings short-lived, while others survive—inscriptions over other inscriptions, messages and traces in combat with other traces.

Another important characteristic of those new urban practices of public space appropriation and collective dissent is that they use information exchanges with the aim of potentially coordinating those who participate in the exchanges. Information is not a flow, in this context, but it is directed toward recipients and returned as a promise of mutual involvement.[2]

The call for the first meeting in Athens's Syntagma Square, which borders the Parliament House, was issued on Facebook on May 20, 2011. Two or three young men had an idea for a rally that would give people the opportunity to express their indignation about the economic crisis (Giovanopoulos and Mitropoulos 2011, 278). There would be no political parties, no organized initiatives, no prearranged demands, no planning—it was just a call. After it was circulated through social media, it had an amazing effect: thirty thousand people gathered on May 25, 2011 in Syntagma Square. Everyone was simply astonished, including the Left and the anarchist movement. This movement was called the *aganaktismeni* [indignant] movement by those who made the initial call as well as by the media.[3]

Emergent 'City of Thresholds,'" *Spatial Justice* 2 (2010). Available at www.jssj.org/archives/02/media/public_space_vo2.pdf.

2.   One of the early examples of such practices was the "*pasalo*" mobilizations in Barcelona and Madrid on March 13, 2004. During the "night of the short messages," people exchanged messages that would overthrow a government. "Liars murderers. Your war our dead. *Pasalo* [Pass it on]": this message was circulated the day before general elections and accused the government of systematically hiding from the people the reasons behind the 2004 Madrid bombings. Huge demonstrations occupied the central squares in Barcelona and Madrid, as these were defined by the messages of protesters as meeting points. In this process, information ("they are not telling us the truth") addressed people as potential actors. Through acts of sharing and participation, information thus acquired a power to mobilize people. See Manuel Castells, Jack Linchuan Qiu, Mireia Fernández-Ardèvol, and Araba Sey, *Mobile Communication and Society: A Global Perspective* (Cambridge, MA: MIT Press, 2007).

3.   *Aganaktismenos* comes from the ancient Greek verb *aganakto*, to become angry because of injus-

The call, of course, did not come out of nowhere. The Tunisian revolution had already ignited. People saw images of common people in revolt on television and in the newspapers. Then came the Tahrir Square occupation in Cairo. Suddenly the Arab world exploded into a stage of public expression with no apparent history, with no recognizable ideological characteristics, with no leaders. Inventive, self-organized, and determined people took to the streets.

The Spanish were the first to incorporate this message into their own social context. *Indignados* occupied major city squares and demanded their lives back. Calls to action made via social media managed to bypass formal opposition parties and trade unions, producing events that gave everyone the means to express their increasing anger against neoliberal austerity policies.

The Spanish *indignados* and the Greek *aganaktismeni* exchanged solidarity messages and loosely coordinated their protests on certain mobilization days. Messages were transmitted through the Internet and were projected on outdoor screens in Syntagma. Tunisian and Egyptian activists were invited to speak in large assemblies, and they were welcomed with great enthusiasm. A loose network of self-organized initiatives developed from this exchange among the squares. And, of course, alternative information media, including the active multimedia team at the Syntagma occupation, contributed to a feeling that things happening around the world can have common characteristics, express common attitudes and dreams, and share a common demand for real, direct democracy.

In contemporary societies, interactive technologies mediate the creation of communities of collective action that are not necessarily composed of people sharing a common identity or common

tice, and is similar to the Spanish *indignados* [the outraged]. In everyday use, the term connotes an attitude of being fed up (comparable to "*ya basta*"), but it was used in the past by the Left to describe aggressive law-abiding citizens with racist or even fascist attitudes. This has caused an understandable unease with the term's current use.

values. These are communities in movement, developed through common action and the sharing of public space.[4]

Opportunities are not created by interactive media. Instead, shared information and meeting points bind people. In a curious reversal, the reterritorialization of politics happens through the active mediation of deterritorializing communication technologies. Communities become located in urban space and develop by redefining and reappropriating their surroundings.

"Common space" as threshold space

Communities in movement form their own space. This is not the public space as we know it, space given from a certain authority to the public under specific conditions that ultimately affirm the authority's legitimacy. Nor is it private space, if by this we mean space controlled and used by a limited group of people excluding all others. Communities create "common space,"[5] space used under conditions decided on by communities and open to anyone. The use, maintenance, and creation of common space does not simply mirror the community. The community is formed, developed, and reproduced through practices focused on common

---

4. The idea of communities in movement echoes Raúl Zibechi's "societies in movement," describing collective practices and events that go beyond the usual definition of social movements. See Raúl Zibechi, *Autonomías y emancipaciones: América Latina en movimiento* (Lima: Universidad Nacional Mayor de San Marcos, 2007); and Zibechi, *Dispersing Power: Social Movements as AntiState Forces* (Oakland, CA: AK Press, 2010).

5. "Common space," according to Marcel Hénaff and Tracy B. Strong, "admits no criteria; it is open to all in the same way. It is not owned or controlled. . . . All can go there to extract from it what is there." Marcel Hénaff and Tracy B. Strong, *Public Space and Democracy* (Minneapolis: University of Minnesota Press, 2001), 4. This is more or less an understanding of common space as preexisting its social uses (including its potential enclosure), whereas common space is primarily and necessarily considered as a social artifact created through practices of space commoning. See also Gigi Roggero, "Five Theses on the Common," *Rethinking Marxism* 22, no. 3 (2010): 357–73, 361–63. For a discussion that compares public and common space, see Massimo De Angelis and Stavros Stavrides, "Beyond Markets or States: Commoning as Collective Practice (a public interview)," *An Architektur*, no. 23 (2010): 4–27, esp. 12. Available at eflux.com/journal.

space. To generalize this principle: the community is developed through commoning, through acts and forms of organization oriented toward the production of the common.

During the occupation, Syntagma Square developed into a network of connected microsquares, each with a distinct character and spatial arrangement. All were contained, or rather territorialized, in the area of what was known to be the main public square in Athens. Each microsquare had its own group of people who lived there for some days, in their tents, who focused their actions and their microurban environment to a specific task: a children's playground, a free reading and meditation area, a homeless campaign meeting point, a "time bank" (services are exchanged, eliminating money and profit), a "we don't pay" campaign meeting point (focused on organizing an active boycott of transportation fees and road tolls), a first-aid center, a multimedia group, a translation group, and so on.

There were various levels on which these microcommunities were connected, and of course, all had to follow the General Assembly's rules and decisions. However, differences in opinion regarding spatial arrangement and expression media (the use of banners, placards, stickers, images, "works of art," etc.) were more than apparent. Although they shared a common cause and a common target (the Hellenic Parliament), each microsquare established different routines and aesthetics and organized different microevents during the occupation.

The organizing structures of the Syntagma Square occupation were developed according to a decentralization-recentralization dialectics. The central assembly, as with most of the assemblies characterizing the Occupy movements, remained an opento-all discussion area, but decisions were made in common by vote (every participant could vote). Every effort was made for decisions to be as widely accepted as possible. This process would have been absolutely pointless without the preparations done in various

The assembly at the Syntagma Square occupation, 2011.

Tent city at the Syntagma Square occupation, 2011.

committees. Those were open too and were created so as to focus on certain issues which the General Assembly would have to think through and decide on.

The dispersion of initiatives and the decentralization of acts and discussions did not result in a loss of the common cause and a weakening of solidarity. Questions were sometimes hotly debated, but no one and no group was allowed to dominate, and nobody was silenced. Interestingly, the procedure of assembly discussions also reflected the decentralization-recentralization dialectics. Many wanted to speak, and so those who actually spoke were chosen by lot in each specific phase of the discussion. Decisions, however, concerned everybody, so proposals were collected by a secretary (who changed every day) in order to put them to vote.

Space commoning in the reappropriated square involved the production and use of in-between spaces. Common spaces emerge as threshold spaces, spaces not demarcated by a defining perimeter. Whereas public space bears the mark of a prevailing authority that defines it, common space is opened space, space in a process of opening toward "newcomers" (Rancière, 2010, 59). Common spaces are porous, spaces in movement, space passages.

Threshold spaces neither define people who use them nor are defined by them. Rather, they mediate negotiations between people about the meaning and use of space. Such spaces thus correspond to a process of identity opening forming, as I've stated previously, "intermediary zones of doubt, ambivalence, hybridity, zones of negotiable values."[6] Syntagma could be considered a miniature city, a "city of thresholds"[7] in which encounters and dispersed initiatives build spaces where people explore a public culture based on solidarity and mutual respect.

6. See Introduction, 9.
7. Ibid.

Community in movement in Syntagma was not created through organizational schemes that presupposed a central decision-making process or through the absolute predominance of a central space. Spaces and decisions were decentralized and recentralized, and so was the process of creating those social bonds that created a community in constant remaking.

Reinventing community

Commoning procedures leave room for differentiated initiatives and individual improvisations. Not everybody came to Syntagma to participate in the assembly. Many came only to shout and express their anger and disapproval. On Sundays, some brought their children along simply to enjoy the air of a public space that was "different."

To search desperately for a locatable common identity that could include all those people was a serious mistake. Sometimes it made participating activists of the Left completely misunderstand the motives, practices, and expressions of all those who participated more or less regularly. Were those, for example, holding "their" national flags (in Syntagma, in Tunis, in Barcelona, and elsewhere) simply nationalists? Was this therefore a potentially dangerous community resurfacing in a period of crisis? If we simply judge using a well-established repertoire of political forms of expression, obviously this is the case. But in the squares people used national symbols in various ways. In Athens a person "wore" the flag as a kind of shield against those who "sell the country" (literally, indeed). Another participant used flag-waving to appeal to an injured collective dignity: "rise up," "wake up," "we are here, as the Spaniards are in their squares, as should be the Italians, the French, and others."

One way to judge the long discussions about real or direct democracy (in assemblies but also in smaller commissions or groups), which were predominant throughout the European squares experience, was to analyze the words and thoughts used. Then one could say that this or that kind of discourse was depoliticized, utopian, ineffective, and so on. Another way was to compare words, acts, and forms of expression. "Real" or direct democracy was performed in various ways in the squares. No matter what observers would say, women's participation in Tahrir Square is a de facto practicing of common space as democratic space. And, people in the squares devised ways to make decisions and to defend themselves against police aggression, which established new forms of direct equalitarian democracy. Just after one such incident—a brutal police incident in which the people had been chased, hit, and tear-gassed—the square of Syntagma was peacefully reoccupied. People formed long human chains that transported, from hand to hand, small bottles of water to clean the square of the poisonous tear gas remains. Collective inventiveness—in order to meet the lack of sufficient water—created a democratic equalitarian solidarity. Those human chains, improvised to face a pressing situation, emblematize a community in movement that reinvents "real" democracy in action. Sometimes those human chains took the form of circle dancing, either to celebrate a victory (as in Tahrir, after the announcement of Hosni Mubarak's fall) or to exorcise fear (in Syntagma, people danced in the square as the police were bombing the area with suffocating gas grenades).

Discourses, practices, and forms of expression can and should be interpreted as acts in movement. Their correspondences are sometimes strengthened, but one should not deduce a preexisting pattern that maps their common ground. Discrepancies, ambiguities, and contradictions are necessary ingredients of a potential community in action, a community of different people who remain different but recognize themselves as coproducers of a common space in the making.

"We"?

A peculiar "we" surfaces in the squares, an ambiguous "we" can condense but can also evaporate in the current uprisings. Is this the "we" that marks the emergence of new political subjects, the emergence of those who did not count before but demand to take part, as Jacques Rancière understands the process of political subjectivation (Rancière 2010, 32–33)?

Here are some examples from writings in the squares. In Barcelona: "We are ordinary people. We are like you, people who get up every morning to study, to work or find a job, people who have families and friends. People who work hard every day to provide a better future for those around us."[8] In Patras, Greece: "We call everybody, working people, jobless people, young people, we call society to fill St. George's Square in Patras. Let's reclaim our lives." Finally, in Syntagma: "For a long time decisions have been made for us, without us. We are workers, unemployed, retirees, youth, who have come to Syntagma Square to fight and struggle for our lives and our future. We are here because we know that the solutions to our problems can come only from us," and "We are nobody."[9]

This is a "we" of common people, an inclusive "we" that demands life and justice. This is a "we" that does not name, differentiate or erect barriers. Most important, perhaps, this is a "we" that is formed in complete opposition to the national or cosmopolitan "we" that the governing elites and the mainstream media attempt to impose. "We are not responsible, you are." "We don't have to pay your debts." "We don't have to fight your wars." "We are not you." Opposed to a recognizable outside, the outside that contains

8. ¡Democracia real YA! Manifesto. Available at http://www.democraciarealya.es/?s=manifesto.
9. Patras Real Democracy, available at http://patras-democracy.blogspot.com/. Patras' *aganaktisme-ni* posted their General Assembly decisions and discussions here. For Syntagma Square General Assembly resolutions, see real-democracy.gr/content/poioi-ei- maste1.

all those who destroy the future, there is a multifaceted "we," a kaleidoscopic "we" full of refractions and always open to new arrangements of difference.

Is it the "we" of the multitude? Perhaps, if the multitude is characterized by heterogeneous multiplicity. But the reasoning behind using multitude to describe the crowd in the current phase of capitalism is based on the idea that the multitude emerges as the productive human force in the period of biopolitical production. The multitude, according to Michael Hardt and Antonio Negri, "is a multiplicity of singularities that produce and are produced in the biopolitical field of the common" (2009, 165).

However, in the squares and in the recent uprisings, the multitude does not present itself as a productive force. Not even if we allow the term production to contain almost every form of human activity, as Hardt and Negri do. True, capitalism attempts to distill out of every human activity its productive power on which the production of value and profit necessarily are based. People in the squares, however, are creating rather than producing.[10] Forms of public sharing and encounter are created while being performed. Can these forms potentially be manipulated by dominant institutions and appropriated by the market by being turned into mechanisms of exploitation?

---

10. Hardt and Negri clearly insist that today "labor cannot be limited to waged labor but must refer to human creative capacities in all their generality." Michael Hardt and Antonio Negri, *Multitude: War and Democracy in the Age of Empire* (London: Hamish Hamilton, 2004), 105. Virno believes that "the dividing line between Work and Action [*poiesis* and *praxis*] . . . has now disappeared altogether." Paolo Virno, "Virtuosity and Revolution: The Political Theory of Exodus," *Radical Thought in Italy: A Potential Politics*, eds. Paolo Virno and Michael Hardt (Minneapolis: University of Minnesota Press, 2006), 189–222; 190. Virno also states, "There is no longer anything which distinguishes labor from the rest of human activities." Paolo Virno, *A Grammar of the Multitude* (Los Angeles: Semiotext(e), 2004), 102. There is, however, a movement that opposes the continuing entrapment of creative action by the logic of capital, which can be recognized in the square's commoning experiences. Perhaps it is more appropriate to speak of a potential temporary emancipation of "doing" in the prospect of an "antipolitics of dignity," as theorized by John Holloway. John Holloway, *Crack Capitalism* (London: Pluto, 2010), 245–249; and John Holloway, *Change the World without Taking Power: The Meaning of Revolution Today* (London: Pluto, 2002).

Yes, but one should not judge only in terms of possibilities. What we know about the present shows us that forms of commoning are directly opposed to the main targets of the dominant politics and to the hegemonic project of governing the crisis.

What the theory of the multitude can offer us, along with other attempts to rethink the political (including Giorgio Agamben's and Jacques Rancière's), is that politics is necessarily linked to processes of collective subjectivation. What these theories attempt to rethink is not simply changes in the definition of political subject but also about the processes of collective subjects' constitution. Agamben uses "whatever singularities" to describe the subjectivities of a coming community (Agamben 1993), and Rancière speaks of the "democratic practice as the inscription of the part of those who have no part—which does not mean the 'excluded' but anybody whoever" (Rancière 2010, 60). Clearly distinguished from the "people" and the "masses," the multitude is for Hardt and Negri an "active social subject" that "although it remains multiple and internally different is able to act in common and thus rule itself" (Hardt and Negri 2004, 100).

Political subjectivation, thus, can be considered as a process that does not move toward the construction of collective identities and unified social bodies but toward new forms of coordination and interaction based on commoning practices that create open communities. These theorizations can only hint toward the possibility of a different society, developing ideas about forms of collective action that can indeed prefigure egalitarian and emancipating social relations. Is this enough today? Probably not. This is why it is so urgently necessary to understand contemporary movements and learn from their actions, discourses, and forms of organization.

One thing we already know is that these events had the power to overthrow governments even in societies with histories of absolutist regimes. And we also know that these events mark the return of people to collective action. There is no obvious common economic or social definition that can include them, though. A crisis of power legitimation unites them, along with a shared feeling of a total absence of justice. Everyone draws experiences from their own life that verify this prevailing injustice. In the Tunisian uprising, this feeling was expressed in a revolt against a corrupt family that ruled the country for many years. In the December 2008 uprising in Athens, this feeling was everywhere in young people's actions; the killing of a young boy by a policeman condensed into a single act all dominant measures, politics, and ideologies that imprison youth in a predetermined future of antagonisms and disappointments. And in the squares, this feeling took the form of a collectively recognized economic injustice (accelerated through austerity measures). This feeling was also behind the 2011 UK riots.

All these events indicate societies in movement. This movement goes beyond any agglomeration of particular demands that are expressed by different social groups in pursuit of their interests. In practices of collective improvisation and collective inventiveness, common spaces are created in which people not only express their anger and needs but also develop forms of life in common. True, those forms are fragile, precarious, ephemeral, and sometimes contradictory in terms of ideological premises or values. But this collective and de facto production of common spaces reinvents dissident politics and gives new form to practices that overstep the boundaries of dominant social roles.

Sharing and solidarity are not introduced as values or ideologically sanctioned imperatives but are experienced in practice; specifically, in solving practical problems and collectively organizing actions of protest. In such a context, there is no difference between the solidarity that supports organizing against state aggression and the solidarity expressed in the collection of garbage in the occupied squares. Solidarity is not simply a force that sustains people in clashes with state forces. Solidarity becomes a creative force.

At Syntagma Square, solidarity developed in practice gave people the means to confront violence in ways that reformulated dilemmas about oppositional action. The occupation declared itself from the beginning a peaceful but determined gathering of angry people. Certain anarchists accused the Syntagma occupiers of being pacifists and nonviolent petit bourgeois ideologues. That said, although there were many proposals to denounce violent attacks on police, banks, and public buildings that came before the General Assembly, they were not accepted. Many have criticized the acts of violence that were exemplary of a self-proclaimed avant-garde, and many tried to limit the results of such acts, while protecting the people from brutal police "responses." Police aggression was so great that sometimes the limits between expressly chosen violent "black bloc" action and spontaneous stone-throwing became blurred. If one wants to understand the Syntagma occupation's attitude to oppositional violence, one has to consider all those ambiguous and perhaps contradictory aspects of this collective experience.

The most urgent and promising task, which can oppose the dominant governance model, is the reinvention of common spaces. The realm of the common is in constant confrontation with state-controlled "authorized" public space. Behind a multifarious demand for justice and dignity, new roads to collective emancipation are tested and invented. As the Zapatistas say, we can create these roads only while walking. But we have to listen, observe, and feel the walking movement. Together.

10

Emerging common spaces
as a challenge to the city of crisis

In today's Athens we can trace the devastating effects the cataclysmic financialization of the capitalist economy has on urban and social reproduction. We can also, however, discover emerging new forms of resistance to the policies of capitalist crisis, which are connected to acts that transform public space. Such acts shape urban space as a means to create new social bonds and to build forms of collective struggle and survival.

Two crucial tasks are laid before a necessary return to politics for the governing elites who imagined that they, at last, could do away with the obstacles labor creates to profit (Midnight Notes 2009). The first one is to ensure that social bonds continue to constitute individuals as economic subjects whose behavior and motives can be analyzed, channeled, predicted, and ultimately, controlled by the use of economic parameters and measures only. The second one is to ensure that people continue to act and dream without participating in any form of connectedness and coordination with others. It is against these dominant policies that people gropingly rediscover the importance of taking their lives in their hands. Creating common spaces is an essential step in this direction.

The December 2008 youth uprising (Stavrides 2010) and the Syntagma Square occupation were catalysts of dissident awareness and urban commoning in Athens. Both events produced collective experiences reclaiming the city as a potentially liberating environment and reshaping crucial questions about emancipatory politics. In this context, the city becomes not just the setting but also the means to collectively experiment on alternative forms of social organization.

For some, the project of autonomy may be described as a process that creates completely independent socio-spatial entities that become capable of reproducing themselves with no recourse to their hostile social and political surrounding. Autonomous areas are meant to create their own rules of self-regulation and people inhabit them by following those rules.

The Greek state wants to sustain the myth of a locatable marginal "outside" of dissent because it can·"surgically" intervene when it chooses to crush any dissident behavior, and at the same time, it gives the impression that these behaviors only exist in secluded enclaves. The December youth uprising has shifted the media and police focus from the allegedly anomic Exarchia enclave to many other neighborhoods in Athens and to other major Greek cities (Stavrides 2010). Thus the state could not present the uprising as one more Exarchia-centered incident of "rioting hooliganism."

Autonomous spaces are imagined as liberated enclaves surrounded by a hostile capitalist environment. Through a powerful spatial metaphor, autonomy is equated to spatial distinctness, to circumscribed areas that are defined by their exteriority to the rest of the city-society.

The occupied Navarinou Park project, as well as many neighborhood initiatives after the Syntagma occupation, hints towards a different imaginary of emancipating autonomy. Always porous and open to new potential users, Navarinou Park may support a spatial experience as well as a spatial metaphor which is beyond and against the experience and metaphor of the enclave (Marcuse and van Kempen 2002; Atkinson and Blandy 2005; Graham and Marvin 2001). The park's porous perimeter is defined by spatial arrangements that acquire the characteristics of a threshold rather than those of a boundary. Actually, the park itself may be considered a multileveled and multiform urban threshold.

Threshold spatiality may host and express practices of commoning that are not contained in secluded worlds shared by secluded communities of commoners. Thresholds explicitly symbolize the potentiality of sharing by establishing intermediary areas of crossing, by opening inside to outside. As mechanisms that regulate and give meaning to acts of passage, thresholds may become powerful tools in the construction of institutions of expanding commoning. Many societies strictly and boldly control symbolic and real thresholds because people may "lose their way" and discover potential common worlds that are beyond the corresponding society's established hierarchies. But, in the process of expanding commoning that directly defies capitalist society's enclosures, thresholds may become both the image and the setting of emancipating experiences of sharing. Thresholds are potential sociospatial "artifices of equality" (Rancière 2010, 92).

Maybe we need to abandon a view of autonomy that fantasizes uncontaminated enclaves of emancipation (Stavrides 2009, 53; Negri 2009, 50). The prevailing experiences of urban enclosures and the dominant imaginary of recognizable identity enclaves colonize the thought and action of those who attempt to go beyond capitalist hegemony. Threshold experience and the threshold metaphor offer a counter-example to the dominant enclave city. Rather than perpetuating an image of the capitalist city as an archipelago of enclave-islands, we need to create spaces that inventively threaten this peculiar urban order by upsetting dominant taxonomies of spaces and life types. Those spaces-as-thresholds acquire a dubious, precarious perhaps but also virus-like existence: they become active catalysts in the presence of potentially explosive chemical compounds.

This is where the problem of the "institutions of commoning" (Roggero 2010, 369) arises. By its very constitution as a tool of social organization, an institution tends to circumscribe a community as a closed world of predictable and repeatable social practices. Thus, institutions of commoning may be employed to define specific commoning practices and the corresponding community of commoners as a closed self-reproducing world too. But this may—and often does—lead to forms of enclosure (De Angelis and Stavrides 2010, 12). For commoning to remain a force that produces forms of cooperation through sharing, it has to be a process which overspills the boundaries of any established community—including if this community aspires to be an egalitarian and antiauthoritarian one. Emerging subjects of commoning actions transform themselves by always being open to "newcomers" (Rancière 2010, 59–60) or by becoming themselves newcomers.

For commoning practices to become important prefigurations of an emancipated society, commoning has to remain a collective struggle to reappropriate and transform a society's common wealth (Hardt and Negri 2009, 251–253). Collective experiences such as those of Syntagma Square's self-managed tent city and the post-December experiments of neighborhood assemblies and initiatives (including the Navarinou Park occupation) construct an inspiring example of a culture based on equality, solidarity, and collective inventiveness only when they remain "infectious," osmotic, and capable of extending egalitarian values and practices outside their boundaries.

Dominant institutions legitimize inequality, distinguishing between those who know and those who do not, those who are affected by decisions and those who must execute them, and those who have specific rights and those who are deprived of them. Thus, dominant institutions focused on the production and uses of public space are essentially forms of authorization that aim at directing the behaviors of public space's users (Stavrides 2012, 589).

There also exist dominant institutions that appear grounded upon an abstract equality: real people with differentiated characteristics, needs, and dreams are reduced to neutralized subjects of rights. Thus, in public space general rules appear addressed to homogenized users who can only have access to a specific place at specific hours of the day (or who are not allowed to "step on the grass," and so on).

Dominant institutions classify and predict types of behavior and deal with only those differences that are fixed and perpetuated through the classifications they establish. Institutions of commoning established in a stable and well-defined community may very well look like the dominant institutions in the ways they regulate people's rights and actions. There are obviously differences in terms of content. For example, an institution that aims at guaranteeing certain forms of equality (no matter how abstract) is different from an institution that openly imposes discriminations.

Institutions of expanding commoning, however, differ from the dominant ones not only in terms of content but also in terms of form. This makes them potentially different "social artifices" which are oriented towards different social bonds. Such institutions establish, first of all, the ground of comparisons between different subjects of action and also between different practices. Subjects of action and practices themselves become comparable and relevant. What is at stake is to invent forms of collaboration based not on homogenization but on multiplicity (Hardt and Negri 2005, 348–349).

However, comparability is not enough. Institutions of commoning need to offer opportunities as well as tools for translating differences between views, actions, and subjectivities, one to the other. If comparability is based on the necessary and constitutive recognition of differences, translatability creates the ground for negotiations between differences without reducing them to common denominators. "An emancipated community is a community of narrators and translators" (Rancière 2009, 17–20 and 22). Obviously, this is quite difficult, since dominant taxonomies tend to block those processes of establishing a socially recognizable common ground that are not based on the predominance of the ruling elites. Translation seeks correspondences but cannot and does not aspire to establish an absolute unobstructed mirroring of one language to the other. So does or should do an institution which keeps alive the expanding potentiality of commoning. Indeed "the common is always organized in translation" (Roggero 2010, 368).

A third characteristic of institutions of expanding commoning has deep roots in the history of human societies. Social anthropologists have well documented the existence of mechanisms in certain societies which prevent or discourage the accumulation of power. Depending on the case, these mechanisms were focused on the equal distribution of collected food, on the ritual destruction of wealth, on the symbolic sacrifice of leaders, on carnivalistic role reversals, etc.

If institutions of commoning are meant to be able to support a constant opening of the circles of commoning they need to sustain mechanisms of control of any potential accumulation of power, either by individuals or by specific groups. If sharing is to be the guiding principle of self-management practices, then sharing of power is simultaneously the precondition of egalitarian sharing and its ultimate target. Egalitarian sharing, which needs to be able to include newcomers, has to be encouraged by an

Occupied City Plaza Hotel: a self-managed common space in Athens.

Occupied City Plaza Hotel: refugees welcome.

always-expanding network of self-governance institutions. Such institutions can really be "open" and "perpetually in flux" (Hardt and Negri 2009, 358–359) but in very specific ways connected to the practices of expanding commoning. Power is first and foremost the power to decide. If, however, the power to decide is distributed equally through mechanisms of participation, then this power ceases to give certain people the opportunity (legitimized or not) to impose their will on others.

Perhaps what the collective experiments in space commoning in Athens during this crisis modestly gesture towards is the possibility of reclaiming the city as a collective work of art (Lefebvre 1996, 174). To devise common spaces means, thus, something a lot more than to succeed in reappropriating small pieces of still available open space. It means, explicitly or implicitly, sometimes in full conscience and sometimes not, discovering the power to create new ambiguous, possibly contradictory but always open institutions of commoning. Actual physical space, but also metaphorical imaginary space, becomes not only the ground that is necessary in order to see these institutions function; space shapes institutions of commoning and is shaped by them.

In the contemporary capitalist city people have to invent forms of life in order to survive. To help release the power of doing (Holloway 2010, 246–247), which capitalism continuously captures and traps in its mechanisms, we need to participate in the creation of spaces and institutions of expanding commoning. If autonomy has any meaning as an anticapitalist venture, then it must be constructed in-against-and-beyond the metropolis, by upsetting the dominant taxonomies of urban spaces as well as of political actions.

11

Urban commoning
and the city of thresholds

To say that the city constitutes a common world for the people
who inhabit it seems almost a tautology. Yet what if the very logic
of inhabiting a common world can be questioned starting precisely from the fact that the city is an apparent concretization of
this world? What if this common world is what is at stake in the
creation of urban communities?

Jacques Rancière suggests that a "common world" is an "always polemical distribution of modes of being and 'occupations'
in a space of possibilities" (2006, 42). A common world can thus
be taken to be the result—always a temporary one—of compet-
ing processes embedded in social antagonisms. Rancière's well-
known distinction between "police" and "politics" (Rancière
1999, 28–29) actually attempts to categorize the limits of this
space of possibilities. "Police" describes a society reduced to a
rigid order, in which the space of possibilities becomes rather narrow. When this order is challenged by people who—by
their very actions—question or defy dominant classifications of
modes of social existence, then "politics" emerges as the opening
of a space of possibilities.

What if the city-as-a-common-world is actually both a well-ordered world which inhabitants learn to recognize as the almost-indisputable proof of an existing social order, and at the same time, a "space of possibilities"—a space not fixed in its form, its meaning and its uses, but open to challenges and acts of interpretation?

If urban space is considered merely as a quantity, and is reduced to a commodity to be distributed amongst the people who inhabit it, then "urban commons" can be reduced to a set of goods or resources, more like water, air, electricity, land, etc. If, however, urban commons are the emergent results of multiple processes of urban commoning (Stavrides 2016), then urban space is revealed to have a crucially important role that differs from most of the goods and services to the distributed in a city. Urban commoning neither simply "happens" in urban space, nor does it simply produce urban space as a commodity to be distributed. Urban commoning treats and establishes urban space as a medium through which institutions of commoning take shape.

We expect an institution to be a mechanism of social organization; a mechanism through which a specific society reproduces itself by ensuring that a certain social order repeats itself. Institutions are mechanisms that guarantee a regulated repeatability and, therefore, predictability of acts. Institutions of commoning, thus, are mechanisms that regulate the corresponding practices of commoning. If, however, commoning is more than a set of practices that produce and distribute goods to all the "commoners," then choices and values connected to this process must express themselves in the form of institutions that sustain the act of commoning itself. Institutions of commoning define subjects of action, and the boundaries of the group inside which commoning takes place.

By its very nature, an institution tends to limit the "space of possibilities" and to circumscribe a community of commoners. But this may—and often does—lead to forms of enclosure (De Angelis and

Stavrides 2010, 12). Those outside the circle see any closed community of commoners as an attempt to limit the dynamics of commoning. In order to prevent the institutions from limiting commoning, a specific politics of commoning must develop.

This is where Rancière's definition of politics may become useful. We can say that politics institutes itself as a challenge to the order established by the institutions of enclosed commoning. Politics, then, is that social force that pushes from the inside to open the boundaries of any social enclosure. Politics activates processes of "political subjectivation." Emerging subjects are not members of an existing community but potential participants in a community created in movement. They are "those who are capable of perceiving, thinking and altering the coordinates of the shared world" (Rancière 2009, 49).

Can the politics of commoning create institutions that continuously open the circles of commoning and in addition guarantee the benefits of social sharing? We know that production in industrial societies has depended heavily upon forms of cooperation in labor that were organized and managed in favor of capital's interests. The factory, as well as the plantation, were spaces of organized and controlled coordination of working bodies and thus contributed to the institutionalization of exploitation. Those spaces were "diagrams of power," because they gave shape to specific asymmetries of power that regulated people's relations at work.

In contemporary societies of neoliberal development, relations between people are not mainly regulated by way of spatial arrangements of power within the workplace, but by way of arrangements of power and forms of coordinated collaboration embedded in everyday metropolitan life. Everyday life is thus diffusely productive and creative at the same time, and many of its products (material but also immaterial as knowledge, skills, communication and survival tactics, etc.) are "captured" by capital (Hardt and Negri

2009). Dominant institutions enclose the products of commoning as well as the resources that commoning attempts to manage. "Dominant institutions corrupt the common" (ibid., 356). More precisely, "capitalist institutionalization is a form of capture and domestication of the institutions of the common" (Roggero 2010, 370). The city becomes important in shaping the institutions of commoning because it molds both the practices of collaboration in the production of social life, and the practices that compete for the appropriation of the commons produced.

In order to arrive at institutions that sustain an ongoing struggle against enclosure, we need to understand them as mechanisms which sustain relations between different groups of people who want to create shared worlds. Rather than being part of a process of homogenization and predictability, these institutions should be generators of continual negotiations of heterogeneity (Stavrides 2016).

In the contemporary metropolis, organized and controlled co-operation through and in urban space produces various forms of common goods and services. Urban metropolitan space is discontinuous and differentiated. In today's "cities of enclaves," many different spatial enclosures correspond to "corrupted" commoning practices of dwelling in which a community of commoners separates itself from the rest of the city. These can either be enclaves of privilege (as in gated communities) or enclaves of stigma (as in ghettos), but they are essentially forms of urban enclosure reproduced by the dominant institutions that regulate the city's form and uses. Common worlds, developed in those enclaves, are guaranteed by site-specific and localized institutions that explicitly treat members of other urban communities as "outsiders."

The sharing between equals and, at the same time, the opening of the circles of sharing towards "outsiders," necessarily implies creating institutions that can manage difference and tolerate unpredictability. In this case, institutions of commoning should shape the negotiations between equals that encourage encounters and offer opportunities for communication. Threshold spatiality contributes to the development of the practices of urban commoning that prevent its enclosure. Threshold spatiality allows forms of self-management of the commoning processes that permit the expansion of commoning circles through a regulated flow that connects "inside" and "outside."

Thresholds, those in-between spaces that separate by connecting at the same time, also allow a comparison between inside and outside. The establishment and comparing of differences is a first step towards the creation of common ground. And common ground, considered as a constantly negotiable in-betweenness, is a primary form of sharing. Sharing between different people who accept others as equals (equally in need and having equal rights to claim existing resources), is based on the creation of a common ground that does not need to be identified exclusively by way of a group of people (Stavrides 2012). Neighborhood kitchens in today's crisis-ridden Athens have created through commoning initiatives organized from below, opportunities of encounter and mutual recognition between different people in need, including immigrants, young precarious workers, and the unemployed.

On a larger scale, in the 2013 popular uprising in Taksim Square in Istanbul, public space was reclaimed as common space in direct confrontation with brutal authorities. In their struggle for democracy, people set in motion practices of urban commoning that expressed the emergence of a common world shaped by the awareness of differences and a will for collaboration between those in protest.

In the Gezi Park protests, public space was transformed to a network of common spaces (Postvirtual 2013) in which no clear limits were visible between the quasi-private personal spaces of those who camped in the occupied park and the spaces for public use. This was a process of reinventing public space through commoning. As one of the groups that contributed to the Gezi uprising explicitly formulates it: "The struggle for Gezi Park and Taksim Square set a new definition of what public space means. Reclaiming Taksim has shattered AKP's [Turkish governing party] hegemony in deciding what a square is supposed to mean for us citizens, because Taksim is now what the Resistance wants it to mean: our public square" (Müştereklerimiz 2013). A mixture of secondhand materials and objects created an anarchic which contributed to the blurring of uses in the occupied public space of Gezi Park. Collective identities were emphatically expressed in the arrangement of different spaces although such a cultural, religious, and political compartmentalization did not erect barriers between different collectivities but rather established forms of encounter and collaboration, even between groups typically hostile to each other. Kemalists and Muslim activists, gay activists and football hooligans, feminists and religious patriarchic family members, anarchists and leftists, Kurds and Turks found through their coexistence and collaboration unexpected common ground (Bektaş 2013, 14–15).

In the occupied public spaces of the so-called "squares movement" (2011–2013), common spaces became alive, albeit temporary, urban thresholds (Stavrides 2012, 2016). Thresholds neither define people who use them nor are defined by them. Rather, they mediate negotiations between people about the meaning and use of the spaces they share. Common threshold spaces correspond with identity-opening processes, like the kind that characterized the squares experience. A miniature city emerged in the form of a "city of thresholds" in which encounters and dispersed initiatives built spaces of negotiation and osmosis by collectively shaping a public culture based on solidarity and mutual respect.

Thresholds can be zones that allow flows to penetrate the perimeter of a defined community. Thresholds can also be bridges, constructions built explicitly to generate a relation between two sides. Bridges and bridge-like spaces connect different sides without eliminating their differences. We could even think of bridge-like spaces as those that help translate one side to the other. The translatability of social practices presupposes the existence of different forms of social life that actively search for common ground beyond homogeneity or monophony. This is why bridge spatiality sustains and encourages the production of new subjects of sharing. In the self-managed occupied squares in Athens, Madrid or Cairo during the squares movement, open assemblies had to devise institutions in order to specify practices of good use and care for a "common space." Those institutions were constantly readjusting to include new users and face unforeseen problems. An urban threshold was maintained by a porous assembly of experimental institutions.

In order to establish institutions of commoning open to comparisons and translations, in order for those institutions to be able to regulate relations between different but equal individuals and groups of people, there is one more precondition of sharing. There is a continuous effort to prevent any accumulation of power and, especially, any situated accumulation of power. Institutions of expansive commoning need to establish and enable the sharing of power.

Zibechi talks about the "dispersing of power" when he interprets the form of organization and action that characterized the struggling communities of El Alto in Bolivia (2010). Rancière suggests that "artifices of equality" may be employed by political subjects in their struggle to "refigure the common of a given world" (2010, 92). Both contribute, thus, to a possible theorizing of mechanisms employed in the sharing of power (i.e., duty rotation, collective and not individual accumulation of goods, democratic accountability, the balanced micro-macro community dialectic of decision-making, etc.).

Commoning, and especially urban commoning, is a process that must open a space of possibilities if it is to counteract the practices of enclosure. Commoning must overspill the boundaries of any given community (and its corresponding milieu), if it is to remain the generator of relations beyond exploitation and hierarchical control. Commoning must allow space for and give opportunities to the emergence of new subjects—potential commoners. And commoning must be a part of "the revolt of creative doing" (Holloway 2010, 225) as a potentially unrestrained force of creation that invents new social bonds, new forms of human and social relations, that run counter to human exploitation and inequality. "The means of doing must be reappropriated" (Holloway 2002, 209). And the city, produced through practices of sharing, can indeed become a collective work of art (Lefebvre 1996, 173). That is, a common world that contains many worlds, one which constantly recreates and reestablishes itself as a common world to be shared.

Reappropriating the power of creativity in common in Havana, Cuba.

References

¡*Democracia real YA!* "Manifesto." Available at democraciarealya.es. Accessed February 5, 2012.

Giorgio Agamben. *The Coming Community*, trans. Michael Hardt. Minneapolis: University of Minnesota Press, 1993.

_____. *Homo Sacer: Sovereign Power and Bare Life*, trans. Daniel Heller Roazen. Stanford, CA: Stanford University Press, 1998.

_____. *Means Without End: Notes on Politics*, trans. Cesare Casarino and Vincenzo Binetti. Minneapolis: University of Minnesota Press, 2000.

_____. "Genova e il nuovo ordine mondiale" *il manifesto*, July 25, 2001.

_____. *State of Exception*, trans. Kevin Attell. Chicago: The University of Chicago Press, 2005.

Michel Agier, "Between War and City: Towards an Urban Anthropology of Refugee Camps," *Ethnography* 3, no. 3 (2002): 317–341.

Rowland Atkinson and Sarah Blandy. "Introduction: International Perspectives on the New Enclavism and the Rise of Gated Communities." In *Housing Studies* 20, no. 2 (2005): 177–186.

_____. "A Picture of the Floating World: Grounding the Secessionary Affluence of the Residential Cruise Liner," *Antipode* 41, no.1 (2009): 92–110.

Marc Augé. *An Anthropology for Contemporaneous Worlds*, trans. Amy Jacobs. Stanford, CA: Stanford University Press, 1999.

_____. *Non-Places: Introduction to an Anthropology of Supermodernity*, trans. John Howe. London: Verso, 1995.

Gaston Bachelard. *The Dialectic of Duration*, trans. Mary McAllester Jones. Manchester: Clinamen Press, 2000.

Mikhail Bakhtin. *Rabelais and His World*, trans. Helene Iswolsky. Bloomington: Indiana University Press, 1984.

Ballard, Richard, Adam Habib, and Imraan Valodia, eds. *Voices of Protest. Social Movements in Post-Apartheid South Africa*. Scottsville: University of KwaZulu-Natal Press, 2006.

Balibar, Étienne and Immanuel Wallerstein. *Race, Nation, Class: Ambiguous Identities*. London: Verso, 1991.

Bauman, Zygmunt. "Desert Spectacular." In *The Flaneur*, ed. Keith Tester.

London: Routledge, 1994, 138–157.

_____. *Globalization: The Human Consequences.*Cambridge: Polity Press, 1998.

Ali Bektaş. "'I've gone to resist, I'll be right back': Against the Dictatorship of Development," in *This is only the beginning: on the Gezi Park resistance* (2013). Available at *https://www.indybay.org/uploads/2014/03/03/this_is_only_the_beginning.pdf.* Last accessed December 17, 2018.

Belinghausen, Hermann, "Homer Shouldn't Have Died," *La Jornada Semanal,* August 22, 2004.

Benjamin Walter. *GesammelteSchriften.* Frankfurt: Suhrkamp Verlag, 1980.

_____. *Charles Baudelaire: A Lyric Poet in the Era of High Capitalism,* London: Verso, 1983.

_____. "A Berlin Chronicle." In *One Way Street and Other Writings.* London: Verso, 1985a.

_____. "Naples." In *One Way Street and Other Writings.* London: Verso, 1985b.

_____. "Theses on the Philosophy of History." In *Illuminations.* London: Fontana Press, 1992a.

_____. "The Work of Art in the Age of Mechanical Reproduction." In *Illuminations.* London: Fontana Press, 1992b.

_____. *The Arcades Project.* Cambridge: The Belknap Press, 1999.

_____. "Expose of 1935." in Benjamin 1999a.

_____. "Expose of 1939" in Benjamin 1999b.

_____. "Experience and Poverty." In *Selected Writings 1927–1934.* Cambridge: The Belknap Press, 1999c.

_____. "The Return of the Flaneur." In *Selected Writings 1927–1934.* Cambridge: The Belknap Press, 1999d.

Berger, John. *Ways of Seeing.* London: Penguin Books, 1972.

Berman, Marshall. *All That is Solid Melts Into Air: The Experience of Modernity.* London: Verso, 1983.

Borden, Iain. "Another Pavement, Another Beach: Skateboarding and the Performative Critique of Architecture." In *The Unknown City,* edited by Iain Borden et. al., 178–199. Cambridge, MA: MIT Press, 2001.

Bourdieu, Pierre. *Outline of a Theory of Practice.* Cambridge: Cambridge University Press, 1977.

_____. *The Logic of Practice.* Cambridge: Polity Press, 1992.

_____. *Pascalian Meditations.* Cambridge: Polity Press, 2000.

Boyer, M. Christine. *The City of Collective Memory*. Cambridge, MA: MIT Press, 1994.

Breytenbach, Breyten. "The Long March from Hearth to Heart." In *Home: A Place in the World*, edited by Arien Mack, 65–80. New York: New York University Press, 1993.

Brighenti, Andrea. M. "On Territorology. Towards a General Science of Territory," *Theory, Culture & Society*, 27 no.1 (2010): 57–72.

Buck-Morss, Susan. *The Dialectics of Seeing: Walter Benjamin and the Arcades Project*. Cambridge, MA: MIT Press, 1991.

_____. *Hegel, Haiti, and Universal History*. Pittsburgh, PA: University of Pittsburgh Press, 2009.

Cacciari, Massimo. *Larcipelago*. Milano: Adelphi, 1999.

Cal, Burguete and Aracely Mayor, B. (ed.) *Indigenous Autonomy in Mexico*. Copenhagen: IWGIA, 2002.

Caldeira, Teresa. "From Modernism to Neoliberalism in Sao Paulo: Reconfiguring the City and its Citizens." In *Other Cities, Other Worlds*, edited by Andreas Huyssen, 51–78. Durham, NC: Duke University Press, 2008.

Castells, Manuel. *The Rise of the Network Society*. Oxford: Blackwell, 1996.

Caygil, Howard. *Walter Benjamin: The Colour of Experience*. London: Routledge, 1998.

Chaplin, Sarah. "Heterotopia Deserta: Las Vegas and Other Spaces." In *Intersections: Architectural Histories and Critical Theories*, edited by I. Bordeu and J. Rendell, 203–220. London: Routledge, 2000.

Cixous, Hélène. *Stigmata*. London: Routledge, 2005.

Coaffee, Jon. "Recasting the 'Ring of Steel': Designing Out Terrorism in the City of London?" In *Cities, War and Terrorism*, edited by Stephen Graham, 276–296. Oxford: Blackwell, 2004.

Cowan, Michael, "The Heart Machine: 'Rhythm' and Body in Weimar Film and Fritz Lang's Metropolis," *Modernism/Modernity*, 14 no.2 (2007): 225–248.

Davis, T. C. "Theatricality and Civil Society." In *Theatricality*, edited by T.C. Davis and Thomas Postlewait, 127–155. Cambridge: Cambridge University Press, 2003.

Davis, Mike. *City of Quartz*. London: Vintage, 1990.

De Angelis, Massimo and Stavros Stavrides. "Beyond Markets or States: Commoning as Collective Practice (a public interview)," *An Architektur*, no. 23 (2010): 4–27. Available at e-flux.com.

de Certeau, Michel. *The Practice of Everyday Life*. Berkeley: University of California Press, 1984.

de Certeau, Michel, Luce Giard and Pierre Mayol. *The Practice of Everyday Life, Vol. 2: Living and Cooking*. Minneapolis: Minnesota University Press, 1998.

Deleuze, Giles. *Foucault*. Minneapolis: University of Minnesota Press, 1988.

Deleuze, Giles and Felix Guattari. *A Thousand Plateaus*. London: Continuum, 2004.

Diderot, Denis. *The Paradox of Acting*. New York: Hill and Wang, 1957.

Dreyfus, Hubert and Paul Rabinow. *Michel Foucault: Beyond Structuralism and Hermeneutics*. Chicago: The University of Chicago Press, 1983.

Elden, Stuart. *Mapping the Present: Heidegger, Foucault and the Project of Spatial History*. London: Continuum, 2001.

Feral, Josette. "Theatricality: The Specificity of Theatrical Language," *SubStance*, 31 no.2/3 (2002): 17–41.

Foster, Susan Leigh. "Walking and Other Choreographic Tactics: Danced Inventions of Theatricality and Performativity." *SubStance* 31, no. 2/3 (2002): 125-46.

Foucault, Michel. *The Order of Things, An Archaeology of the Human Sciences*. New York: Vintage Books, 1973.

_____. "The Subject and Power." In *Michel Foucault: Beyond Structuralism and Hermeneutics*, edited by Hubert Dreyfus and Paul Rabinow, 208–228. Chicago: Chicago University Press, 1983.

_____. "Space, Knowledge and Power." In *The Foucault Reader*, edited by Paul Rabinow, 239–256. New York: Random House, 1984.

_____. *The History of Sexuality. Volume 1: An Introduction*. New York: Vintage Books, 1990.

_____. *Discipline and Punish*. New York: Random House, 1995.

_____. *History of Madness*. London: Routledge, 2006.

_____. "Of Other Spaces." In *Heterotopias and the City: Public Space in Postcivil Society*, edited by Livien De Cauter and Michiel Dehaene, 13–30. London: Routledge, 2008.

Franck, Karen and Quentin Stevens (eds.) *Loose Space: Possibility and Diversity in Urban Life*. London: Routledge, 2007.

Freud, Sigmund. "The Uncanny." In *Freud Standard Edition Volume 17*, London: Hogarth Press, 1919[1975].

Garcia, Jose Alejos. "Ethnic Identity and the Zapatista Rebellion in Chiapas." In *National Identities and Sociopolitical Changes in Latin America*, edited by M. F. Daran-Cogan et al. New York: Routledge, 2001.

Gell, Alfred. *The Anthropology of Time.* Oxford: Berg, 2001.

Genocchio, Benjamin. "Discourse, Discontinuity, Difference: The Question of Other Spaces." In *Postmodern Cities and Spaces*, edited by Sophie Watson and Katherine Gibson. London: Blackwell, 1995.

Gilloch, Graeme. *Myth and Metropolis: Walter Benjamin and the City.* Cambridge: Polity Press, 1997.

Giovanopoulos, Christos and Dimitris Mitropoulos. Από τους δρόμους στις πλατείες. Δημοκρατία *Under Construction (Democracy Under Construction)* Athens: A/synexeia Editions, 2011.

Gossen, Gary. *Telling Maya Tales: Tzotzil Identities in Modern Mexico.* London: Routledge, 1999.

Gove, Philip Babcock. *Webster's Third New International Dictionary.* London: Encyclopædia Britannica, 1981.

Graham, Steve and Simon Marvin. *Splintering Urbanism.* London: Routledge, 2001.

Hardt, Michael and Antonio Negri. *Multitude: War and Democracy in the Age of Empire.* London: Hamish Hamilton, 2004.

_____. *Commonwealth.* Cambridge: The Belknap Press, 2009.

Harvey, David. *Justice, Nature and the Geography of Difference.* Cambridge: Blackwell, 1996.

Hastrup, Kristen. *Action. Anthropology in the Company of Shakespeare.* Copenhagen: Museum Tusculanum Press, 2004.

Hénaff, Marcel and Tracy B. Strong, eds. *Public Space and Democracy.* Minneapolis: University of Minnesota Press, 2001.

Hetherington, Kevin. *The Badlands of Modernity: Heterotopia and Social Ordering.* London: Routledge, 1997.

Heynen, Hilde. *Architecture and Modernity: A Critique.* Cambridge: MIT Press, 1999.

Holloway, John. *Change the World Without Taking Power.* London: Pluto Press, 2002.

_____. *Crack Capitalism.* London: Pluto Press, 2010.

Iveson, Kurt. "Beyond Designer Diversity: Planners, Public Space and a Critical Politics of Difference." *Urban Policy and Research*, 18 no. 2 (2000): 219–238.

_____. "The City versus the Media? Mapping the Mobile Geographies of Public Address," *International Journal of Urban and Regional Research*, 33 no. 1 (2009): 241–245.

Jankelevitch, Vladimir. *Lironie*. Paris: Flammarion, 1996.

Kracauer, Seigfried. *From Caligari to Hitler: A Psychological History of the German Film*. Princeton: Princeton University Press, 2004.

Laclau, Ernesto. *New Reflections on the Revolutions of Our Time*. London: Verso, 1990.

Lakoff George and Mark Johnson. *Metaphors We Live By*. Chicago: University of Chicago Press, 1980.

Lascano, Sergio Rodriguez, "El Zapatismo: un Puente a la Esperanza," *Rebeldia*, 2002(1).

Le Bot, Yvon. *Subcomandante Marcos: El sueno Zapatista*. Barcelona: Plaza and Janes editors, 1998.

Lefebvre, Henri. *Writings on Cities*. Oxford: Blackwell, 1996.

_____. *Rhythmanalysis: Space, Time and Everyday Life*. London: Continuum, 2004.

Lévi-Strauss, Claude. *The View from Afar*. London: Peregrine Books, 1985.

Macrae, David. "Ruttman, Rhythm and 'Reality': A Response to Siegfried Kraccauer's Interpretation of Berlin: The Symphony of a Great City." In *Expressionist Film: New Perspectives*, edited by Dietrich Scheunemann, 251–270. Rochester: Camden House, 2003.

Maffesoli, Michel. *The Time of the Tribes*. London: Sage, 1996.

Marcos (Subcomandante). *Our Word is Our Weapon: Selected Writings*. New York: Seven Stories Press, 2002.

_____. *Ya Basta: Ten Years of Zapatista Uprising*. Oakland: AK Press, 2004.

Marcuse, Peter. "Not Chaos but Walls: Postmodernism and the Partitioned City." In *Postmodern Cities and Spaces*, edited by Sophie Watson and Katherine Gibson. London: Blackwell, 1995, 243–253.

Marcuse, Peter and Ronald Van Kempen, eds. *Of States and Cities: The Partitioning of Urban Space*. Oxford: Oxford University Press, 2002.

Massey, Doreen. *For Space*. London: Sage, 2005.

Menninghaus, Winifried. "Walter Benjamin's Theory of Myth." In *On Walter Benjamin*, edited by Gary Smith, 156–174. Cambridge, MA: MIT Press, 1991.

Mertes, Tom. (ed.) *A Movement of Movements*. London: Verso, 2004.

Midnight Notes Collective. *Promissory Notes: From Crisis to Commons*.

Brooklyn: Autonomedia, 2009. Available at midnightnotes.org.

Mills, Catherine. *The Philosophy of Agamben.* Montreal & Kingston: McGill-Queen's University Press, 2008.

Minton, Anna. *Ground Control: Fear and Happiness in the Twenty-First-Century City.* London: Penguin Books, 2009.

Montalbán, Manuel Vázquez. *El señor de los espejos. Madrid: Aguilar, 1999.*

Müştereklerimiz, "Today We Are All Someone New" *OpenDemocracy.* June 3, 2013. Available at: opendemocracy.net. Accessed June 19, 2014.

Nash, June. *Mayan Visions: The Quest for Autonomy in an Age of Globalization.* New York: Routledge, 2001.

Negri, Antonio, "On Rem Koolhaas." *Radical Philosophy* 154 (2009) 48–50.

Nemeth, Jeremy and Justin Hollander. "Security Zones and New York City's Shrinking Public Space," *International Journal of Urban and Regional Research,* 34 no.1 (2010): 20–34.

Norris, Andrew (ed.) *Politics, Metaphysics and Death. Essays on G. Agamben's Homo Sacer.* Durham, NC: Duke University Press, 2005.

Patras Real Democracy blog, patras-democracy.blogspot.com.

Pickvance, Christopher G. "Where Have Urban Movements Gone?" In *Europe at the Margins: New Mosaics of Inequality,* edited by Costis Hadjimichalis and David Sadler, 197–217. London: J. Wiley and Sons, 1995.

PostVirtual blog, "Historical Atlas of Gezi Park." June 27, 2013. Available at: postvirtual.wordpress.com.

Rancière, Jacques: *Disagreement.* Minneapolis: University of Minnesota Press, 1999.

_____. *The Politics of Aesthetics.* London: Continuum, 2006.

_____. *The Emancipated Spectator.* London: Verso, 2009.

_____. *Dissensus: On Politics and Aesthetics.* London: Bloomsbury, 2010.

Rayner, Alice. "Everywhere and Nowhere: Theatre in Cyberspace." In *Of Borders and Thresholds,* edited by Michal Kobialka, 278–302. Minneapolis: The University of Minnesota Press, 1999.

Robins, Kevin. *Into the Image: Culture and Politics in the Field of Vision.* London: Routledge, 1996.

Roggero, Gigi. "Five Theses on the Common," *Rethinking Marxism,* 22 no. 3 (2010) 357–73.

Samatas, Minas. "Security and Surveillance in the Athens 2004 Olympics: Some Lessons from a Troubled Story." *International Criminal Justice Review* 17 no.3 (2007)

Scott, James. *Domination and the Arts of Resistance*. New Haven: Yale University Press, 1990.

Schechner, Richard. *Between Theater and Anthropology*. Philadelphia: University of Pennsylvania Press, 1985.

Sennett, Richard. *The Fall of Public Man*. London: Faber and Faber, 1977.

_____. *The Conscience of the Eye*. London: Faber and Faber, 1993.

Simmel, Georg. "Bridge and Door." In *Rethinking Architecture: A Reader in Cultural History*, edited by Neil Leach. London: Routledge, 1997a.

_____. "The Metropolis and Mental Life" in Leach N. (ed.) *Rethinking Architecture*. London: Routledge, 1997b.

Soja, Edward. *Thirdspace. Journeys to Los Angeles and Other Real and Imagined Places*. Oxford: Blackwell, 1996.

_____. *Postmetropolis*. Oxford: Blackwell, 2000.

Starobinski, Jean. *Portrait de l'Artiste en Saltimbanque*. Geneve: Skira, 1970.

Stavrides, Stavros. "Especialidades de emacipacion y 'La Ciudad De Umbrales.'" In *Pensar a Contrapelo. Movimientos Sociales y Reflexión Crítica*, edited by John Holloway, Fernando Matamoro and Sergio Tischler. Buenos Aires: Herramienta, 2009.

Stavrides, Stavros. "The December 2008 Youth Uprising in Athens: Spatial Justice in an Emergent 'City of Thresholds'" *Spatial Justice* 2 (2010). http://www.jssj.org/archives/02/ media/public_space_vo2.pdf

Stavrides, Stavros. Από την πόλη οθόνη στην πόλη σκηνή (*From the City-Screen to the City-Stage*), Athens: Ellinika Grammata, 2002.

Stavrides, Stavros. "Square in Movement," *South Atlantic Quarterly* 111 no. 3 (2012): 585-596.

Stavrides, Stavros. *Common Space: The City as Commons*. London: Zed Books, 2016.

_____. "En las huellas de una heterotopia," In *La Jornada Semanal*, 2004, 494.

_____. "Heterotopias and the Experience of Porous Urban Space." In *Loose Space: Possibility and Diversity in Urban Life*, edited by Karen Franck and Quentin Stevens. London: Routledge, 2007.

Svoronos, Nicolas. *Histoire de la Grece Moderne*, Paris: Presses Universitaires de France, 1972.

Tafuri, Manfredo. *The Sphere and the Labyrinth: Avant Gardes and Architecture from Piranesi to the 1970s*. Cambridge MA: MIT Press, 1990.

Taussig, Michael. *Defacement: Public Secrecy and the Labor of the Negative*. Stanford: Stanford University Press, 1999.

Thompson, E.P. *Customs in Common*. New York: The New Press, 1993.

Tiedemann, Rolk. "Dialectics at a Standstill." In *The Arcades Project*. Cambridge: The Belknap Press, 1999.

Tisdall, Caroline and Angelo Bozzola. *Futurism*. London: Thames and Hudson, 1984.

Todorov, Tzvetan. *On Human Diversity*. Cambridge, MA: Harvard University Press, 1993.

Turner, Bryan. "The Enclave Society: Towards a Sociology of Immobility," *European Journal of Social Theory* 10 no. 2 (2007): 287-304.Turner, Victor. *The Ritual Process*. Ithaca, NY: Cornell University Press, 1977.

_____. *From Ritual to Theatre*. New York: PAJ, 1982.

Urbach, Henry. "Writing Architectural Heterotopia," *The Journal of Architecture* 3 no. 4 (2010): 347- 354.

Van Gennep, Arnold. *The Rites of Passage*. London: Routledge and Kegan Paul, 1960.

Vecchi, Benedetto. "Zona Rossa." In *La Sfida al G8*, edited by Arturo Di Corinto. Roma: Manifestolibri, 2001.

Vernant, Jean Pierre and Marcel Detienne. *Cunning Intelligence in Greek Culture and Society*. Atlantic Highlands, NJ: Humanities Press, 1978.

Vidler, Anthony. *The Architectural Uncanny*. Cambridge, MA: MIT Press, 1992.

Virilio, Paul. *Open Sky*. London: Verso, 1997.

Virno, Paolo. "Virtuosity and Revolution: The Political Theory of Exodus." In *Radical Thought in Italy: A Potential* Politics, edited by Paolo Virno and Michael Hardt, 189–222. Minneapolis: University of Minnesota Press, 2006.

Virno, Paolo. *A Grammar of the Multitude*. Los Angeles: Semiotext(e), 2004.

Wacquant, Loïc. *Urban Outcasts: A Comparative Sociology of Advanced Marginality*. Cambridge: Polity Press, 2008.

Weigel, Sigrid. *Body-and Image-Space: Re-reading Walter Benjamin*. London: Routledge, 1996.

Weizman, Eyal. "Hollow Land: The Barrier Archipelago and the Impossible Politics of Separation." In *Against the Wall*, edited by Michael Sorkin, 224–253. New York: The New Press, 2005.

Zibechi, Raúl. *Autonomías y emancipaciones: América Latina en movimiento*. Lima: Univ. San Marcos y Bajo Tierra, 2007.

_____. *Dispersing Power. Social Movements as AntiState Forces*. Oakland, CA: AK Press, 2010.

Index

About the Author

Stavros Stavrides is an architect and professor teaching at the National Technical University of Athens on housing and public space design as well as on the meaning of metropolitan experience. Stavrides's work on political autonomy in contemporary crises-governed cities provides timely urban theory to theorize forms of emancipating spatial practices and urban commoning, illuminated by an experience and knowledge of protest and rebellion in Athens since 2008.

In addition to *Towards the City of Thresholds*, he has published six books and numerous articles. His recent books include: *The Symbolic Relation to Space* (1990), *Advertising and the Meaning of Space* (1996), *The Texture of Things* (1996), *From the City-as-Screen to the City-as-Stage* (2002), *Suspended Spaces of Alterity* (2010), *Common Space: The City as Commons* (2016), as well as *Common Spaces of Urban Emancipation* (2019).

About Common Notions

Common Notions is a publishing house and programming platform that advances new formulations of liberation and living autonomy.

Our books provide timely reflections, clear critiques, and inspiring strategies that amplify movements for social justice.

By any media necessary, we seek to nourish the imagination and generalize common notions about the creation of other worlds beyond state and capital. Our publications trace a constellation of critical and visionary meditations on the organization of freedom. Inspired by various traditions of autonomism and liberation—in the U.S. and internationally, historically and emerging from contemporary movements—our publications provide resources for a collective reading of struggles past, present, and to come.

Monthly Sustainers

These are decisive times, ripe with challenges and possibility, heartache and beautiful inspiration. More than ever, we are in need of timely reflections, clear critiques, and inspiring strategies that can help movements for social justice grow and transform society. Help us amplify those necessary words, deeds, and dreams that our liberation movements and our worlds so need.

Movements are sustained by people like you, whose fugitive words, deeds, and dreams bend against the world of domination and exploitation.

For collective imagination, dedicated practices of love and study, and organized acts of freedom.
By any media necessary.
With your love and support.

Monthly sustainers start at $5, $10 and $25.

At $10 monthly, we will mail you a copy of every new book hot off the press in heartfelt appreciation of your love and support.

At $25, we will mail you a copy of every new book hot off the press alongside special edition posters and 50% discounts on previous publications at our web store.

Join us at commonnotions.org/sustain.

More From Common Notions

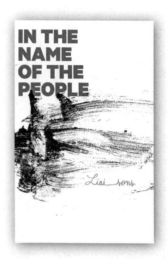

In the Name of the People
Liaisons

978-1-942173-07-6
$18.00
208 pages

The ghost of the People has returned to the world stage, claiming to be the only force capable of correcting or taking charge of the excesses of the time. This truly internationalist and collectivist publication boldly examines the forms of right and left-wing populism emergent in the fissures of the political world. Experimental in both form and analysis, *In the Name of the People* is the commune form of thought and text.

More From Common Notions

Writings from a Greek Prison
By Tasos Theofilou
Translated by Eleni Pappa
Preface by Ben Morea

978-1-942173-12-0
$15
144 Pages

Writings from a Greek Prison is a literary work of biting realism. Tasos Theofilou gives testimony on the brutality of prison life, and its centrality in contemporary capitalism, through a blur of memoir, social commentary, free verse, and a glossary of the idiom used by inmates in Greek prisons.

A political prisoner in Greece from 2012 to 2017, Theofilou's work centers on exposing the conditions of widespread exploitation and social struggle that persist in Greece as a result of the debt crisis—in prisons as well as across society.

More From Common Notions

Abolishing Carceral Society
Abolition Collective

978-1-942173-08-3
$20.00
256 pages
20 Illustrations

Beyond border walls and prison cells—carceral society is everywhere. *Abolishing Carceral Society* presents the bold and ruthlessly critical voices of today's revolutionary abolitionist movements.

Abolition Collective masterfully assembles this collection of essays, poems, artworks, and interventions to create an inciteful articulation and collaboration across communities, movements, and experiences embattled in liberatory struggle. In a time of mass incarceration, immigration detention and deportation, rising forms of racialized, gendered, and sexualized violence, and deep ecological and economic crises, abolitionists everywhere seek to understand and dismantle interlocking institutions of domination and create radical transformations.

More From Common Notions

Grupo de Arte Callejero:
Thoughts, Practices, and Actions
Grupo de Arte Callejero

978-1-942173-10-6
$22.00
320 pages

Grupo de Arte Callejero: Thought, Practices, and Actions tells the
profound story of social militancy and art in Argentina over
the last two decades and propels it forward. For Grupo de Arte
Callejero [Group of Street Artists], militancy and art blur together
in the anonymous, collective, everyday spaces and rhythms of life.
Thought, Practices, and Actions offers an indispensable reflection on
what was done and what remains to be done in the social fields of
art and revolution.

More From Common Notions

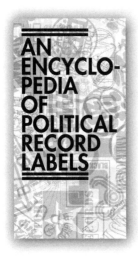

An Encyclopedia of Political Record Labels, 3rd edition
Josh MacPhee

978-1-942173-11-3
$24.95
208 pages

From A-Disc (the record label of the Swedish Labor Movement) to Zulu Records (the label of free jazz pioneer Phil Choran), *An Encyclopedia of Political Record Labels* is a compendium of information about political music and radical cultural production. Focusing on vinyl records and the labels that released them, this groundbreaking book traces the parallel rise of social movements in the second half of the twentieth century and the vinyl record as the dominant form of music distribution.